W9-ANK-271

Contradictions in Teacher Education and Society: A Critical Analysis

The Wisconsin Series of Teacher Education

General Editor: Professor Carl Grant, School of Education, University of Wisconsin-Madison, Wisconsin, USA.

Welcome to the Wisconsin Series of Teacher Education. This series is, dedicated to providing a forum for scholars in Teacher Education to debate, critique and illuminate the problems and challenges facing Teacher Education. Present reform efforts, past neglects and tomorrow's challenges in teacher education are demanding that we encourage and articulate the best ideas and arguments, and the most compelling alternatives, that we can. These contributions, I would argue, should not be constrained by ideology or tied to past formulations of what worked. The discourse expected and needed in the series is one that will foster critical inquiry, provide thoughtful and provocative discussions and encourage debate that has been previously neglected or shut out, regarding the many and varied problems and challenges facing Teacher Education. For example, one of the central ideas that demands further examination is the relationship between colleges of education and the public schools. The history of reform in teacher education is largely composed of attempts to legislate change from universities and colleges, which is then superimposed on schools and teachers. This model of reform is not only unlikely to produce progressive changes in schools, but it also reflects the tendency for educational change to be undertaken in ways that maintain existing differentials of power and control. Such differentials of power are rejected in this series, which seeks to forge alliances between schools and universities in improving educational quality.

In an 1894 report to the Board of Regents at the University of Wisconsin the following words were written:

> 'Whatever may Be the Limitations Which Trammel Inquiry Elsewhere, We Believe That The Great State University of Wisconsin Should Ever Encourage That Continued and Fearless Sifting and Winnowing By Which Alone The Truth can be Found.'

The Wisconsin Series of Teacher Education is dedicated to just such 'sifting and winnowing', that which leads to critical inquiry and scholarship and which widens the base for dialogue.

Carl A. Grant
University of Wisconsin-Madison
Series Editor

The Wisconsin Series of Teacher Education

Contradictions in Teacher Education and Society: A Critical Analysis

Mark B. Ginsburg
University of Pittsburgh

 The Falmer Press
(A member of the Taylor & Francis Group)
London • New York • Philadelphia

CARNEGIE LIBRARY
LIVINGSTONE COLLEGE
SALISBURY N C

120808

UK   The Falmer Press, Falmer House, Barcombe, Lewes, East Sussex, BN8 5DL

USA   The Falmer Press, Taylor & Francis Inc., 242 Cherry Street, Philadelphia, PA 19106-1906

© Copyright M. B. Ginsburg 1988

All rights reserved. No part of this publication may be reproduced, stored in a retrieval system, or transmitted in any form or by any means, electronic, mechanical, photocopying, recording or otherwise, without permission in writing from the Publisher.

First published 1988

Library of Congress Cataloguing in Publication Data is available on request

ISBN 1 85000 362 9
ISBN 1 85000 367 X (pbk.)

Jacket design by Caroline Archer

Typeset in 11/13 Bembo by
Mathematical Composition Setters Ltd, Ivy Street, Salisbury

Printed in Great Britain by Taylor & Francis (Printers) Ltd, Basingstoke

Contents

Series Editor's Introduction

As the debates about Teacher Education rage concerning what the problems are, what changes should be made in curriculum and program structure, and how these changes should be made, it is becoming increasingly obvious that penetrating critical examination is required. Mark Ginsburg's *Contradictions in Teacher Education and Society: A Critical Analysis* provides such an examination. Professor Ginsburg's discussion illuminates how the processes and content of teacher education tend to reproduce social stratification by encouraging future teachers to accept particular perspectives and interpretation of teachers, schooling, society and children; and also how teacher education in many respects contradicts that reproduction. Using both historical and ethnographic data Professor Ginsburg describes how teacher education is constrained *and* enabled by unequal race, class and gender relations, while at the same time teacher education serves to legitimate *and* challenge these unequal social relations. This analysis is particularly useful and telling as more teacher educators are being encouraged or forced by educational reform efforts to examine and change existing program policies and practices.

The work is also especially insightful and provocative because the author takes the analysis into the infrastructure of teacher education. He employs the concept of contradiction and uses ethnographic methodology to explain contradictions in how university professors experienced their own proletarianization and professionalization and how the students constructed their career identities based in part upon the contradictory messages presented in the formal and hidden curriculum. Ginsburg's contribution does not end there. Using the production metaphor he provides a revealing account and analysis of the development and implementation of a competency-based teacher education (CBTE) program at the University of Houston. He also traces the link between the dynamics in social class and gender relations and the historical development of teacher education in the United States.

Professor Ginsburg concludes his book by proposing critical praxis as a critical theorizing and critical practice 'tool' that could be used by educators of teachers to bring about needed social transformation in teacher education and society. He critiques much of what is occurring in the reform debates and argues for what needs to be done at the policy, ideological, curricular and practice levels in teacher education.

Contradictions in Teacher Education and Society: A Critical Analysis is a much needed analysis of teacher education. Educators interested in a serious examination of the complex relationship between social stratification and teacher education will find this book a rich and valuable resource.

Carl A. Grant
University of Wisconsin-Madison

Wisconsin Series Advisory Board
Michael W. Apple, University of Wisconsin-Madison
Jean Erdman, University of Wisconsin-Oshkosh
Martin Haberman, Dean, Department of Educational Opportunity
Fred M, Newmann, University of Wisconsin-Madison
Johh Palmer, Dean, School of Education, University of Wisconsin-Madison
Thomas S. Popkewitz, University of Wisconsin-Madison
Christine E. Sleeter, University of Wisconsin-Parkside
Robert B. Tabachnick, University of Wisconsin-Madison
Sam Yarger, Dean, School of Education, University of Wisconsin-Milwaukee
Kenneth Zeichner, University of Wisconsin-Madison

Preface

Here I am in Houston, making what I hope will be the final revisions on this book manuscript in between various tasks associated with my impending move to the University of Pittsburgh. I recall discussions I had with Kit Newman in 1979. These dialogues in some ways constitute the onset of the intellectual and political project that is contained in this book, even though Kit's move to California in 1981 reduced the extent of our collaboration before completion of the fieldwork. As 1979 was my first year at the University of Houston, it strikes me that in part this volume reflects my experience during the UH phase of my career.

There are obviously a number of colleagues and students at the University of Houston to whom I owe part of whatever 'academic capital' is accumulated by this publication. Let me first note those who will remain anonymous because of research conventions and because the list is too long. I refer here to the university faculty, guest lecturers, and students who during my ethnographic fieldwork let me share in their lives and at the same time taught me so much. Special mention goes to the students who agreed to be interviewed on a semesterly basis, and whose comments are illustrated in Chapters 4–6, and to those colleagues, who through being interviewed helped me develop a portrait of the College of Education in the decade before my arrival that is presented in Chapter 3. Other UH colleagues and students to whom I am indebted should be mentioned here. They include Abdul Al-Sharbari, Beatriz Arias-Godinez, Linda Bain, Bob Blomeyer, Gricelle and Lorenzo Cano, Johnnie Carter, Janet Chafetz, David Chao, Kowsar Chowdhury, Renee Clift, H. Paul Cooper, John Croft, Tom De Gregori, Rick Duschl, Gary Dworkin, Barbara Foorman, Jerry

Freiberg, William Georgiades, Joanne Giles, Jane Haglund, John Hart, Bob Howsam, Steve Huber, Joe Kotarba, Bruce Kimball, Margaret Le Compte, Dov Liberman, Shirley McFaul, John McNamara, Margarita Melville, Sarath Menon, Darla Miller, Michael Olivas, Jong-Hub Park, Jim Pearson, Bob Randall, Hossein Razi, George Reiter, Nestor Rodriguez, Monika Reuter-Echols, Marilyn Rothman, Jeff Sammons, Judy Sands, Paul Secord, Linda Spatig, Susan Stilley, Masih Shokri, Monty Tedwell, Hersh Waxman, Donnie Wilson, and John York. Our discourse provided me with ideas and energy that helped produce this book.

Despite this book being, in many ways, an effort at the University of Houston, I would be seriously remiss in not acknowledging the contributions of other colleagues, many others of whom are referenced in the notes at the end of various chapters. In a number of ways, the work reported here builds on discussions and research that Bob Meyenn, Henry Miller and I engaged in during our collaboration at the University of Aston in Birmingham, England, as well as the conversations I had with David O'Shea during my graduate program at UCLA and subsequently. Without the encouragement, the example, and the constructive criticisms of the following people, the value of this book would be significantly reduced: Phil Altbach, Jean Anyon, Michael Apple, Ann Berlak, Marvin Berlowitz, Kathryn Borman, R. Connell, Michael Connelly, Sara Delamont, Joe Farrell, Henry Giroux, Carl Grant, Gail Kelly, Nancy King, Joe Kretovics, Tom La Belle, Margali Larson, Peter McLaren, Linda McNeil, Bill Phelan, Tom Popkewitz, Mara Sapon-Shevin, Ed Silva, Sheila Slaughter, Robert Tabachnick, Steve Tozer, Geoff Walford, Don Warren, Lois Weis, Philip Wexler, and Ken Zeichner.

A special thank you is directed toward Tessa Jo Shokri, who word-processed the manuscripts on which this book is based and whose editorial suggestions and sarcastic humor helped me frequently to make progress on this project.

In addition, there are a number of people whom I have come to know through progressive political work in Texas, who helped me think about and act upon some of the issues presented herein, put this project in proper perspective, and have otherwise served as sources of moral support and inspiration. While it is not conventional to acknowledge such non-academic mentors, this would not be the first convention I have violated. Appreciation is thus given to Nancy Cole, Claire and Ken Crouch, Joan Dusard, Ada Edwards, Angie Grindon, Beverly Harper, Brenda Hart, Janis Heine, Bob Henschen, Larry Jones,

Omowali Lithuli, Travis Morales, Susan Murphy, Ed Nelson, Willie Reid, Jeannie Ritter, David Rossie, John Sarge, Pete Seidman, Arthur Shaw, Carol Shattuck, Ted Weisgal, Marilyn White, and Mara Youngdahl.

In addition, this book would not have been possible without the support of my family. My wife, Barbara, and our three children, Jolie, Kevin and Stefanie, have been a source of love and encouragement as well as providing me with an important reminder that life is about people as well as social structures and ideologies. My parents, brothers and sister, as well as my in-laws have also contributed in different ways to who I am and how I have created this book. Finally, I want to thank my Grandfather, Fred Burg, who challenged me during my youth through our conversations and with the books he lent me from his library, and who has continued to encourage me in my scholarly and political endeavors.

This book is dedicated to the children, many of whom are as yet unborn, who depend on us to struggle in schools and society in order to transform this world into one of equality, justice and peace, without destroying it in the process.

Mark B. Ginsburg
University of Houston

Chapter 1

On Developing a Critical Sociology of Teacher Education[1]

Teacher education is a disputed territory of conflicting tendencies: on one hand, there is the tendency to maintain and
reproduce the pattern of traditional ways of valuing, thinking
and organizing; on the other, there is a tendency to promote
innovation and reform. ... The aims of teacher education are
problematic insofar as the society and the role on which they are
focused reflect contradictory tendencies.[2]

Introduction

This is a book about teacher education, its organizational structure,
curricular content and lived experience. We will examine the process of
preservice teacher socialization, that is, the process of formally preparing to become a teacher. In order to contextualize this discussion based
on two years of ethnographic fieldwork in one institution, we shall also
analyze the development of institutionalized forms of teacher education.
This will entail a general focus on the historical development of teacher
education programs in the United States as well as a more specific focus
on the development and implementation of the 'competency-based'
teacher education program, which served as the site for the ethnography, during the decade preceding my fieldwork.

The current period seems like a propitious one to write a book
about teacher education. The mid-1980s have witnessed an increased
interest in teacher education. Following in the wake of reports[3] on
public schools in the US, identifying what are seen as its 'problems' and

proposing what are viewed as needed 'reforms', there has been a wave of analyses of and reform proposals for teacher education.[4] As we will learn in the next chapter, the contemporary surge in interest in and debate about teacher education is not without historical precedent. Nevertheless, when discussions concerning teacher education are splashed across the front pages of daily newspapers, the situation is afloat with opportunities to communicate. At least someone may be paying attention.

Besides wanting to add my own to the sea of voices in commenting on teacher education, why am I writing this book? Why would a comparative sociologist of education, who is concerned about unequal social relations, focus his interest on the education of teachers? What, you may be asking yourself, does the reproduction (perpetuation and legitimation) of inequalities in wealth, power and status along social class, racial/ethnic and gender divisions have to do with teacher education?

Why Teacher Education and Reproduction?

Discussions about the relationship between education and social inequalities are well known to those who labor in the field of social foundations of education and curriculum theory, though less a part of the consciousness of teacher educators, let alone other educational workers (e.g., teachers and administrators) and the public. Over the last ten to fifteen years an increasing number of critical theorists in Europe and the United States have offered explanations of how and why the organization and processes of schooling function to reproduce unequal social structures. The explanations have varied in their focus and include: curriculum knowledge and relations of pedagogy,[5] teacher evaluative actions and perspectives,[6] and student culture[7].

In much of this discourse concerning reproduction, implicit and explicit allusions have been made to the potential significance of teacher socialization. The point is that given teachers' central, but not independent, role in constructing the schooling experience, it is crucial to understand how and where they 'obtain the categories which enable them to make sense of their working lives'.[8] This concern brings us quickly to a formal strand of their socialization, preservice teacher education, although we must not forget the salience of their prior and subsequent experiences in schools and society.[9]

A number of writers have drawn attention to the broader, supraindividual implications of teacher socialization.[10] Generally, in these writings, teacher education is *not* conceived as a neutral enterprise *vis-à-vis* the unequal social structure, in that it 'articulates not only "skill" competence, but communicate(s) ways of reasoning about teaching that contain principles of authority, legitimacy and control'.[11] As Giroux argues:

> Charged with the public responsibility to educate teachers to enable future generations to learn the knowledge and skills necessary to build a principled and democratic society, [teacher education programs] represent a significant agency for the reproduction and a legitimation of a society characterized by a high degree of social and economic inequality.[12]

For the most part, however, these claims have not been associated with 'thick descriptions' of the web of meaning and action[13] involved in the process of becoming a teacher, nor informed by a well developed historical perspective. Nevertheless, on the basis of one of the more comprehensive studies to address issues of the societal functions of teacher education — an impressive study, limited, because of its cross-national focus, by its reliance on documents and other more distal forms of data — Lynch and Plunkett's analysis reinforces the basic contention of others' theorizing, that:

> If educational systems do function to reproduce in learners the dominant values of a culture, or to legitimate for them the status generally accorded to those values, then this function could be expected to be most clearly observable in teacher education.[14]

Why the Concept of Contradiction?

We want to be careful, however, not to fall into an overly deterministic approach to studying the relationship between teacher education and social structure. For example, some of the work referenced above might be interpreted as following the strongly criticized path of Bowles and Gintis,[15] who are said to have promoted a 'correspondence theory' in which the economy was characterized as totally determining human thought and action. While taking as a major problematic the question of how unequal social relations are perpetuated and legitimated, I do not posit that either schooling or teacher education perfectly or automatically reproduces the extant unequal class, race/ethnic, and gender relations.

Rather, the approach adopted here posits a notion of relative autonomy of the cultural level and provides space for human agency, that is, people's relatively autonomous acts of resistance, contestation and struggle.[16] Thus, my approach is informed by Giddens'[17] concept of 'duality of structure' — that the 'logic' of the macro political, economic and ideological spheres both constrains and enables human action and consciousness, while at the same time this context is reproduced, challenged, or sometimes transformed by human thought and action. Moreover, because human agency is a factor and because social formations (at the societal and world system levels) contain contradictions, the potential for social transformation or change. 'however trivial or minor' is 'inherent in all moments of reproduction'.[18]

The concept of contradiction has been seen as a particularly promising corrective to an overly-deterministic model, without according undue weight to voluntarism, which can sometimes occur with over-zealous celebrations of resistance, contestation and struggle. For example, Apple comments on Bowles and Gintis' conceptualization:

> While correct to a point, correspondence theory cannot do complete justice to the complexity of school life; the actual and often contradictory conditions which tie education to an unequal society, or to struggles and contradictions that exist in the school, the work place, and ... in the state.[19]

Interestingly, Bowles and Gintis reached a similar conclusion in reflecting upon their earlier work. They contend that:

> ... by standing in our approach as the only structural link and by its character as an inherently harmonious link between the two, the correspondence principle forced us to adopt a narrow and inadequate appreciation of the contradictions involved in the articulation of the educational system within the social totality.[20]

It is rather paradoxical, though, that there have been relatively few efforts among critical theorists in education to incorporate systematically the notion of contradiction in their analyses,[21] given 'the centrality of the category of contradiction for any Marxist analysis'[22] or that, as Mao notes, the 'law of contradictions in things, that is, the law of unity of opposites, is the basic law of materialist dialectics'.[23]

My theoretical approach, then, is grounded in the Marxist notion, here expressed by Mao, that 'the unity of opposites, ... contradiction, exists in the process of development of all things',[24] i.e., 'nature as well as social and ideological phenomena',[25] but that the 'particular essence of each form of motion is determined by its own particular contradiction'.[26] This is not to argue, however, that social structures and ideologies are completely isolated regions of contradiction. It is only to clarify the relative autonomy of, for example, the ideologies of social mobility/reproduction, professionalism, or curriculum from extant class, race/ethnic or gender relations and to indicate that ideologies and structures may stand (at any historical conjuncture and with respect to any particular aspects) in a relation of correspondence or contradiction.[27]

We need to consider two kinds of contradictions: internal (e.g., within ideology, within education, or within the political economy) and external (e.g., between ideology and the political economy). As Carter explains:

> Any set of structures is said to be internally contradictory if it tends to produce by its own functioning conditions which hamper its own reproduction ... Similarly, two relatively autonomous structures are said to be [externally] contradictory if either produces conditions that hamper the reproduction of the other.[28]

We must also note, following Carter, that contradictions internal to the political economical system may initially be latent or mediated temporarily by other institutions [or ideologies] in society[29] and, partly because of this, 'reproduction of existing structures can proceed despite the existence of contradictions of both types'.[30] Alternatively, ideologies, for example, may serve to expose and thus provide the basis for challenging the contradictory relations of the political economy, or at least hamper the reproduction of extant political economic relations, for example.[31] In either case, contradictory ideologies and social relations can be seen to inform the thought and action of people — for instance, teacher educators or preservice teachers — involved in the construction of teacher education and the socialization of teachers.

Contradictions and the Socialization of Teachers[32]

The concept of contradiction not only provides a promising corrective for discussions about social reproduction and social transformation. It

also helps to clarify issues in the general field of occupational socialization and its more specific subfield, the socialization of teachers. These
issues, which have erupted in debates between adherents of 'functionalist' models and proponents of 'phenomenological' or 'symbolic
interactionist' models of the process of occupational socialization,
revolve around the question of whether people learning to be members
of some occupation — for example, preservice teachers — are passive
recipients or active agents in this process.

Traditionally, studies of occupational socialization have been
based, however implicitly, on a model which emphasized the role of
training programs (and the other less formal occupational socialization
experiences) in molding and shaping the ideas and behavior of
prospective occupational incumbents.[33] This functionalist model of
socialization is perhaps best illustrated by Brim and Wheeler's statement
about socialization after childhood: 'The function of socialization is to
transform the human raw material of society into good working
members'.[34] This image of the future occupation member as a passive
recipient of a given occupational role is also evidenced in Merton,
Reader and Kendall's discussion of the 'student physician':

> [Socialization is] ... the process through which individuals are
> inducted into their culture. It involves the acquisition of atti-
> tudes and values, of skills and behavior patterns making up
> social roles established in the social structure.[35]

as well as by Eddy's comments about teacher socialization during the
induction year: novice teachers 'receive the lasting imprint which
shapes their perspectives and behaviors as teachers'.[36]

While the functionalist view of occupational socialization seems to
have remained influential, especially among people who are responsible
for developing and coordinating training programs, its assumptions of
passive acquisition of occupation roles has been challenged by an
alternative model with roots in social phenomenology and symbolic
interactionism. According to this alternative model, which seeks to
avoid an 'oversocialized conception'[37] of human existence:

> Socialization is not merely the transfer from one group to
> another in a static social structure, but the active creation of a
> new identity through a personal definition of the situation.[38]

Adherents of this symbolic interactionist/phenomenologically
informed model of occupational socialization suggest that even though
trainees may (at times and with respect to certain ideas and behaviors)

be shaped and moulded by the program, in general they are 'not passive recipients of messages from their accorded agents of socialization';[39] rather they are 'persons engaged in choice making'.[40]

While the disagreements between these two perspectives on the *process* of occupational socialization are sharp, they seem to share a conception of the *content* of socialization as being without contradictions. The major issue of debate is whether trainees absorb and internalize versus select and filter the messages sent to them, for example, in the formal and hidden curriculum of a teacher education program. However, if the messages transmitted in each of these curricular channels contain contradictory messages, or, as has been suggested,[41] the hidden curricular messages contradict those available through the formal curriculum, then the passive-active dichotomy becomes more difficult to apply. Is the active agent merely internalizing available messages that contradict what might be seen as dominant in the formal curriculum of a program? Is the passive recipient really actively selecting to incorporate the messages that the organizers of the program or researchers perceive as dominant?

Because of this problem, I want to re-emphasize the point I made earlier, drawing on Giddens' concept of 'duality of structure'.[42] Human action and consciousness are mutually constitutive with social structure and ideology. Not only are what people do and think constrained and enabled by existing social relations and ideologies, but their thoughts and actions help to produce social structures and ideologies. We should also stress that existing social structures comprise what Giddens terms the 'rules and resources'[43] that are both constitutive of and constituted by human activity. The contradictions thus provide the tension through which the dynamics of social life are set in motion. But it is the real people — teacher educators or preservice teachers, among others — who individually or collectively move themselves in the context of these contradictions in directions to either reproduce or transform existing social relations and ideologies.

Class, Race, and Gender Contradictions in Society and in Education

In this section we will discuss some of the major contradictions of class, race, and gender within the political economy (i.e., the society) and within education. In Chapters 2–6, this discussion will be drawn upon in identifying how such contradictions inform the thoughts and actions of teacher educators, preservice teachers and others involved in constructing the relations of teacher education, while concomitantly helping to mask (and thus mediate) or expose (and thus provide the basis to challenge) extant contradictory class, race, and gender relations.

Our concern here with class, race, and gender is not primarily about characteristics or background factors of individuals as 'independent variables'. Rather, the focus is on the structural phenomena of class, race, and gender *relations*, the dynamic through which groups are mutually implicated.

Class relations are conceived as 'the set of relationships between ... groups which centre on property, wealth, the employment relation and the labour market as a means of organising the society's production of resources and deciding their distribution'.[44] Conflict and struggle are seen as inherent in such relations. Within capitalist political economies, for instance, there is the fundamental contradiction that although production is a social activity, the ownership and control of the means of production is privately concentrated.[45] Also relevant is the contradiction that production takes place for profit accumulation by capitalists rather than to satisfy the needs of workers, who constitute the vast majority of people. Moreover, another contradiction arises because of the profit motive to reduce labor costs and increase productivity; this is that while many workers experience deskilling/proletarianization and thus became less expensive workers and more easily replaced by other humans or machines, a few workers undergo reskilling/professionalization as they can be seen to enhance the design or control of the work process.[46] Associated with this latter contradiction is another one between mental and manual forms of labor, that a few people are seen to engage in work of the mind, while the majority are viewed to engage in work of the hand, leg, back, etc.

In the context of schooling and teaching, these contradictions surface in a slightly different form. First, there is the contradiction that many educators teach, while a few occupy management positions. Second, although schooling may be provided for the masses, that available only on a selective basis is considered of higher status. Third, knowledge and skill with 'mental work' is contrasted with and given higher value than knowledge and skill associated with 'manual work.'

In terms of teachers' participation in class relations, teachers are in some sense members of the middle class(es). From a Weberian, status group perspective, they might be conceived as part of a buffer group, protecting the upper or dominant class(es) from challenges by the lower or subordinate class(es), either as examples of the 'open' contest system of status mobility or as more explicit agents of some control (via physical force or ideological transmission). Alternately, they might operate as activist intellectuals working with subordinate groups to bring about fundamental changes in schools and society. From a Marxist, class conflict perspective, the class location of teachers as intellectuals and situated in the middle class(es) is no less ambiguous and contradictory.[47] Within this viewpoint, teachers' economic functions are seen to include, to varying extent, aspects of both the global function of capital and the function of the collective labourer; thus, teachers share, in part, the class relational experience of both the bourgeoisie and the proletariat. Generally, similar to workers, teachers do not own or control the means of production (or even the means of 'educational production') and work for wages or salary. However, similar to the bourgeoisie, they live (some would argue barely) off the wealth created by productive workers and to some degree operate as managers/socializers of future workers.

This is not to suggest that we can somehow read educators' political stance from their economic class location.[76] The point is that public school or university teachers are intimately and complicatedly involved in class relations (in the context of the state), and, thus, questions of how they act and how they characterize their actions (e.g., in terms of curriculum knowledge, professionalism, or social mobility/reproduction) are important to examine for their political economic consequences.

Race or ethnic group relations pertain to the division of labor; the distribution of power, wealth, status; and residential and interaction patterns among groups that have come to be seen as 'physically' or 'culturally' different.[49] In racially stratified societies there is the fundamental contradiction that some groups are over-represented and other groups are under-represented in positions of wealth, status and power. Related to this as well as to issues of residential and other interaction patterns is the contradiction in society discussed by Schermerhorn[50] as *centripetal* versus *centrifugal* tendencies. These are tendencies, characteristic of group efforts and products of intergroup dynamics, that refer, respectively, to movement toward common institutional participation and lifestyles versus movement toward separate (horizontally or, more significantly, vertically related) structural positions and cultural attributes.

With respect to schooling and teaching, there is the contradiction that although a mass schooling system may be in operation, groups differ in their length of attendance, amount and status of knowledge received, and quality of facilities available. Similarly, there is the contradiction that despite schools being an 'equal opportunity' employer, teachers are not equally representative of respective adult or student populations across groups.[51] Also, educators from different groups vary in the holding of administrative positions and in the quality and status of the institutions in which they work.[52]

As with class relations, teachers occupy a contradictory role *vis-à-vis* race relations. Regardless of their own race or ethnicity, educators in public schools and universities, as agents of the state, may function as a buffer group, deflecting criticisms of and challenges to schools and society from dominated groups or they may act as a catalyst and become involved in struggle for social transformation.

We will follow Connell here in defining gender relations as the set of social relationships, including:

> ... the sexual division of labour, the power relations between men and women, ... institutions like the family, the social relations of child rearing, and the social movements and political struggles connected with issues such as sexual morality, the family, abortion rights, violence against women, [and political and economic participation and power].[53]

Within patriarchal societies, the fundamental contradiction is that although women normally constitute at least half of the population, political and economic power is concentrated in the hands of relatively few (elite) men. Related to this contradiction are the ideological notions that women 'belong' in the home, while men 'belong' in the public sphere, and that males specialize in emotional detachment required for authority positions, while females specialize in emotional engagement necessary for nurturant/caretaking positions.[54]

With respect to schooling and teaching, we should note the contradiction, which arose along with a mass education system in the United States, that although education (particularly at the primary level) is predominantly a 'feminine' pursuit, the vast majority of those who control the means and manage the process of educational production — school board members and educational administrators, respectively — are men.[55] Historically, the sexual division of labor enabled schools boards and administrators 'to maintain bureaucratic control of their employees and of the curriculum and teaching practices',[56] because 'the managerial aspects of education were removed from the job of teaching and the new solely managerial positions of principal and superintendent were created'.[57]

The connection of these developments with patriarchy and the ideology of domesticity was explicitly made by some of the Victorian era's leading proponents of women entering teaching — Catherine Beecher, Mary Lyon, Zilpah Grant, Horace Mann, and Henry Barnard, who argued that women, because of their 'natural' qualities of nurturance and patience, would be ideal teachers, but not managers; that teaching was an ideal preparation for women's most appropriate role, motherhood;[58] and that women would 'willingly' work for less money than men.[59] It is this historical context, as well as subsequent developments in education and in the political economy, which leads Acker to conclude that the 'sexual division of labor among teachers contributes to the reproduction of patriarchal and/or capitalist social order, especially in providing models to students of male/female relations'.[60]

As in the case of class relations, however, teachers' involvement in the gender relations of educational work is marked by contradictions. That is, educators may operate either to perpetuate and legitimate or to critique and challenge gender-based relations of domination and subordination. Moreover, educators confront the (stereotypically) gender-linked contradiction in the role of teacher: the 'opposing requirements' of emotional detachment and emotional engagement in relation to students as well as to their parents.

Organization of the Book and Research Methods

This section provides information about the data collection and data analysis procedures used in building the discussions in Chapters 2–6. A brief overview of the major theoretical and substantive points discussed in each of these chapters and the concluding one, Chapter 7, is also presented.

Chapter 2: Teacher Education in the United States:
A Critical Review of Historical Studies[61]

In this chapter, we will contrast evolutionary, functionalist and status competitive approaches to explaining developments in the history of teacher education in the U.S. with the approach adopted here focusing on structural and ideological contradictions in class and gender relations.[62] We will go on to analyze the discourse, organizational forms, and instructor and student characteristics associated with normal schools, teachers colleges, and college or university departments/ schools/colleges of education from the early nineteenth century through the late 1960s. The discussion is based on a critical review of an extensive bibliography of book, book chapter, and article accounts of time-period or institutional-type focused histories of teacher education as well as case studies of particular institutions. The content analysis of history of teacher education literature was undertaken using a set of procedures I normally follow in analyzing fieldnotes, printed matter artifacts, and interview data in ethnographic studies. Following Spradley,[63] domains of meaning were identified based on an initial reading of the teacher education histories. Quotes and other notes taken on these readings were then classified into one or more relevant domains. Elements in a given domain were then compared and contrasted, through procedures similar to Spradley's taxonomic and componential analyses, with other elements in the same and other domains. From this process more general themes were identified. Three major themes, derived from the content analysis of these texts, will be discussed: (1) normal schools and teachers colleges versus universities as contexts for teacher education programs, (2) education versus arts and science faculties in universities, and (3) curriculum responses to class and gender contradictions in teaching, schooling and society.

Chapter 3: On Producing a Competency-Based Teacher Education Program[64]

This chapter begins by elaborating theoretically on a major contradiction within (at least) capitalist societies: proletarianization versus professionalization. Using these concepts as a theoretical lense, we proceed to a contextualized case history of the development and initial implementation of a 'competency-based' teacher education (CBTE) program at the University of Houston between the mid-1960s and the late-1970s.

The descriptive account is based on an analysis of data collected through interviews and from documents identified with the assistance of interviewees. During January 1985, nine individuals, who had played key roles in supporting or critiquing the CBTE development process, were interviewed in depth about their perceptions and interpretations of events and activities in the College of Education during the relevant period. Two other informants, who were similarly involved, discussed the issues with one of the researchers during more informal conversations. Interviewees were either identified after pre-liminary examination of relevant documents or nominated by individuals who were interviewed initially. Respondents represented major groups within the College, including four of the five departments and those who were participant-supporters, participant-critics, non-participant-supporters, and non-participant-critics.

Tape-recorded interviews were semi-structured with open-ended questions. The questions were designed to elicit when respondents came to the University, if and when they were involved in concept-ualizing or implementing the CBTE program, and whom they viewed as key actors in these processes. Respondents were also asked to trace the key events and debates associated with the development of the CBTE program. They were also queried concerning other dynamics of relevance which occurred during the time period in the College, University, the City of Houston, the State of Texas, the United States, or the world. The interview data were analyzed employing an approach adopted from Spradley[65] in which domains, taxonomies and themes are identified.

A variety of documents were also examined. These included: meeting minutes, memos, institutional reports (e.g., to the National Council for the Accreditation of Teacher Education), reports to funding agencies, unpublished manuscripts on which presentations were based, published articles and books written by College faculty, and a mono-graph[66] based on research on CBTE at the University conducted during the mid-1970s by a German visiting scholar. These were reviewed initially to develop probes for the interviews and content analyzed subsequently to identify domains, taxonomies and themes which replicated or extended the analysis of the interview data.

The case history reveals a process oriented toward 'professionaliz-ing' school teaching as an occupation, while at the same time driven by a quest to accumulate what I term 'academic capital', the coin of the realm in universities. By analyzing the developments from a perspective focused on the labor process and relations of production, we are not only able to see how some faculty members profitted from the production of the program — they acquired significant amounts of academic (and financial) capital and became more professionalized. We are also able to note how others experienced a process similar to the proletarianizatiorn and deskilling of craft workers. We additionally examine the forms of resistance that emerged from the latter group of faculty and discuss the ideological and structural factors limiting such struggle.

An Ethnography of a Teacher Education Program

Chapters 4–6 are based on the analysis of data collected in conjunction with a longitudinal participant observation study conducted in the context of the secondary education certification component of the Professional Teacher Preparation Program at the University of Houston between September 1980 and May 1982. The secondary education certification program consisted of eighteen semester hours of coursework in the College of Education which was usually taken over a three-semester period. The first semester involved students in two, three-hour courses: (social, historical, philosophical, and psychological) 'Foundations of Education for Teaching' and 'Introduction to the Profession of Teaching'. During the Fall 1980 semester when the data collection began there were nine sections of the first course, which also contained students from the elementary and all-level (health, physical education, art, and music) certification components of the program, and three sections of the latter course. During the second semester of the program, secondary education students were normally enrolled in 'Generic Teaching Competencies', of which there was one section in the Spring 1981 semester, and 'The Structure and Process of Teaching', which was divided into sections according to students' major teaching area (e.g., social sciences, mathematics, science, English, foreign language). The final semester of the program consisted of a student-teaching assignment and a weekly student teaching 'seminar', which variably included class sessions for 100–150 students from secondary as well as elementary and all-level programs, smaller class sessions for all secondary education students only, and even smaller (more seminar-like) class sessions for subject-matter groups of secondary education students.

As a faculty member in this College of Education but with teaching responsibilities at the time including only graduate-level courses, I enrolled informally as a student in one section of the 'Introduction to the Teaching Profession' course during Fall 1980 and the only section of the 'Generic Teaching Competencies' course the second semester. Participation involved attending class sessions, doing reading and other class assignments, being involved in class discussions and exercises (including peer micro-lesson teaching), taking quizzes and exams, and accompanying students on school observation visits. Informal conversations were held periodically (primarily during breaks and before and after class) with individual and groups of students as well as instructors and guest speakers. During the student teaching phase of the program,

14

informal conversations continued. Participant observation, however, was limited to attending weekly student-teaching 'seminars'. Partly because of this more limited involvement in the students' experience and because some students with whom I had been attending class opted to skip a semester between the second and the final student-teaching phase of the program, I attended the 'seminars' during both Fall 1981 and Spring 1982 semesters.

Fieldnotes were compiled based on observations and informal conversations.[67] For the analyses presented in Chapters 4–6 fieldnotes, as well as assigned textbooks, other readings, and handouts, were carefully scanned for relevant entries.[68] Following an approach adopted from Spradley,[69] domain, taxonomic, componential and, finally, theme analyses were performed on these excerpts from the fieldnotes. I accumulated from my fieldnotes, textbooks, other readings and handouts, all material relevant to conceptions of curriculum, professionalism, and social mobility/reproduction.

In addition, individual tape-recorded interviews — focusing on a variety of topics[70] — were conducted with a sample of students enrolled in the course observed each semester. A random sample of ten students in the first semester class were interviewed at the beginning and eight of them were interviewed at the end of that semester. Due to dropout after the first semester, a new (second semester) interview sample was identified consisting of ten students: three of whom had been in the first semester sample, the only other five students from the first semester class (in which I observed) who continued in the program, and two students who had been in another section of the first semester course. All ten of these were interviewed at the end of the second semester.[71] Eight were interviewed after their student teaching experience and three after their first semester employed as a teacher. Interviewees have been given pseudonyms for purposes of presenting the data. The transcribed interview protocols were content-analyzed following an approach adapted from Spradley, identical to one employed with fieldnote and printed matter artifact data.[72]

Chapter 4: Conceptions of Curriculum and the Anticipatory Deskilling of Preservice Teachers[73]

One of the thematic areas derived from the ethnography is conceptions of curriculum. The chapter opens with a discussion of three of Berlak and Berlak's[74] curriculum dilemmas or contradictions: knowledge as given versus knowledge as problematical, public knowledge versus personal knowledge, and knowledge as molecular versus knowledge as holistic. After explaining these concepts in relation to other relevant work in curriculum theory, I employ them to explore the messages in the formal and hidden curriculum of the teacher education program studied. How preservice teachers' evolving conceptions of or orientations to curriculum knowledge interact with these messages is also analyzed. While not all students in the program could be so described, many of them can be seen as being anticipatorily deskilled, thus helping to mediate the deskilling/reskilling contradiction, especially as it is encountered by women. They were never really helped to develop curriculum decision-making skills nor oriented toward viewing such skills as integral to the teacher's role. Thus, it is argued, they may be less likely to resist the trend toward deskilling of teachers' work upon which Apple and others[75] have commented.

Chapter 5: Ideologically Informed Conceptions of Professionalism[76]

The chapter emphasizes the need to view professionalism as an ideology rather than as some objective or scientific construct that can be used to stratify occupations. The conceptions of professionalism held by preservice teachers are thus analyzed not only in relation to the messages about professionalism in the formal and hidden curriculum of the teacher education program, but also in relation to broader ideologies of professionalism.[77] Three major themes about professionalism are derived from the analysis of the ethnographic data: remuneration/service ideal, power, and individual attitude/behavior. These themes are illustrated and shown how the preservice teachers' differing conceptions of professionalism, and the related messages encountered in the program, can be seen to either mask, and thus mediate, or illuminate, and thus provide the basis for challenging, contradictions associated with class, race, and gender relations.

Chapter 6: Ideologically Informed Conceptions of Social Mobility and Social Reproduction[78]

Preservice teachers encounter one of the major contradictions in stratified societies in which the education system plays a prominent role in selecting, sorting, and credentialing future workers and citizens. This 'warming-up' versus 'cooling-out' contradiction[79] involves the dilemma that at almost every level of education some students must be motivated to achieve, while others need to be discouraged from seeking 'success', and both tendencies need to operate without significantly undermining the legitimacy of the system for either group of students or others in society. In this chapter, we investigate the ideologically informed conceptions of social mobility and social reproduction espoused by prospective teachers during the ethnographic study. The focus is on how these perspectives interact with the contradictory messages in the formal and hidden curriculum of the teacher preparation program. The future teachers' varying conceptions of social stratification and schooling are also shown to offer a foundation for masking, as well as illluminating, the warming-up versus cooling-out contradiction in capitalist, patriarchal and racially stratified societies.

Chapter 7: What Is To Be Done? Critical Praxis by Educators of Teachers

The final chapter provides a summary of the major findings from the research discussed in Chapters 2–6. This serves as the basis for revisiting the theoretical issues (reproduction, contradiction, and socialization) introduced in Chapter 1. In addition, the contemporary debates and reform proposals are reviewed in light of the insights derived from the historical and ethnographic research. I also outline goals and strategies that we as educators of teachers, whether we work in education or arts and sciences in universities, in schools or elsewhere, must consider seriously in terms of our programmatic efforts. Finally, I discuss how we can become involved as activist intellectuals in broader struggles for social transformation at the levels of the community, the nation and the world. That is, I sketch the strategies we might employ to construct a critical praxis, conjoining critical theory and practice, in teacher education. These strategies not only may help us to 'focus on those limitations which make a particular social formation ... seem inevitable',[80] but also to act individually and collectively to expose, challenge and transform unequal and contradictory class, gender and race relations.

Notes

1   Revised version of paper presented at the American Educational Research Association annual meeting, Washington, DC, April 20–24, 1987.

Sincere appreciation is expressed to Tessa Jo Shokri for word-processing this manuscript.

2 LYNCH, J and PLUNKETT, H., *Teacher Education and Cultural Change: England, France and West Germany* (London, Allen and Unwin, 1973), pp. 171 and 173.

3 Perhaps the report having the broadest circulation, *Nation At Risk: The Imperative for Educational Reform*, National Commission on Excellence in Education, (Washington, DC, US Department of Education, 1983), actually seems to echo many of the concerns expressed in the Green Paper in Britain in 1977, DEPARTMENT OF EDUCATION AND SCIENCE, *Education in Schools a Consultative Document* (London, HMSO). My use of the aquatic metaphor in this and subsequent sentences is a take-off on the *Nation At Risk's* references to the 'rising *tide* of mediocrity', but does not reflect my agreement with the terms of debate set out therein.

4 Some of the more widely discussed reform proposals are included in CARNEGIE TASK FORCE ON TEACHING AS A PROFESSION, *A Nation Prepared: Teachers for the 21st Century* (Hyattsville, MD, Carnegie Forum on Education and Economy, 1986); HOLMES GROUP, *Tomorrow's Teachers: A Report of the Holmes Group* (East Lansing, MI, Holmes Group, Inc., 1986); NATIONAL COMMISSION FOR EXCELLENCE IN TEACHER EDUCATION, *A Call for Change in Teacher Education* (Washington, DC, NCETE, 1985); NATIONAL CONSORTIUM FOR EDUCATIONAL EXCELLENCE, *An Agenda for Educational Research*: *A View from the Firing Line* (Nashville, TN, Vanderbilt University, 1985).

5 For example, see APPLE, M., *Ideology and Curriculum* (Boston, Routledge and Kegan Paul, 1979); BERNSTEIN, B., 'On the classification and framing of educational knowledge', in *Class, Codes and Control* (London, Routledge and Kegan Paul, 1975), pp. 85–115; BOURDIEU, P. and PASSERON, J. C., 'Reproduction' in *Education, Society and Culture* (Beverly Hills, Sage, 1977); BOWLES, S. and GINTIS, H., *Schooling in Capitalist America* (Boston, Routledge and Kegan Paul, 1976); GIROUX, H., *Ideology, Culture and the Process of Schooling* (Philadelphia, Temple University Press, 1981); YOUNG M. (Ed.), 'An approach to the study of curricula as socially organized knowledge', in *Knowledge and Control* (London, Collier-Macmillan, 1971), pp. 19–46.

6 For example, see CONNELL, R., *Teachers' Work* (Sydney, Allen and Unwin, 1985); GRACE, G., *Teachers, Ideology and Control* (London, Routledge and Kegan Paul, 1978); SHARP, R. and GREEN, A., *Education and Social Control* (London, Routledge and Kegan Paul, 1975).

7 See EVERHART, R., *Reading, Writing and Resistance* (Boston, Routledge and Kegan Paul, 1983); LONDON, H., *Culture of a Community College* (New York, Praeger, 1978); MCLAREN, P., *Schooling as Ritual Performance* (Boston, Routledge and Kegan Paul, 1986); WEIS, L., *Between Two Worlds: Black Students in an Urban Community College* (Boston, Routledge and Kegan Paul, 1985); WILLIS, P., *Learning to Labour* (London, Saxon House, 1977).

8 SALTER, B. and TAPPER, T., *Education, Politics and the State* (London, Grant McIntyre, 1981), p. 76.

9   See LORTIE, D., *School Teacher: A Sociological Analysis* (Chicago, University of Chicago Press, 1975); MARDLE, G. and WALKER, M., 'Strategies and structure: Some critical notes on teacher socialization', in WOODS, P. (Ed.) *Teacher Strategies*, (London, Croom Helm, 1980).

10 See Bourdieu and Passeron, p. 32; Bowles and Gintis, p. 36; GREENE, M., 'The matter of mystification: Teacher education in unquiet times', in *Landscapes of Learning* (New York: Teachers College Press, 1978), pp. 53–73; HARNETT, A. and NAISH, M., 'Technicians or social bandits? Some moral and political issues in the education of teachers', in WOODS, P. (Ed.) *Teacher Strategies* (London, Croom Helm, 1980), pp. 254–73; POPKEWITZ, T. 'Ideology and social formation in teacher education', in *Critical Studies in Teacher Education: Its Folklore, Theory and Practice* (Lewes, Falmer Press, 1986).

11 POPKEWITZ, T., TABACHNICK, R., and ZEICHNER, K., 'Dulling the senses: Research in teacher education', *Journal of Teacher Education* 30 (1979), p. 58.

12 GIROUX, H., 'Teacher education and the ideology of social control', in *Ideology, Culture and the Process of Schooling* (Philadelphia, Temple University Press, 1981), p. 143.

13 See GEERTZ, C., 'Thick descriptions: Toward an interpretive theory of culture', in *Interpretations of Cultures* (New York, Basic Books, 1973).

14 J. Lynch and H. Plunkett, p. 62.

15 Bowles and Gintis.

16 See, for example, ANYON, J., 'Intersections of gender and class: Accommodations and resistance by working class and affluent females to contradictory sex roles', in BARTON, L. and WALKER, S. *Gender, Class and Education* (Lewes, Falmer Press, 1983), pp. 19–38; APPLE, M., *Education and Power* (Boston, Routledge and Kegan Paul, 1982); APPLE, M. and WEIS, L. (Eds.) *Ideology and Practice in Schooling* (Philadelphia, Temple University Press, 1983); BERLAK, A. and BERLAK, H., *Dilemmas of Schooling: Teaching and Social Change* (New York, Methuen, 1981); GINSBURG, M. and ARIAS-GODINEZ, B., 'Nonformal education and social reproduction/transformation: Educational radio in Mexico', *Comparative Education Review* 28 (1984), pp. 116–27; GINSBURG, M. and GILES, J., 'Sponsored and contest modes of social reproduction in selective community college programs', *Research in Higher Education* 21 (1984), pp. 281–99; KARABEL, J. and HALSEY, A., 'Educational research: A review and interpretation', in *Power and Ideology in Education* (New York, Oxford University Press, 1977), pp. 1–86; MALMSTAD, B., GINSBURG, M., and CROFT, J., 'The social construction of reading lessons: Resistance and reproduction', *Journal of Education* 165 (Fall, 1983), pp. 359–74; WILLIS, P., 'Cultural production is different from cultural reproduction is different from social reproduction is different from reproduction', *Interchange* 12 (1981), pp. 48–67.

17 GIDDENS, A., *Central Problems in Social Theory: Action, Structure and Contradictions in Social Theory* (Berkeley, University of California Press, 1979).

18 *Ibid.*, p. 114.

19   APPLE, M., 'Reproduction and contradiction in education: An introduction', in *Cultural and Economic Reproduction in Education: Essays on Class, Ideology and the State* (Boston, Routledge and Kegan Paul, 1982), p. 8.
20   GINTIS, H. and BOWLES, S., 'Contradiction and reproduction in educational theory', in BARTON, L., MEIGHAN, R., and WALKER, S. (Eds.) *Schooling, Ideology and the Curriculum*, (Lewes, Falmer Press, 1980), p. 53.
21   But see ANYON, J., 'Social class and school knowledge', *Curriculum Inquiry* 11 (1981), pp. 3–42; CARNOY, M., 'Education, economy and the state', in APPLE, M. (Ed.) *Cultural and Economic Reproduction in Education*, (Boston, Routledge and Kegan Paul, 1982); MCNEIL, L., *Contradictions of Control: School Structure and School Knowledge* (Boston, Routledge and Kegan Paul, 1986); WEXLER, P., 'Educational change and social contradiction: An example', *Comparative Education Review* 23 (1979), pp. 240–55.
22   JAMESON, F., *The Political Unconscious* (Ithaca, New York, Cornell University Press, 1981), p. 94.
23   MAO TSE-TUNG, *Selected Readings from the Works of Mao Tse-Tung* (Peking, Foreign Language Press, 1971), p. 85.
24   *Ibid.*, p. 91.
25   *Ibid.*, p. 96.
26   *Ibid.*, p. 96.
27   BERNSTEIN, B., 'Aspects of the relation between education and reproduction', in *Class, Codes and Control, Volume 3: Towards a Theory of Educational Transmissions* (London, Routledge and Kegan Paul, 1975).
28   CARTER, M. 'Contradictions and correspondence: Analysis of relations of schooling to work', in CARNOY, M. and LEVIN, H. (Eds.) *The Limits of Educational Reform*, (New York, Longman, 1976), p. 59.
29   *Ibid.*, p. 54.
30   *Ibid.*, p. 59.
31   This is not to argue that educational or political economic structures are solely or primarily reproduced or challenged by dynamics at the ideological level. I am not positing an idealist notion that if we just altered people's ways of thinking and talking, a classless, as well as race- and gender-equal society would appear. Certainly, individual and collective human action is shaped by material reality and the extant political economic distribution of wealth and power. This is only to claim that the ideologies of social mobility/reproduction, professionalism, and curriculum warrant attention as a source support for unequal and unjust social relations. This conception of ideology is consonant with that of Jameson (p. 52), who argues that a Marxian theory of ideology is not 'one of false consciousness, but rather one of structural limitation and ideological closure.' Jameson illustrates his point by referring to Marx's discussion about petit-bourgeoisie intellectuals, who 'in their own minds ... cannot get beyond the limits' of the petit-bourgeoisie class location and, thus, are 'driven theoretically to the same problems and solutions to which material interest and social position drive' the petit-bourgeoisie. See MARX, K., *The Eighteenth Brumaire of Louis Bonapart* (New York, International Publishers, 1963), pp. 50–51.
32   Elsewhere, in collaboration with colleagues, I have developed the notion

of passive versus active models of occupational socialization. See LEC-
OMPTE, M. and GINSBURG, M., 'How students learn to become teachers:
An explanation of alternative responses to a teacher training program', in
NOBLIT, G. and PINK, W. (Eds.) *Schooling in Social Context: Qualitative
Studies*, (Norwood, NJ, Ablex, 1987), pp. 3–22; SPATIG, L., GINSBURG,
M. and LIBERMAN, D., 'Ego development as an explanation of passive and
active models of teacher socialization', *College Student Journal* 16 (1982),
pp. 315–25. For other useful treatments of teacher socialization, see
LACEY, C., *The Socialization of Teachers* (London, Methuen, 1977); Mardle
and Walker; Popkewitz, Tabachnick, and Zeichner.

33 Oleson and Whittaker observe that 'sociologists concerned with professional socialization [often use] concepts suffused with implicit [determin-
istic] models from childhood socialization'; see OLESON, V. and
WHITTAKER, E., *The Silent Dialogue: A Study of the Social Psychology of
Professional Education* (San Francisco, Jossey-Bass, 1968), p. 89. This has
occurred despite the fact that some studies of childhood socialization have
raised questions about the validity of the images of the child as an empty
vessel, a passive agent and of the process as a 'one-way, parent-to-child',
form in influence; see LEWIS, J. and ROSENBAUM, L., *The Effects of Infant
on Its Caregiver* (New York, Wiley, 1974).

34 BRIM, O. and WHEELER, S., *Socialization After Childhood* (New York,
Wiley, 1966), p. 5.

35 MERTON, R., READER, G., and KENDALL, P., *The Student Physician:
Introductory Studies in the Sociology of Medical Education* (Cambridge, MA,
Harvard University Press, 1957), pp. 40–41.

36 EDDY, E., *Becoming a Teacher: The Passage to Professional Status* (New York,
Teachers College Press, 1969), p. vi.

37 See WRONG, D., 'The over-socialized conception of man in modern
sociology', *American Sociological Review* 26 (1961), pp. 183–93.

38 REINHARZ, S., *On Becoming a Social Scientist* (San Francisco, Jossey-Bass,
1979), p. 374.

39 BUCHER, R. and STELLING, J., *Becoming Professional* (Beverly Hills, Sage,
1977), p. 134.

40 Oleson and Whittaker, p. 208.

41 See BARTHOLOMEW, J. 'Schooling teachers: The myth of the liberal
college', in WHITTY, G. and YOUNG, M. (Eds.) *Explorations of the Politics of
School Knowledge*, (Nafferton, Driffield, England, Nafferton Books, 1976),
pp. 114–24; DALE, R., 'Implications of the rediscovery of the hidden
curriculum for the sociology of teaching', in GLEESON, D. (Nafferton,
Driffield, England, Nafferton Books, 1977), pp. 44–54; Mardle and
Walker.

42 GIDDENS, A., *Central Problems in Social Theory*.

43 *Ibid.*

44 Connell, p. 8.

45 That this is increasingly true in the United States is indicated by a 1986
report of the Joint Economic Committee of Congress. As reported in the
Houston Chronicle (Saturday, July 26, 1986, Section 1, Page 1), in 1983,
'The "super rich" — the top one-half of 1 per cent of the population —

held 35.1 per cent of the nation's wealth [compared to 25.4 per cent in 1963] ... The super rich also controlled most of the nation's business assets: ... 58 per cent of the unincorporated businesses and 46.5 per cent of corporate stock, owned by individuals, [and] ... 62 per cent of state and local bonds'.

46 See BRAVERMAN, H., *Labor and Monopoly Capital: The Degradation of Work in the Twentieth Century* (New York, Monthly Review Press, 1974); Carter. For further discussion of proletarianization and professionalization of teacher educators and of the ideologies associated with these dynamics, see Chapters 3 and 5.

47 See CARCHEDI, G., 'On the economic identification of the new middle classes', *Economy and Society*, 4 (1975), pp. 361–417; HARRIS, K., *Teachers and Classes: A Marxist Analysis* (London: Routledge and Kegan Paul, 1982); JOHNSON, T., 'What is to be known: The structural determinism of social class', *Economy and Society*, 6(2) (1977), pp. 194–233; NADEL, S., *Contemporary Capitalism and the Middle Classes* (New York: International Publishers, 1982); POULANTZAS, N., *Classes in Contemporary Capitalism* (London: New Left Review Books, 1975); SARUP, M., *Marxism/Structuralism/Education* (Lewes: Falmer Press, 1984); WRIGHT, E., 'Intellectuals and the class structure of capitalist society', in WALKER, P. (Ed.) *Between Labor and Capital*, (Boston: South End Press, 1979), pp. 191–212.

48 Connell (p. 15) appropriately criticizes those who engage in 'the trigonometrical excerises of calculating a "location" on an *a priori* set of theoretical axes, and reading off the political consequences'. I concur that examining the class location or economic functions of teachers does not lead to an unambiguous determination of what role they will take in the class struggle (see also Sarup, p. 117). However, if we juxtapose teachers' class position with their role as intellectuals, having a special connection to producing and reproducing ideas (and thus ideologies), we can discern more clearly to what extent teachers' actions can be shaped by (hegemonic or counter-hegemonic) ideologies. Regardless of whether one concurs that dominant ideologies primarily function to consolidate the capitalist class (see for example, ABERCROMBIE, N., HILL, S., and TURNER, B., *The Dominant Ideology Thesis* [London, Allen & Unwin, 1980] and 'The domination ideology thesis', *British Journal of Sociology* 29(2) (1978), pp. 149–70), or that such ideologies have their most important impact in fostering acceptance of the status quo among the proletariat (see for example, ROOTES, C., 'The dominant ideology thesis and its critics', *Sociology*, 15(3) (1981), pp. 436–44, it seems very clear that dominant ideologies (even with their contradictory nature) are crucial to understanding the thoughts and actions of the middle class(es), and particularly intellectuals such as teachers. Not only do teachers constantly work with ideas, but given their contradictory economic functions, ideologies are especially important in shaping their current and future action. If their economic position was more clearly constructed, ideologies could serve primarily to reinforce this position, even if the position was antithetical to their interests. With an ambiguous economic class position, teachers and others in the middle class(es) have less strong structural constraints on

their consciousness and action and, thus, ideology may have more of an influence in swaying them toward coalitions with either the bourgeoisie or the proletariat.

49 I am combining two concepts, race and ethnicity, that could perhaps more adequately be dealt with separately. The biological or genetic concept of race focuses on inherited physical characteristics, while the concept of ethnicity deals with cultural characteristics of language, customs, beliefs, and traditions. In combining race and ethnicity here I am merely wanting to emphasize that physical and/or cultural characteristics may serve as the basis for typifications of 'differences', and thus form the boundaries of a group in relation to other groups.

50 SCHERMERHORN, R., *Comparative Ethnic Relations* (New York, Random House, 1970). A series of case studies on educational policy issues built on Schermerhorn's conceptualization is offered in LABELLE, T. and HAWKINS, J., *Education and Intergroup Relations: An International Perspective* (New York, Praeger, 1985).

51 See RICHARDS, C. and ENCARNATION, D., 'Race and educational employment', Institute for Research on Educational Finance and Governance Project Report No. 82–A46 (School of Education, Stanford University, December, 1982).

52 For example, see RODMAN, B. 'For women and minorities, the path to leadership is strewn with hurdles', *Education Week*, 10 June 1987, pp. 16–7. EQUAL EMPLOYMENT OPPORTUNITY COMMISSION, *Job Patterns of Minorities and Women in Public Elementary and Secondary Schools*, Research Report No. 51 (Washington, DC, US Government Printing Office, 1976).

53 Connell, pp. 8–9.

54 See Connell; HOCHSCHILD, A., *The Managed Heart: Commercialization of Human Feeling* (Berkeley, University of California Press, 1983).

55 See ACKER, S., 'Women and teaching: A semi-detached sociology of a semi-profession', in WALKER, S. and BARTON, L. (Eds.) *Gender, Class and Education*, (Lewes, Falmer Press, 1983), pp. 123–39; APPLE, M., 'Teaching and "women's work": A comparative historical and ideological analysis', in GUMBERT, E. (Ed.) *Expressions of Power in Education*, (Atlanta, Center for Cross-Cultural Education, Georgia State University, 1984), pp. 24–49; EQUAL EMPLOYMENT OPPORTUNITY COMMISSION, *Job Patterns of Minorities and Women in Public Elementary and Secondary Schools*: RODMAN, B. 'For women and minorities...', SCHMUCK, P., 'Differentiation by sex in educational professions', in STOCKARD, J., SCHMUCK, P., KEMPNER, K., WILLIAMS, P., EDSON, S., and SMITH, M. (Eds.) *Sex Equity in Education*, (New York, Academic Press, 1980), pp. 79–97; STROBER, M. and TYACK, D., 'Why do women teach and men manage?', *Signs* 3 (1980), pp. 494–503.

56 Apple, 'Teaching and "women's work",' p. 37.

57 Strober and Tyack, p. 499.

58 In this regard, it is interesting to note the following links between class position, individualism, patriarchy and professionalism: 'Even the virtual confinement of nineteenth century married middle class women to the

home was seen as a consequence of individual choice: such women merely chose to develop their special gifts and sensitivities in the professionalization of domesticity' (S. ACKER, p. 132).

59 Apple, 'Teaching and "women's work",' p. 36; Strober and Tyack, p. 496.

60 Acker, p. 134

61 This chapter was developed from GINSBURG, M., 'Teacher education and class and gender relations: A critical review of historical studies', *Educational Foundations* 2 (1987), p. 4–36. This is a revised version of a paper presented at the American Educational Research Association annual meeting, Pittsburgh, 29 October - 2 November, 1986.

62 See discussion in Chapter 2 regarding the absent presence of race in most histories of teacher education, and thus contradictions in race relations are not scrutinized in this review of historical studies of teacher education.

63 SPRADLEY, J., *Participant Observation* (New York, Holt, 1980).

64 Chapter 3 is a revised version of GINSBURG, M. and SPATIG, L., 'Proletarianization of the professoriate: The case of producing a competency-based teacher education program', paper at the annual meeting of the American Educational Research Association, 31 March–4 April, 1985.

65 SPRADLEY, J., *The Ethnographic Interview* (New York, Holt, 1979).

66 VOGEL, D., *Professional Teacher Preparation Program of the [University of Houston] College of Education* (Bielefield, Germany, Institut fur Didaktik der Mathematik de Universitat Bielefield, 1978).

67 For useful treatments of ethnographic research methodology, see BOGDAN, R. and BIKLEN, S., *Qualitative Research for Education* (Boston, Allyn and Bacon, 1982); GOETZ, J. and LECOMPTE, M., *Qualitative Design in Educational Research and Evaluation* (New York, Academic Press, 1984).

68 The specific domains used in the analysis of fieldnotes, printed matter artifacts, and interviews are discussed in Chapters 4–6.

69 Spradley, 1980.

70 Details about the topics raised during interviews are presented in Chapters 4–6. For a systematic treatment of interview research procedures, see GORDEN, R., *Interviewing: Strategies, Techniques, and Tactics* (Homewood, IL, Dorsey Press, 1985).

71 Given the alterations in what was originally a randomly sampled group of respondents, it may be useful to note how those interviewed compared with the population of students in the two cohorts of students in the secondary education programs whom we surveyed by administering an 'Autobiographical Information' form as well as semesterly questionnaires. As can be seen in Table 1, the students in the secondary education program whom we interviewed are remarkably similar to the overall student population in the program with respect to sex, age, marital status, race, mother's education, and father's education. The one noticeable exception to this point is that the second semester interview sample contains fewer single individuals (20 per cent versus 52.6 per cent) than overall student population.

72 See Spradley, 1979.

Table 1:   *Comparison of Interview Samples and Population of Secondary Teacher Education Students on Selected Background Variables*

Variable	Population (N = 76)	First Semester Sample (N = 10)	Second Semester Sample (N = 10)
SEX (% Female)	75	80	70
AGE (X years)	25	25.6	25.7
MARITAL STATUS			
(% single)	52.6	50	20
RACE (% white)	85.3	50	70
MOTHER'S EDUCATION			
(X years)	13.2	12.3	11.9
FATHER'S EDUCATION			
(X years)	14	13.3	12.8

73   This chapter is a revision of GINSBURG, M., 'Reproduction, contradictions, and conceptions of curriculum in preservice teacher education', *Curriculum Inquiry* 16 (1986), pp. 283–309.

74   Berlak and Berlak, *Dilemmas of Schooling.*

75   For example, see APPLE, M., 'Curricular form and the logic of technical control', in APPLE, M. and WEIS, L. (Eds.) *Ideology and Practice in Schooling*, (Philadelphia, Temple University Press, 1983); BUSWELL, C., 'Pedagogic change and social change', *British Journal of Sociology of Education* 1 (1980), pp. 293–306.

76   This chapter is developed from two manuscripts: GINSBURG, M., 'Reproduction, contradiction and conceptions of professionalism: The case of preservice teachers', in POPKEWITZ, T. (Ed.) *Critical Studies in Teacher Education: Its Folklore, Theory and Practice*, (Lewes, Falmer Press, 1986) and GINSBURG, M., 'Reproduction and contradictions in preservice teachers' encounters with professionalism', paper presented at the American Educational Research Association annual meeting, New Orleans, 23–27 April, 1984.

77   See LARSON, M., *The Rise of Professionalism* (Berkeley, University of California Press, 1977).

78   This chapter is revised from GINSBURG, M., 'Teacher education and ideologies of social mobility and social reproduction', paper presented at the American Educational Studies Association annual meeting, Atlanta, 6–9 November, 1985. A discussion of some of the issues contained herein, based on early phases of the fieldwork, is presented in GINSBURG, M. and NEWMAN, K., 'Social inequalities, schooling and teacher education', *Journal of Teacher Education* 36 (1985), pp. 49–54.

79   On the issues of 'warming-up' and 'cooling-out', see HOPPER, E., *Social Mobility: A Study of Control and Insatiability* (Oxford, Basil Blackwell, 1981).

80   BARNETT, S. and SILVERMAN, M., *Ideology and Everyday Life* (Ann Arbor, University of Michigan, 1979), p. 22.

Chapter 2

Teacher Education in the United States:
A Critical Review of Historical Studies[1]

Teacher educators vary in their sensitivity to underlying forces
which move society. Yet inevitably they reflect these forces, and
their thoughts [and actions] must be judged accordingly.[2]

Introduction

In this chapter, we explore the relationship between the development of
institutionalized forms of teacher preparation and broader social forces,
notably unequal social class and gender relations characteristic of a
capitalist and patriarchal society, the United States.[3] By examining this
relationship from a critical historical perspective, we should have a
clearer conception of the historical context within which the analyses in
Chapters 3, 4, 5, and 6 can be located. Moreover, we should be in a
position to comprehend more fully some of the broader ideological and
structural phenomena connected with the current 'debates' about the
proposed 'reforms' of teacher education (see discussion in Chapters 1
and 7). This should help us to see what, at another level, the contemporary discourse concerning teacher education is also about.

Approaches in the History of Teacher Education

Traditional histories of teacher education, like traditional histories of
schooling, have tended to stress an evolutionary, functionalist perspective. Normal schools, teachers colleges, and university departments/

colleges/schools of education all emerged, it is argued, when there was a need for their contribution, and they changed over time as the need shifted. From this perspective, people were involved in this process but primarily in terms of enacting a script. For example, it is said that normal schools were created because there was a need for teachers for the common schools, which in turn had been developed to meet the 'needs' of an evolving society. As Beggs describes it:

> As capitalism, the industrial revolution, the inroads of scientific inquiry, and the resurgence of learning of all kinds gradually altered the structure of Western society, formal education came to be recognized as one of the basic ingredients *necessary* to the successful operation of the complicated cultural machinery. ... [This notion was] paralleled with a new interest in the process of training teachers for the schools.[4]

Similarly, it has been argued that the 'normal school, by a *natural evolutionary process*, adapted itself to changing economic and social situations'.[5] That is, according to Pangburn:

> While the schools under conditions of local control were slowly adapting themselves to meet the *needs* of [industrial] society, the teacher training institutions were reorganizing to meet the *needs* of the schools.[6]

There are at least two problems with this evolutionary, functionalist approach to teacher education history. The first is that society is treated as unproblematic; it is seen to have evolved naturally into a formation characterized by consensus and a mutually beneficial association of all or most of its members. The second problem with the evolutionary, functionalist approach is the lack of attention to social struggle, resistance and contestation. There is, as noted above, a view of people's involvement in the process, but usually it is a role that is 'given' and thus they do what needs to be done. It is as if there is only one need or problem to address and there is only one mutually agreed upon course to follow, and someone merely has to volunteer to lead in that direction.

This consensual assumption may appear to be challenged by the centrality of the concepts of professionalism and professionalization in the history of teacher education literature. For instance, Herbst discusses his analysis of the development of teacher training in Wisconsin as involving a struggle between common school educational leaders and the general population of tax-paying worker/citizens:

The former wanted to create single-purpose institutions for training a corps of professionals; the latter desired practical and inexpensive opportunities for their sons and daughters to acquire post-elementary education.[7]

However, most of the time professionalization has been treated as an evolutionary process in itself, one that is not only compatible with the general evolution of society, but also functions in the best interests of all members of society. This evolutionary notion is evidenced in one of the factors Snarr cites as leading to the transformation of university departments of education into university schools/colleges of education: 'recognition by the ... universities of teaching as a profession analogous to other professions'.[8] The same unproblematic, evolutionary conception of professionalization is contained in Pangburn's discussion of the metamorphosis from normal schools to teachers colleges:

> The changes incident to the transformation of the normal schools into teachers colleges reveal ... the growing realization that the educational practitioner has a need of prolonged, highly specialized technical preparation for his professional career.[9]

Making teaching a profession was the 'battle cry' for many of the actors in the efforts to institute and then develop formal programs for the preparation of teachers. As Borrowman reports:

> The word 'professional' became the symbol of the new gospel, and the need to make teaching a 'true profession' was invariably cited as one of the prime reasons for the normal school movement.[10]

Johnson and Johanningmeier also make reference to the fact that the 'by now obvious requirement of professionalization in the teaching force was to be focused primarily on the normal school'.[11] The professionalization banner was also unfurled by those developing teacher education in the context of universities. For instance, James Earl Russell, who served as the first dean of Teachers College, Columbia University (1897–1927), built his case for university preparation of school teachers, explaining that 'teachers capable of such service [in schools] would be truly professional workers and would take their place alongside professional experts in law, medicine, and engineering'.[12] Moreover, professionalization efforts within universities were often viewed more favorably than similarly labeled efforts in normal schools. William H.

Payne, who was appointed in 1879 to the first US university pro-fessorship in education at the University of Michigan:

> ... contended that normal schools' stress on 'mechanical exactness and expertness' produced a 'machine' rather than teachers of 'freedom and versatility'. ... True professionals were taught to do by knowing. Only quacks professed dogma that one learned to do by doing. [13]

This last point signals another approach to explaining the develop-ment of teacher education in the United States. This approach focuses on status competition between what Borrowman[14] terms proponents of the 'technical' and the 'liberal' in teacher education. The competition was played out by normal school people and university people, respectively, but also took place in universities between education faculty and arts/science faculty, respectively.[15] A similar dynamic appears to operate within colleges of education, involving curriculum and instruction faculty and foundations of education faculty.[16]

Such competitive relations, however, do not occur in isolation or within some political, economic and ideological vacuum. And it is not sufficient to fill the vacuum with some notion of the ambiguity or uncertainty of education as an academic field of study or as a profession as Johnson and Johanningmeier or Powell do,[17] for this is but another version of the professionalization approach. Rather, what is needed is an approach to studying the history of teacher education that system-atically takes into account broader social, structural and ideological phenomena. Institutional arrangements and curricular programs for the formal preparation for teachers do change over time, and status competition and professionalization projects[18] are salient dimensions of these processes. But such dynamics are related to structural and ideological features of society.

The thesis here, though, assumes a more complex dynamic than is suggested in Lanier and Little that 'variables associated with ... the larger society are *simply mirrored* in ... colleges and departments of education'.[19] As discussed in Chapter 1, the concept of contradiction will be employed in our analysis in order to avoid such an overly-deterministic 'correspondence theory' approach.[20] Thus, we will focus on how contradictions in class and gender relations have informed the thought and action of those involved in construction of teacher education practice, while such ideas and actions have served to mask and thus mediate or to expose and thus challenge the contradictions imbedded within unequal class and gender relations. (See Chapter 1 for details on the theoretical issues involved.)

Analysis of Histories of Teacher Education

The discussion below is based on a critical analysis of a wide range of historical studies of teacher education. It is organized around three interrelated themes derived from that analysis. (See Chapter 1 for details on research procedures.) The first two can be termed: (1) normal schools and teachers colleges versus universities and (2) education versus arts/sciences faculties in universities. Implicit in these themes is a sense of competition or conflict and a concern about professionalization. However, I intend to demonstrate that the competition/conflict and professionalization dynamics reflected in these themes must be understood (at least in part) in terms of their connection to contradictions in unequal class and gender relations. The final theme to be explored is: (3) curriculum responses in teacher education to class contradictions and to gender contradictions.

An overview of the history of institutionalized forms of teacher preparation may be helpful to place subsequent discussion in perspective. The first teacher training institution in the United States evolved in 1821 from the Troy (New York) Female Seminary (founded by Emma Willard in 1814), although, most historians cite the academy Samuel R. Hall opened in 1823 in Concord, Vermont.[21] The first private 'normal school' was opened by James Carter in Lancaster, Massachusetts, in 1827, with the first public (i.e., state-funded) normal schools, institutions created solely for training teachers, began operating as of 1839 at Lexington, as well as Barre, Massachusetts. The first 'collegiate-level' department of education was created at Washington College in Pennsylvania in 1831.[22] Departments of 'normal instruction' were approved initially at the University of Missouri (1846), University of Wisconsin (1849), and the University of Iowa (1855),[23] though the departments of education at the University of Iowa (1873) and the University of Michigan (1879) are more often cited as the beginnings of university-level instruction in education. Between 1899 and 1929, normal schools were transformed into teachers colleges (and later into state colleges/universities) and, during a similar period (1905–1930), university departments of education underwent a metamorphosis, emerging as schools/colleges of education.[24]

Normals/Teachers Colleges Versus Universities

Although some, e.g., J.P. Harrison (in 1836), initially proposed 'normal schools ... for the instruction of men',[25] normals almost from their origins became female-dominated institutions, especially in terms of their student population,[26] if not with respect to faculty.[27] In contrast, university students have until recently been predominantly male, and men remain in the majority as professors.

The feminization of normal schools, in part, reflects the feminization of (particularly elementary) school teaching. With the expansion of the public school system, women increasingly entered the field of teaching. Because of greater restrictions on their educational and career options, women (compared to men) not only could be recruited for less pay and with fewer demands for authority, but also could be induced into pursuing normal school training in connection with an occupation with such relatively low status, power and remuneration.[28]

There was a voluntary aspect to this recruitment for 'exploitation', in that young women could, by pursuing work as a teacher, escape their greater subordination in the home. However, despite this liberatory moment, women were really invited into a hierarchical career modeled on the patriarchal structure of the family. A way had been found 'to advance women into the public sphere without disturbing the dominance of patriarchal authority'.[29] Ideas attributed to Horace Mann and Calvin Stowe, key figures in the normal school movement, reinforce this point. Mann is said to have preferred public normal schools over private seminaries because the former would 'assure that men would have charge of educating women teachers'[30] and Stowe 'thought that bringing women into teaching might deflect feminist urges to speak at public meetings and hold elective office'.[31]

University and normal school students were also different in terms of social class background. Normal school training in the early years was linked with positions in the common elementary schools. Given the pay, working conditions, and status of such work,[32] it is not surprising that normalites (compared to university students) more often came from 'modest social backgrounds'[33] or 'lower economic and social classes'[34] and had more limited educational and occupational opportunities.[35] Compared to universities, 'normal schools ... never attracted students in any numbers from the wealthy and professional classes' and that normal school students decreasingly came even from the 'middling social class of self-sufficient farmers and mechanics', while increasingly they were 'sons and daughters of hostlers, teamsters, sailors and gate-tenders'.[36] Similar inter-institutional comparisons have been made of the class composition of teachers colleges versus state or private universities.[37]

Thus, the student populations of normal schools/teachers colleges versus universities can be seen as stratified along gender and social class dimensions. Moreover, class and gender relations also entered into the antagonisms and competition between these sets of institutions. This occurred both explicitly and implicitly, through the theme of liberal versus technical education for teachers, during the two major phases of the relationships between these sets of institutions. At first normal schools rushed into the scene to provide formal preparation for common elementary school teachers — a scene that universities generally ignored or disdained.[38] The second phase, beginning in about 1890, involved more frequently a head-to-head competition to recruit and prepare secondary school teachers.[39]

Some viewed the move by normals to train secondary school teachers as a move on their part to abandon or de-emphasize the preparation of elementary teachers.[40] While perhaps true, we should note that normal schools initially undertook training teachers for the expanding high school system because universities were seen not to be sufficiently discharging this responsibility.[41] Nevertheless, although some more 'elite' universities looked askance on preparing any level of school teachers, preferring instead to focus on the training of administrators or developing a science of education,[42] many universities did become involved in educating high school teachers.[43]

The competition between normal schools/teachers colleges and universities in programs to prepare high school teachers was governed partly by quests for enrollment and funds, either state allocations or private philanthropy.[44] For example, the University of Illinois' relations with the normal schools/teachers colleges in that state were thus characterized:

> An interesting brand of academic imperialism thus resulted from [University of Illinois College of Education's Dean Thomas Elliott] Benner's tendency to argue that the College [of Education] ought to be enlarged in order to prevent the old normal schools — now teachers' colleges — from enlarging themselves.[45]

In the context of this competition, the normals tended to be 'suspicious and narrowly defensive' and the universities were 'frequently maddeningly condescending'.[46] Often normals were 'held in contempt' by the universities.[47] This can be explained in terms of normals' association with the common elementary schools[48] and the not unrelated differences in the social class and gender compositions of their student bodies.[49]

In terms of class relations, Mattingly discusses how Henry Barnard worked to establish normal instruction as a 'legitimate collegiate enterprise' and observes: 'Had he succeeded, the collegiate prejudices against normal schools would likely never have sharpened into the social class divisions of the early twentieth century'.[50] High school teachers and principals often reinforced the social class related distinctions between the two types of institutions in conjunction with their own professionalization project.

> Male high school principals perceived a growing educational and *social-class chasm* between their own ambitions and the reality of the normal school.[51]

With respect to gender relations, concerns about the 'peril of women' teachers in public secondary schools in the US were drawn upon in the competition between normals and universities.[52] Once again, the sought-after client played a significant role in highlighting gender divisions.

> High school men wished to avoid the normals' low admission standards and growing accessibility to persons of low social status, their emphasis on practical techniques, and their rapid *feminization*.[53]

As the reference (in the quote above) to normals' 'emphasis on practical technique' indicates, the competitive relationship between the institutional types derived from, and concomitantly engendered, an ideological struggle concerning where secondary school teachers could be most appropriately trained.[54]

> The collegiate [or university-level] institutions entertained grave fears regarding the ability of the normal schools to properly equip teachers for the high schools, while the normal school was certain that the failure to provide practice teaching and the need of adapting subject matter to the mind of the high school pupil rendered collegiate education inadequate.[55]

The ideological struggle that transpired should be conceived of not only in terms of 'liberal' versus 'technical',[56] but also in relation to 'mental' versus 'manual' — terms which have a clearer association with social class relations. The terms of the debate also connect with gender relations, although not explicitly in terms of 'mental' versus 'emotional' labor.[57] The connection with gender relations is suggested by the parallels in themes articulated in the normals versus universities debates and those in the higher education for women versus men debates. In the latter, the focus was on training females for the 'emotional' and 'technical' work of *housekeeping* versus liberally educating males for the 'mental' work of the 'professions', business and political leadership. In the former debate, training for the 'emotional' and 'technical' work of *schoolkeeping* was distinguished from liberally educating men for the 'mental' work of the 'professions', business and political leadership.[58]

Although some proponents of normal schools stressed the need for a liberal education, understanding, and developing the 'culture of the mind',[59] and although state universities created out of the 1862 Morrill Act were at least initially conceived of as having a practical and technical orientation,[60] the technical versus liberal distinction was one that became clearly associated with contrast between normal schools and universities.[61] Whether the polarized labels were validly assigned, perhaps, is less important than the fact that those involved in the rivalry between the normals and universities made use of such a conception.[62] For example, William H. Payne, the first university professor of education in the United States, argued, as noted above, that 'normal schools' stress on 'mechanical exactness and expertness' produced a 'machine' rather than ... '[t]rue professionals',[63] and that:

> the technical training appropriately offered to immature students in normal schools, who could only be expected to become competent craftsmen, at best, was fundamentally different from the liberal-professional education offered potential educational leaders in the university.[64]

Clearly, normal school people were more oriented to addressing immediately the practical, daily problems as school teachers viewed them.[65] And in this sense, unlike universities, normal schools and later teachers colleges:

> sought only to be a 'peoples college', tied closely to the local community and eager to serve students without any special desire for the high-brow culture of the traditional [universities and] colleges.[66]

It was, however, this association with less elite members of the population — working class, farmers, and women — which helped to locate normal schools at the 'lower' end of the liberal-technical hierarchical relations.

Normals' image also suffered in some groups' eyes because of the form of their organization and programs. Normal schools were often promoted as 'inexpensive' alternatives to university preparation of teachers.[67] Moreover, the 'normal school was doomed to modest beginnings', because Horace Mann 'apparently failed to perceive' that 'Prussian teacher education had a social class basis'; thus, although Mann was impressed with the status of the more elite, civil servant schoolmasters in Prussia, he imported the form of teacher education used in Prussia 'to train teachers from the lower class for the lower class'.[68] Moreover, the apprenticeship model of practice teaching, originated in the normals and only later, after considerable resistance, adopted in university settings, because it was 'associated with lower class occupations, ... had the disadvantage of maintaining the inferior status'.[69]

Given the contradictory nature of class and gender relations, however, we should expect what developed in teacher education to be more complex than this, merely corresponding to or mirroring the hierarchical relations of class and gender. Two examples are provided below of how the contradictions in class and gender relations informed the normal school/teachers college versus university dynamics. First, we should note that despite how vehemently normal school people argued against the liberal education model of universities as an inappropriate context for the preparation of teachers, over the years normals developed a liberal arts curriculum like the universities in their search for academic respectability and degree-granting status.[70]

> In the efforts which have been put forth to elevate the normal schools to collegiate status, the tendency has been toward the creation and exploitation of courses which would secure the approval of the colleges and universities.[71]

What occurred, of course, parallels what happens to groups at the bottom of an unequal relationship: 'To judge the normal school in light of discrete disciplinary [i.e., university liberal arts] criteria', is to ensure that normal schools would be 'always judged to be second rate, in a sense which they could escape only by denying [and eschewing] their central commitment'.[72] Normal schools thus were mobile; they were upgraded to degree-granting institutions, but in a way that did not really challenge the hierarchical relations in which they were imbedded, nor the ideological notions that legitimated such relations.

Contradictory class and gender relations are also implicated in the fact that many universities, despite their rhetoric against teacher education as being too low status, due at least in part to the social class and gender composition of teacher education students, moved over time to incorporate teacher education as a major, if not central, function.[73] This was done partly because of market considerations — to recruit sufficient numbers of students and, especially for public institutions, to improve public relations.[74] But as we shall see in the next section, this boundary-spanning effort was not done in a manner that really challenged unequal class or gender relations. Indeed, it can be seen as a 'logical' response to contradictions in class and gender relations. That is, while the working class and women have less status and power, they do not constitute a minority of the potential students, consumers, tax-payers, and citizens.

Arts and Sciences Versus Education

Overlapping in time with competition and debates between normal schools/teachers colleges and universities, debates and competition of a similar form occurred *within* universities. Not unexpectedly, perhaps, the social class and gender compositions of these two antagonists parallel those evidenced in contrasting normals and universities. In terms of social class, students in education (either education majors or arts and science majors pursuing teacher certification) and faculty in education have tended to have lower social class backgrounds than other university students and faculty.[75]

With respect to gender, although initially faculty positions in education, especially in 'elite' institutions, have tended to be occupied by men,[76] and although males have continued to predominate numerically among education faculty,[77] compared to arts and sciences faculty, the gender ratio in education has continued to be closer to unity. For students, the picture has been similar. Initial reluctance to admit female undergraduate students at the Universities of Michigan, Indiana, and Wisconsin, for example, was followed by an uncomfortable, but an increasing feminization of university teacher education programs.[78] Parallel dynamics are reported for Harvard University and Teachers College, Columbia University.[79] However, in these institutions and many others, including Stanford and Chicago, the thrust toward graduate education programs for school administrators was, at least until recently, associated with efforts to masculinize university schools and colleges of education.[80] According to Lanier and Little, 'the student pool now seeking initial certification has a growing proportion of women'.[81] Thus, even as females become a slight majority of university students as a whole, education programs continue to be characterized by a higher female/male gender ratio, greater than three to one.

Within the university context, education and the arts/sciences not only attracted students and faculty whose characteristics were located at different levels of status, wealth and power, but the relations between these two components of the university tended to be hierarchical and conflict laden as well.[82] Education's situation within the university has been described in terms of a 'chronic inferiority complex', being in a state of 'perpetual disfavor', being the target of 'contempt' and 'hostility', and being able to enter only through the 'back door'.[83]

Relations between education and the arts and sciences can be viewed as a 'historical power struggle'[84] divided into at least two periods: 1890–1907, when universities resisted inclusion of professional-technical training in education, and after 1907 when arts/sciences faculties' views ranged from acceptance with critique or mild support.[85] While the dates are somewhat different, the case of the University of Illinois, Harvard, Stanford, and Teachers College, Columbia University provides ample evidence of such struggle.[86] The degree of animosity directed toward education by faculty in the arts and sciences is strikingly communicated by James Bryant Conant, who recalls his views about education prior to his assuming the presidency of Harvard in 1933:

> Early in my career as a professor of chemistry ... I shared the views of most of my colleagues or the faculty of arts and sciences that there was no excuse for the existence of people who sought to teach others how to teach. ... When any issues involving benefits to the graduate school of education came before the faculty of arts and sciences, I automatically voted with contempt upon the school of education.[87]

To what can these hierarchical and conflict-laden relations be attributed? Similar to that discussed regarding normal schools/teacher colleges relations with universities, part of the explanation resides in the association of the departments/schools/colleges of education with the 'lower' schools.[88] However, there is also an important, more direct contribution of class and gender relations.[89] As Lanier and Little conclude with reference to class relations:

> The social context of teacher education in higher education may
> be better understood when the typically underplayed issues of
> social status, power, and displaced class conflict are taken into
> account.[90]

That the issues were not simply academic ability or the perceived
sophistication of the knowledge content in education, but rather a
question of social class, is evidenced by James Earl Russell's comments
in 1912 about a proposal to raise admission standards at Teachers
College, Columbia University: 'the proposed standards ... made us
dependent upon ... a *class* that never before entered any [US] training
school for teachers'.[91]

Gender relations also played an explicit role in education-
arts/sciences relations in universities. As Clifford notes:

> Gender was an acknowledged factor in the low esteem of many
> schools of education, a chronic threat to their status. ... In the
> response [restricting the numbers of women students and
> faculty] to their version of the 'women problem', ... the
> education faculty was in concord with the rest of the university.
> Yet this was a joining of prejudices more than a meeting of
> minds.[92]

As early as 1837, the University of Michigan created 'branches' for
normal training, in which women were enrolled, at least partly in
response to resistance, which lasted until 1850, to admit women to the
University.[93] In 1887 and 1892 proposals by Nicholas Murray Butler
and James Earl Russell, respectively, to establish a formal link between
New York College for the Training of Teachers (later Teachers
College) and Columbia University were rebuffed because of a University policy against women enrollments.[94] Even after Teachers
College was incorporated into Columbia University, arts/sciences
faculty continued to have hostile attitudes toward the presence of
women at Teachers College, which was derogatorily referred to as
'hairpin alley'.[95] Similar stories can be told at least about Chicago, Yale,
Stanford, and Berkeley.[96] And although Harvard's School of
Education:

> was an authentic pioneer in securing Harvard opportunities for
> women, the fear of the feminized enclave was ever present.
> [Henry] Holmes[97] had little doubt that the School's reputation

and success within Harvard was directly proportional to its dominance by males.[98]

As we discussed in the section on normal school–university relations, unequal class and gender relations informed ideologically the action and discourse of educators in an indirect manner through the issue of liberal versus technical education. And as Weiss indicates:

> Because many struggles were necessary to establish the professional education of teachers at college or university level, teacher education has become more identified with [the technical phase associated with normals] than with the general or liberal aspects.[99]

As with normal schools, the attraction to the technical aspect was encouraged by university educationists' association with and dependence upon school people. Although initially university educationists scorned 'technical problems of serious concern to classroom teachers',[100] they were still pulled more in this direction than their colleagues in the arts and sciences faculties. At Harvard, for example, 'Holmes distinguished sharply between the fundamental [i.e., liberal] and technical field of study within the education curriculum ... [preferring to emphasize the former]. But he knew that the best way to attract experienced teachers was to expand the technical or practical side of the curriculum'.[101]

During the 1920s at Harvard, Education Dean Holmes struggled with University President Lowell to secure a place for Education in the university. 'Protracted discussions had ensued about whether "technical" knowledge in education was as intellectually mature as Holmes claimed or as rudimentary as Lowell believed',[102] but at the same time, the hierarchical, liberal-technical distinctions between education and the arts/sciences were reinforced. These struggles had real consequences for faculty in education, as Lowell refused to appoint, promote, or tenure those who focused their energies, with the encouragement of Dean Holmes, on technical aspects of education and program development at the expense of liberal traditions of scholarship.[103]

In more recent eras we have witnessed the liberal versus technical debate in the late-1940s through mid-1950s, recapitulated in the publications of Arthur Bestor's *Educational Wastelands* and Albert Lynd's *Quackery in the Public Schools.*[104] Education as a field was criticized for being 'anti-intellectual', by which was meant that educationists tended not to fully adopt an Aristotelian notion of the liberal function of education, that is:

> to produce a free man — a *man* who, *relieved from the need to produce goods or* artisan *services* directly, could spend his time in speculative thought concerning the problems of philosophy and government. [105]

About a decade later, perhaps catalyzed by the Soviet Union's successful launch of Sputnik, similar debates raged again. [106] These discourses entangled in the liberal *vs.* technical question were reflected in and refuelled by Koerner's *The Miseducation of Teachers* and, more so, despite its less provocative title, by Conant's *The Education of American Teachers.* [107] The latter debates, especially, also evidenced the conflict and competition between arts/sciences and education faculties for control over the 'life space' of teachers — life space that could be filled with liberal or technical curricular content, and that had student enrollment and funding implications for both parties.

Given this competition, and because of the hierarchical, class and gender related hierarchies implicit in the liberal-technical distinction, university schools and colleges of education have tended to 'ape' the liberal arts and sciences tradition and standards. [108] Sometimes, usually at the more 'elite' institutions, this meant the abandonment of teacher training and the development of 'academically respectable' graduate programs to train educational leaders and to develop the science of or liberal scholarship in education. [109]

This effort to fuse the training of superintendents and principals with science and university liberal education traditions [110] can be seen in part as a strategy to 'professionalize' educational administrators at the expense of teaching as an occupation. [111] Thus, university educationists both depended on the increasing hierarchical relations in the public schools, but also helped to perpetuate and legitimate them. University educationists could make claims for enhancing their own status by being associated more so with school administrators, who had greater power and status than teachers. [112] Educationists often found it in their own best interests:

> to confirm a career structure in which the central practitioner role of teacher became perceived by the profession itself as less desirable and more transient than managerial roles held by a few and characterized by the absence of contact with clients. [113]

By doing so, university educationists helped to 'continue, and to rationalize, the existing dual pattern — setting one program for leaders and a second for followers'.[114]

Such strategies, of course, were not unrelated to extant class and gender relations. By devoting more attention to preparing school administrators than to educating school teachers, university departments and later schools/colleges of education were able to attract a more masculinized and higher social class student body.[115] Professors of education, especially at the 'elite' universities, came to concentrate their efforts on preparing prospective school administrators in order:

> to contain 'the woman problem' ... [since] the school adminis-
> tration fraternity had learned strategies by which to close the
> field to aspiring women. By doing so, it retained male
> hegemony in the better-rewarded and better-regarded profes-
> sions, saving school administration from the disgrace of 'femin-
> ization'.[116]

However, despite this capitulation, educationists' strategy did not resolve 'their troubled relations with their academic fellows'.[117]

The status-enhancement strategy of developing the psychological, research methodological, and social/historical/philosophical foundations of education had similar consequences. It tended to increase the proportion of male faculty and students, while reinforcing the curriculum knowledge 'foundations' upon which arts/science faculty built their higher status. Moreover, it provided a status of marginality in the university for the faculty in such fields — neither in the liberal disciplines nor in the technical-professional field.[118]

The case of Harvard's Graduate School of Education is interesting and relevant here. Efforts were made by Dean Holmes and others to obtain education's independence from the faculty of arts and sciences by offering 'professional' degrees — MEd and EdD. While some 'believed the new degrees would celebrate the liberation of professionalism from the "skirts of the philosophical faculty",' as things developed, it appears that the 'new degree[s] [were] given for essentially the same work as the PhD' and MA.[119] As may be the case with many universities where only the 'professional' degrees are offered in education, Harvard's programs tended often to celebrate the liberal tradition, although not fully becoming recognized as a full member of this 'esteemed' group.

The development of competency-based teacher education programs serves as an important illustration of educationists' response to arts and sciences' criticism of teacher education.[120] Professors of education had a problem in that:

they had no claim to an esoteric area of knowledge that professors of science and arts did not also have a claim to. In attempting to define such an area they identified specific [technical] pedagogical skills which teachers required. In this way it was hoped that a teacher education programme could be developed that was designed to give prospective teachers the minimum competence essential to be a teacher through competency-based teacher education. [121]

But as with other strategies in educationists' struggles with colleagues in the arts and sciences, the liberal education and positivistic science traditions were accorded legitimacy, while education remained viewed as occupying terrain more toward the technical end of the continuum.

Professors of sciences and the arts have not been unwilling to view the teacher as a pedagogical technician who transmits knowledge, but does not have any control over its generation and selection. [122]

While educationists were seeking status and respectability by 'aping' the arts and sciences, the liberal arts faculty groups were dealing with the contradiction that despite women and working and middle classes being considered 'lower' on the hierarchy, such populations constituted a relatively large base of potential public support and a sizeable source of student enrollment. This is why 'despite such opposition and skepticism, college and university presidents reluctantly gave in to the trends of the times' and developed departments and then schools and colleges of education. [123] As Clifford explains, universities in the US:

launched their initially modest ventures in professional education because it served their own interests. First, there was the public relations move: ... educating a few teachers could project an image of contributing to the public weal, [thus justifying] ... tax support. ... Second, there was the motive of attracting more students to ... higher education. ... By admitting women and by assisting their plans to teach, higher education might double its potential pool of applicants. [124]

Curriculum Responses to Gender and Class Contradictions

In the two previous sections we have explored how the contradictory nature of unequal social class and gender relations connect with the competition between and debates about different organizational arrangements for the education of teachers. In this section, we examine how such contradictory relations constrained and enabled curricular developments within teacher education programs.

It has been argued that 'curriculum revision has been a constant feature of the preparation of teachers in the United States',[125] and that such curricular changes in teacher preparation programs must be understood as derived in part from 'society and its problems' or 'our complex and contradictory civilization'.[126] The situation is more complex, though, because teacher education can be seen not only as responding directly to problems and crisis in the broader society generated because of fundamental social contradictions, but also as responding to analogous developments in the schools, and thus indirectly to societal dynamics.[127] However, teacher education 'in no way' is seen to be 'merely a responding organism'[128] or merely some sort of 'a holding company for the solution of ad hoc problems defined by outside forces'.[129] Rather those who have constructed and reconstructed teacher education have operated in the context where the rules and resources which constrain and enable their action are informed by problems and crises arising out of social contradictions.[130]

In the United States during the nineteenth century, the transformations in the economy from an agricultural production through a cottage industry operation to large-scale capitalist industrial organization had a profound impact on social class and gender relations.

> As capital accumulated in the hands of those who [oversaw the building of] the new railroads and factories, income distribution became more highly differentiated, and a sharper class structure began to emerge. ... The cottage industries that had permitted women to work within their own homes diminished as machinery drew labor into the factories. ... [I]n the new urban centers like Massachusetts and New York, there was no place for independent women. ... [D]instinctions ... developed between the culture of the home and that of the workplace and it was expressed in differing expectations of the men, women and children who spent their days in those spaces. Women were detained in their kitchens and nurseries. ... [The 'ideal' mother] was to exert moral pressure on a society in whose operations she had little part, and to spend money — or have it spent on her — in an economy she [did not control].[131]

It is in the context of these changing social relations and contradictions, seen by some in conjunction with the ethnic make-up and size of immigration as a source of destabilizing crisis in the US,[132] that common elementary and secondary schooling as well as normal school and university programs for teacher education emerged and initially developed. And as especially the high schools were shaped around 1880 in ways that sometimes mediated these contradictions by offering skill and value training programs in domestic and industrial arts, it is said that 'specialized preparation of teachers became necessary'.[133] The curriculum of teacher education programs was developed in large part to prepare domestic arts and industrial arts teachers.

Perhaps the most interesting example, because of the link with the high status institution, Columbia University, is that of the Kitchen Garden Association, which later evolved into the Industrial Education Association and then the New York College for the Training of Teachers before being named Teachers College. A key figure in these institutional efforts, Grace Hoadley Dodge, was:

> deeply concerned over slum conditions and their deleterious effects upon homes. The struggle of young housewives, ignorant of cooking and sewing and any kind of budgeting, to hold their families together evoked her special interest.[134]

These organizations, which began in the last decades of the nineteenth century, primarily as philanthropic entities to support the development of school programs in manual and domestic arts for boys and girls, respectively, whose living conditions concerned Grace Dodge so deeply, but over time increasingly took on the task of training teachers for these and other school programs. It should be noted that these curricular areas for high school students or the training programs for their teachers were not defined primarily in terms of technical skill development, but rather focused on socialization for the roles of urban worker and urban housekeeper. For instance, Grace Dodge:

> had quietly resolved to improve the schools of New York City in the direction of a more 'practical' education with emphasis not upon academic but rather upon moral and spiritual values.[135]

The economic panic of 1893 and the increased antagonism between capital and labor around the turn of the twentieth century reflected problems derived from the contradictions of social class relations in the US (and more globally). We saw above some aspects of the efforts (i.e., via industrial arts and domestic arts education) by educationists and others to deal with these contradictory relations as they intersected with gender relations. Additionally, it was in the context of this 'growing class conflict' at the end of the nineteenth century, that led Paul Henry Hanus, Professor in the History and Art of Teaching at Harvard, to focus on social concerns and social objectives in his teacher preparation courses as well as in courses being developed for a new emphasis on training school administrators. Some sense of how Hanus and others like him conceived of the role of education as a 'social force' and how they were likely to orient educators is evidenced in Powell's discussion:

> Schooling should equip youth to resist entrapment by the 'prey of demagogues and the social agitator'. It was essential to foster a 'wise conservatism' to promote suspicion of 'plausible but fallacious solutions' to social problems. The 1896 election results mandated education to combat anarchistic license and socialist utopianism. [136]

The social crisis of the period as it affected educationists' concerns directly and indirectly (through philanthropic opportunities) facilitated schools/colleges of education — particularly, but not solely, those in private, 'elite' institutions like Harvard and Columbia, in becoming 'active in shaping a variety of specialized [courses] and careers aimed at the social and vocational adjustment of [non-college going] adolescents'. [137] These specialty areas included vocational guidance, industrial and commercial education, play, recreation, physical education, and testing and measurement.

Capitalist economies in the US and elsewhere in the world experienced another crisis point — termed the Great Depression — as evidenced by the 1929 US stock market crash. Again we can see teacher education being reshaped in the context of crises and problems developing from contradictory class relations. As Snarr explains it, seemingly from a different theoretical and political perspective:

> the ... depression ... with its accompanying financial, economic, industrial and social dislocations ... brought into relief significant problems in education, problems implying new practices in teacher education. [138]

And as was the case four decades earlier, social (versus psychological) dimensions in education and teacher education were highlighted, [139] but in this case, these were couched more frequently in 'social change' rather than 'social amelioration' terms. As Borrowman reports:

The function of the teacher in respect to social change and stability was greatly emphasized during the depression and war years. Moreover, the concept of democratic school administration which made the teacher an active participant in making decisions about curriculum, discipline, and other crucial matters gained currency.[140]

This is the period in which George Counts and colleagues at Teachers College, Columbia University, initiated more critical discussions about education and society than had previously been found within departments/schools/colleges of education. Through the journal they started, *Social Frontier*, and through their personal associations and influence, such ideas became somewhat generally available. Cremin, Shannon, and Townsend described the developments this way:

> The depression everywhere did more than cause financial distress; it jarred to the core the nation's social, political and economic attitudes. The spectacle of the virtual collapse of their economy caused the ... people [in the US], especially the intellectuals, to reexamine their political views, to question their social and philosophical assumptions, and to cast about ... for a social outlook better fitted for a world of rapid change and uncertainty. Such social-intellectual ferment was bound to affect educational thought and practice.[141]

There is clearly more evidence of how educational thought (as compared to programs and curriculum) was shaped in this context, at least in teacher education. In addition to the pages of *Social Frontier*, take, for example, George Counts' 1932 published speech, 'Dare the Schools Change the Social Order'. Nevertheless, we know that at least at Columbia the interdisciplinary foundations of education course focused on a 'host of social political, economic and personal issues formerly considered alien to the educator's scope — or even vision'.[142] Moreover, from 1932 until 1938 'New College', an experimental elementary and secondary level teacher education venture at Teachers College, was being pursued. Importantly, it is claimed that:

> The whole experiment reflected the social ferment that came in response to the Great Depression ... [and thus it was believed that it was the] peculiar privilege of the teacher to play a large part in the development of the social order of the next generation. ... The faculty, fearing an ivory tower attitude [given the relatively elite backgrounds of the students enrolled], attempted to foster political activity among the students.[143]

As the spectre of fascism in Germany and Italy became more clear, as World War II punctured the bubble of isolationism in the US, and with the advent of the 'cold war', McCarthyism and the post-war economic expansion, the reform and social transformation orientation characteristic of some educationists' endeavors during the 1930s dissipated. The problem of social stratification and concerns about a 'free and classless society' were 'almost forgotten'.[144] The shift is partly explainable in terms of faculty perceptions being altered by the new social structural dynamics, but one must also take account of the role of federal and foundation funding. For example, in 1938, when Teachers College's 'New College' teacher education program was being phased out, Columbia received a sizeable, five-year grant from the General Education Board to create a Commission on Teacher Education methods and to develop a cooperative teacher education program with Barnard College.[145] The GI Bill, which infused many programs with 'mature' students ready to be trained quickly so they could get on with their careers and lives, should also be mentioned as should the war-related and post-war stimulated 'neutral', social scientific research and development projects in education.[146]

The crisis in the cities (and society, more generally) of the mid- to late-1960s, having a basis in contradictions in class, gender and race relations, provided some shift in efforts associated with teacher education curriculum. This was partly indicated by the trends in educational research. As Powell notes about this period:

> Although some employed research designs consistent with social science methodology, others were not 'research' in the sense of dispassionate controlled inquiry. They celebrated moral passion, social activism, and optimistic reforms of a new sort. The principal themes were urban education and the limits of formal schooling.[147]

With respect to curricular developments in teacher education, we should note the emergence and at least rhetorical adoption of curricular foci on multicultural education and concerns about sexism in textbooks and teachers' practice.

In many colleges/schools of education, however, these curricular thrusts were incorporated in processes associated with competency-based teacher education (CBTE). Thus, such topics became translated into cognitive or behavioral objectives, allowing, if not prescribing, a relatively superficial treatment of questions related to class, race, and gender relations (see Chapter 6). I suggested (towards the end of the previous section) how the CBTE movement can be conceived of as an example of a strategy by educationists to enhance their stature within universities by appealing to norms of 'scientism'. But CBTE must also be seen as a set of ideas and practices which arose in the context of social crises, developed with the financial support of the federal government and the states, and served to mediate, at least temporarily, contradictions in class and gender (as well as race) relations.

Conclusions

Based on a critical review of published historical accounts of teacher education in the United States, I have attempted to illustrate how trends in normal schools, teachers colleges and university departments/schools/ colleges of education can be seen to be related to contradictions in class and gender relations. With respect to normal school-university relations and arts/sciences-education relations within the university, I identified how unequal class and gender relations were drawn upon by various actors in the debates and competitive struggles that ensued.

Often these dynamics have, in a sense, depended on the fact that working class members and females have less power and status than the bourgeoisie (or even middle class members) and males. Thus, the hierarchical relations evidenced in teacher education were to some extent constituted by and constitutive of broader, unequal class and gender relations. Nevertheless, we also identified how, because of contradictions in these broader relations, teacher education developed in ways that could not be predicted solely on the basis of the greater power and status of, say, males. This was particularly evident in the 'decisions' to develop programs for the less powerful and lower status students, if only to increase enrollments and financial support.

I have also indicated how at least part of the explanation of changes in teacher education curricular emphases must be located in crises and problems that occur in society deriving from contradictory social relations. Sometimes the crises were 'read' directly (but not necessarily fully or accurately) by teacher educators, who then developed curriculum in response to the crises. Other times there was a more indirect route via the response of school officials or educators to the interpretations of what the crises or problems consisted. In any case, although it was the officials or educators who acted, their actions were frequently stimulated and shaped by others whose ideological work, philanthropic activity, and/or control of the state power enabled and constrained certain courses of action.

Parts of this critical analysis of historical studies of teacher education are sketchy and suggestive rather than detailed and conclusive. We should remember, however, that the historical writings upon which this chapter is based do not, for the most part, take class and gender relations, let alone contradictions therein, as their central problematic. Thus, the additional details that may exist in primary sources were not available in this analysis. Clearly, there is a need to further test the thesis presented herein through an in-depth historical analysis of primary sources of data.

Nevertheless, this analysis should encourage us to be cautious about current debates about and proposals for 'reforms' in teacher education.[148] In Chapter 7, we will discuss the issues raised in these debates and proposals, drawing not only on the critical review of historical studies presented in this chapter, but also on the ethnographic findings identified in the intervening chapters. In the next chapter, we continue in our effort to understand the context of the ethnographic research. Taking off where we concluded this chapter's critical analysis of the history of teacher education, we move to examine how the Competency-Based Teacher Education program was developed and implemented at the University of Houston in the decade prior to my ethnographic fieldwork.

Notes

1   This chapter is adapted from GINSBURG, M., 'Teacher education and class and gender relations', *Educational Foundations* 2 (1987), pp. 4–36, which is a revision of paper presented at the American Educational Studies Association, Pittsburgh, 29 October–2 November, 1986. I wish to thank Maria Jose Alio for her assistance in identifying and reviewing some of the literature referenced herein. Gratitude is also due to Tessa Jo Shokri for her cooperation in word processing this document. Helpful comments on an earlier draft of this manuscript by Renee Clift, Richard Duschl, William Georgiades, Bruce Kimball and Linda Spatig are gratefully acknowledged.
2   BORROWMAN, M., *The Liberal and the Technical in Teacher Education* (Westport, CT, Greenwood Press, 1956), p. 27.
3   I believe that race relations must also be considered in attempting to understand fully the connections between society, schooling and teacher education. The omission, or better, the 'bracketing' of race relations in this paper primarily reflects the extant historical literature on teacher

education. Race and ethnicity seem to occupy an 'absent presence' in much of the writing analyzed and cited herein. Sometimes, as will be discussed later, the issue surfaces in the context of society and schools responding to the 'flood of immigrants' or 'urban problems' but the race of the prospective educators to be educated, for example, is rarely a focus of attention. For exceptions to this general conclusion, see JONES, L., *The Jeanes Teacher in the United States, 1908–33* (Chapel Hill, NC, University of North Carolina Press, 1937); TYACK D., and LOWE, R., 'The constitutional movement: Reconstruction and black education in the south', *American Journal of Education* 94 (1986), pp. 236–56; WHITE, W., 'The decline of the classroom and the Chicago study of education, 1909–29'. *American Journal of Education* 90 (1982), pp. 144–74.

4 BEGGS, W., *The Education of Teachers* (New York, The Center for Applied Research in Education, 1965), p. 7 (emphasis added).

5 HARPER, C., *A Century of Public Teacher Education: The Story of State Colleges as They Evolved from Normal Schools* (Westport, CT, Greenwood Press, 1939), p. 129 (emphasis added).

6 PANGBURN, J., *The Evolution of the American Teachers College* (New York, Bureau of Publications, Columbia University, 1932), p. 2 (emphasis added).

7 HERBST, J., 'Beyond the debate over revisionism: The educational past writ large', *History of Educational Quarterly* 20 (1980), p. 134.

8 SNARR, O., *The Education of Teachers in the Middle States: An Historical Study of the Professional Education of Public School Teachers as a State Function* (Moorehead, MN, Moorehead State Teachers College, 1946), p. 262.

9 Pangburn, p. 126; see also Harper, p. 70.

10 BORROWMAN, M., *The Liberal and the Technical*, p. 59.

11 JOHNSON, H., and JOHANNINGMEIER, E., *Teachers for the Prairies: The University of Illinois and the Schools, 1868–1945* (Urbana, IL, University of Illinois Press, 1972), p. 29.

12 CREMIN, L., SHANNON, D., and TOWNSEND, E., *A History of Teachers College, Columbia University* (New York, Columbia University Press, 1954), pp. 28–29.

13 POWELL, A., *The Uncertain Profession: Harvard and the Search for Educational Authority* (Cambridge, Harvard University Press, 1980), p. 41.

14 Borrowman, *The Liberal and the Technical*.

15 See Cremin, Shannon and Townsend; Johnson and Johanningmeier.

16 See Chapter 3 in this volume.

17 Johnson and Johanningmeier; Powell. *The Uncertain Profession*.

18 See LARSON, M., *The Rise of Professionalism: A Sociological Analysis* (Berkeley, University of California Press, 1977) for a discussion of 'professionalization projects' and other issues concerning professions and the ideology of professionalism.

19 LANIER, J., and LITTLE, J., 'Research on teacher education', in WITTROCK, M., (Ed.) *Handbook of Research on Teaching* (3rd edition), (New York, Macmillan, 1986), p. 535.

20 See BOWLES, S., and GINTIS, H., *Schooling in Capitalist America* (Boston, Routledge and Kegan Paul, 1976).

21 SPRING, J., *The American Schools, 1642–1985* (New York, Longman, 1986), p. 114.

22 CREMIN, L., 'Background of teacher education for US public schools', in RICHARDSON, C., BRULE, H., and SNYDER, H., (Eds.) *The Education of Teachers in England, France, and the USA.*, (Westport, CT, Greenwood Press, 1953), p. 234.

23 See Snarr.

24 *Ibid.*, p. 273.

25 *Ibid.*, p. 96.

26 See Borrowman, *The Liberal and the Technical*; Harper; MATTINGLY, P., *The Classless Profession: Schoolmen in the Nineteenth Century* (New York, New York University Press, 1975); White.

27 TYACK, D., 'The education of teachers and the teaching of education', in TYACK, D., (Ed.) *Turning Points in American Education History*, (Lexington, MA, Xerox College Publishing, 1967), p. 43.

28 See BORROWMAN, M., *Teacher Education in America: A Documentary History* (New York, Teachers College Press, 1965); GRUMET, M., 'Pedagogy for patriarchy: The feminization of teaching', *Interchange* 12 (1981), pp. 165–84; Mattingly; RICHARDSON, J., and HATCHER, B., 'The feminization of public school teaching, 1870–1920', *Work and Occupations* 10 (1983), pp. 81–99; Spring.

29 Grumet, p. 171.

30 MELDER, K., 'Training women teachers: Private experiments, 1820–1840' (ERIC Document, ED 180 936, undated), p. 13.

31 WARREN, D., 'Learning from experience: History and teacher education', *Educational Researcher* 14 (1985), p. 9.

32 During the 1776–1823 period, many teachers, who were indentured servants working off their bondage by apprenticing for teaching, ran away because teaching and life conditions were so poor. See LEMLECH, J., and MARKS, M., *The American Teacher: 1776–1976* (Bloomington, IN, Phi Delta Kappa, 1976), pp. 12–13; WEISS, R., *The Conant Controversy in Teacher Education* (New York, Random House, 1969), p. 14.

33 See CLIFFORD, G., 'The formative years of schools of education in America: A five institution analysis', *American Journal of Education* 94 (1986), pp. 427–46.

34 See Borrowman, *The Liberal and the Technical*.

35 See Borrowman, *Teacher Education in America*.

36 Mattingly, pp. 143 and 163.

37 See Cremin, Shannon and Townsend; Harper.

38 See Clifford; Harper; Johnson and Johanningmeier; SARASON, S., DAVIDSON, K., and BLATT, B., *The Preparation of Teachers: An Unstudied Problem in Education* (New York, Wiley, 1962); Snarr.

39 Mattingly, p. 143.

40 See MONROE, W., *Teaching-Learning Theory and Teacher Education: 1890–1950* (Urbana, IL, University of Illinois Press, 1952); Pangburn.

41 See Pangburn; Snarr; TROW, M., 'The second transformation of American secondary education', *International Journal of Comparative Sociology* 2 (1961), pp. 144–66.

42 See Clifford; PALMER, J., 'Teacher education: A perspective from a major public university', in CASE, C., and MATTHES, W., (Eds.) *Colleges of Education: Perspectives on Their Future*, (Berkeley, McCutchan, 1985), pp. 51–70; White.
43 See Johnson and Johanningmeier; Pangburn.
44 See Cremin; Harper; Monroe; Tyack.
45 Johnson and Johanningmeier, p. 326.
46 *Ibid.*, p. 246.
47 Beggs, p. 9.
48 See Harper. The disdain that many university protagonists directed toward normal schools was not merely because of their association with the 'lower' branches of knowledge. Liberal arts college and university faculty 'seriously doubted' that elementary school teaching 'was anything more than a somewhat skilled occupation' (Sarason, Davidson, and Blatt, p. 21).
49 Lanier and Little.
50 Mattingly, p. 163.
51 Powell, *The Uncertain Profession*, p. 31 (emphasis added).
52 Clifford; Richardson and Hatcher.
53 POWELL, A., 'University schools of education in the twentieth century', *Peabody Journal of Education* 54 (1976), p. 5 (emphasis added).
54 See Cremin; ELSBREE, W., *The American Teacher: Education of a Profession in Democracy* (New York, American Book Company, 1939); Monroe; Snarr; White.
55 Pangburn, p. 52.
56 Borrowman, *The Liberal and the Technical*.
57 Emotional labor, defined as the 'management of feeling to create a publicly observable facial or bodily display' (Hochschild, p. 7), can be seen in the friendly, caring attitude characteristic of, say, a flight attendant as well as in the threatening, demanding attitude exhibited by a bill collector. Like other forms of labor, emotional labor can be sold for a wage. It is possible to see the work of teachers as comprising both types of emotional engagement.
58 See also Grumet.
59 See BUETOW, H., 'Historical overview of Catholic teacher training in the US', *School and Society*, 100 (1972), pp. 165–72; Lemlech and Marks; Monroe.
60 See Borrowman, *Teacher Education in America*; Johnson and Johanningmeier.
61 See Lanier and Little; Sarason, Davidson and Blatt; SEARS, J., and HENDERSON, A., *Cubberly of Stanford and His Contribution to American Education* (Stanford, CA, Stanford University Press, 1957); Tyack; Weiss.
62 See Borrowman, *The Liberal and the Technical*, p. 63; Cremin, Shannon and Townsend, p. 244; Snarr, p. 244.
63 Powell, *The Uncertain Profession*, p. 41.
64 Borrowman, *Teacher Education in America*, p. 13.
65 See BOGNER, C., 'Teaching — progress?', *Journal of Teacher Education*, 29 (1978), pp. 58–60; Johnson and Johanningmeier.

66 Borrowman, *Teacher Education in America*, pp. 19–20. Here I am not arguing that normals actually served the real interests of the 'common people'. Indeed, in a manner different from the universities, they may have functioned equally well, though by no means perfectly, to reproduce class (and gender) relations. Moreover, by drawing on Borrowman's work here, I am not accepting his notion about the 'anti-intellectualism ... amongst the rural groups and the lower economic and social classes from which students of the normal schools, and later the teachers colleges, were largely recruited' (Borrowman, p. 33). Rejecting 'classical' aristocratic traditions of the liberal arts, or even their 'modern' bourgeois version that has come to dominate universities in the US, is not, in my view, tantamount to being anti-intellectual.

67 See Snarr.

68 Borrowman, *The Liberal and the Technical*, pp. 46–47.

69 Weiss, p. 15.

70 See Harper; Monroe; Sarason, Davidson, and Blatt.

71 Pangburn, p. 68.

72 Johnson and Johanningmeier, p. 464.

73 Similarly, the American Institute of Instruction (AII), which provided an alternative form of teacher preparation to normal schools and university departments of education, began in 1826 with a male and higher class biased population of students. In 1837, however, the AII changed its meetings to locations outside of Boston so as to become accessible to less economically advantaged teachers, at least in part because of a drop in membership (Mattingly, pp. 96–97). Moreover, beginning in 1867, the first female teachers were admitted as full participants in AII, reflecting renewed concerns about membership declines, due partly to loss of potential male members during and after the Civil War (Mattingly, pp. 110–111).

74 See Clifford; Mattingly; Snarr.

75 See Lanier and Little. In characterizing the class membership distinctions of education versus arts and sciences students and faculty, I am *not* assuming, as Lanier and Little seem to, that many 'teachers and teacher educators come from home and family backgrounds whose academic roots are often shallow and which are, therefore, not likely to engender strong and ingrained intellectual propensities' (p. 565). Such an assumption is at best a gloss on the complex relations between social class, culture, schooling and cognition, and at worst a blatant example of blaming-the-victim.

76 See Clifford; Powell; White.

77 See Lanier and Little.

78 See Snarr.

79 See Powell, *The Uncertain Profession*; Cremin, Shannon and Townsend.

80 See Sears and Henderson; White.

81 Lanier and Little, p. 538.

82 See Lanier and Little, p. 530; Palmer, p. 152; SCHNEIDER, B., 'Tracing the provenance of teacher education', in POPKEWITZ, T., (Ed.) *Critical*

Studies in Teacher-Education (New York, Falmer Press, 1987), pp. 211–41.

83 Respectively, Clifford, p. 439; Warren, p. 11; Beggs, p. 9; Powell, *The Uncertain Profession*, p. vii; and Johnson and Johanningmeier, p. 454.

84 Weiss, p. 187.

85 See Monroe.

86 See Johnson and Johanningmeier; Powell, *The Uncertain Profession*; Sears and Henderson; and Cremin, Shannon and Townsend; respectively. It is interesting, particularly as it parallels the case of the University of Houston (see Chapter 3), how significant the provision of funds for a building for colleges/schools of education was as a symbol of victory or defeat in the education-arts/sciences struggle at Teachers College, the University of Illinois, and Harvard.

87 CONANT, J., *The Education of American Teachers* (New York, McGraw-Hill, 1963), pp. 1–2.

88 See Weiss, p. 20.

89 See Clifford, p. 433; Conant, p. 12; Lanier and Little, p. 530.

90 Lanier and Little, p. 558.

91 Cremin, Shannon and Townsend, pp. 60–61 (emphasis added).

92 Clifford, p. 441.

93 See Snarr, pp. 43–44.

94 See Cremin, Shannon and Townsend, pp. 19 and 30.

95 *Ibid.*, p. 70.

96 See Clifford; White. A recent development at the University of North Carolina at Chapel Hill indicates that concerns about women as university students are with us today. It is reported that some UNC trustees 'believe the campus has too many women ... [and] fear alumni contributions, as well as the university's political influence, may suffer under the current enrollment pattern of three women for every two men'. GREENE, E., 'Too many women? That's the problem at Chapel Hill, say some trustees; Feminist students chagrined', *Chronicle of Higher Education* 28 January, 1987), p. 27.

97 It should be noted that Henry Holmes, the long-term Dean of the Graduate School of Education (GSE) whose name has been appropriated by the Holmes Group currently at the center of controversies in teacher education, proposed in the late 1920s that a new building be constructed to house the GSE and attract residential students, none of whom would be women. His concern to bar women was based on the notion that 'somehow the presence of women seemed inconsistent with the spirit of community and colleagueship he longed to establish'. For him, the 'ultimate emulation of the Harvard professional ideal — proposed in deepest secrecy — was to abolish women's unique eligibility for Harvard degrees' (Powell, *The Uncertain Profession*, p. 169).

98 *Ibid.*, p. 154.

99 Weiss, p. 9.

100 Borrowman, *The Liberal and the Technical*, p. 30.

101 Powell, *The Uncertain Profession*, p. 144.

102 *Ibid.*, p. 9.
103 *Ibid.*, pp. 145 and 169. See Chapter 3 for discussion of similar developments at the University of Houston in the 1970s.
104 BESTOR, A., *Educational Wastelands* (Urbana: University of Illinois Press, 1953) and LYND, A., *Quackery in the Public Schools* (Boston: Little, Brown & Co., 1953). For a discussion of debates during this period, see Borrowman, *The Liberal and the Technical*: Johnson and Johanningmeier; Spring; Tyack.
105 Borrowman, *The Liberal and the Technical*, p. 3 (emphasis added). The quote clearly illustrates the link between the liberal-technical question and class relations — liberal pertaining to education for elite non-workers or for 'a man of leisure' (*Ibid.*, p. 133). Although the gender-biased language may simply be a usage, common in the 1950s, by males to refer to human beings of both sexes, it may also reflect the link between the liberal-technical question and gender relations.
106 See Sarason, Davidson and Blatt; TURNER, D., 'Education in the USA', in HOLMES, B., (Ed.) *Equality and Freedom in Education*, (London, Allen and Unwin, 1985), pp. 105–34.
107 KOERNER, J., *The Miseducation of American Teachers* (Boston, Houghton-Mifflin, 1963); Conant.
108 See Clifford.
109 See CREMIN, L., 'The Education of the Educating Professions', Nineteenth Charles W. Hunt Lecture presented at the 30th meeting of the American Association of Colleges for Teacher Education, Chicago, February 21 (Washington, DC, AACTE, 1978); Lanier and Little; Powell, *University Schools of Education*, Sears and Henderson; White.
110 See Mattingly.
111 See White.
112 See Clifford; Johnson and Johanningmeier, p. 121; White.
113 Powell, *University Schools of Education*, p. 19.
114 Borrowman, *The Liberal and the Technical*, p. 102.
115 See Johnson and Johanningmeier; Lanier and Little; Monroe; Sears and Henderson; White.
116 Clifford, p. 442.
117 *Ibid.*, p. 428; see also Lanier and Little, p. 559.
118 See Borrowman, *The Liberal and the Technical*, p. 171; Clifford; Powell, *The Uncertain Profession*; Tyack. Ironically, perhaps, it is the foundations of education faculty which help develop the liberal-technical debate within the context of the schools and colleges of education. See also Chapter 3 for a more recent case study of the implications of foundations of education faculty's cultural identity being connected with liberal education traditions.
119 Powell, *The Uncertain Profession*, p. 137.
120 For a provocative example of such critique, see Conant.
121 Turner, p. 119.
122 *Ibid.*, p. 119.
123 Elsbree, p. 320. See also Beggs; Cremin, Shannon, and Townsend, p. 195; Lanier and Little; Monroe; Powell, *The Uncertain Profession*, p. 18.

124 Clifford, pp. 436–37.
125 Pangburn, p. 79.
126 Harper, p. 155.
127 See Monroe, p. 242.
128 Cremin, Shannon and Townsend, p. 271.
129 Powell, *The Uncertain Profession*, p. 274.
130 For further discussion of these points, see GINSBURG, M., 'Problems, conflicts and contradictions in urban education', *The Review of Education*, 11 (1985), pp. 111–116.
131 Grumet, pp. 168–73.
132 See Borrowman, *The Liberal and the Technical*, p. 34.
133 Snarr, p. 286.
134 Cremin, Shannon and Townsend, p. 11.
135 *Ibid.*, p. 14. This emphasis on value socialization and *training* for the domestic (as well as manual) arts versus educating in the liberal arts academic subjects gives different meaning to Lanier and Little's discussion about how the early attempts by teacher educators 'to have professional schools for teachers reflect specific attitudes of intellectual discipline ... were displaced as women and members of the lower social classes came to compose a majority of the teaching force' (p. 532). Here the issue may not be the 'quality' or even the preferences of the students as much as the designs that more powerful groups had for them in the social order.
136 Powell, *The Uncertain Profession*, p. 67.
137 Powell, *University Schools of Education*, p. 8.
138 Snarr, p. 214.
139 See Johnson and Johanningmeier; Monroe.
140 Borrowman, *The Liberal and the Technical*, pp. 210–11.
141 Cremin, Shannon and Townsend, p. 143.
142 *Ibid.*, p. 152.
143 *Ibid.*, pp. 222–26.
144 Powell, *The Uncertain Profession*, p. 260.
145 Cremin, Shannon, and Townsend, pp. 195–96.
146 Powell, *The Uncertain Profession*.
147 *Ibid.*, p. 276.
148 Some of the more widely discussed reform proposals are included in CARNEGIE TASK FORCE ON TEACHING AS A PROFESSION, *A Nation Prepared: Teachers for the 21st Century* (Hyattsville, MD, Carnegie Forum on Education and Economy, 1986); HOLMES GROUP, *Tomorrow's Teachers: A Report of the Holmes Group* (East Lansing, MI, Holmes Group, Inc.,1986); NATIONAL COMMISSION for EXCELLENCE in TEACHER EDUCATION, *A Call for Change in Teacher Education* (Washington, DC, NCETE, 1985); NATIONAL CONSORTIUM FOR EDUCATIONAL EXCELLENCE, *An Agenda for Educational Research: A View from the Firing Line* (Nashville, TN, Vanderbilt University, 1985); SOUTHERN REGIONAL EDUCATION BOARD, *Improving Teacher Education: An Agenda for Higher Education and the Schools* (Atlanta, SREB, 1985).

Chapter 3

On Producing a Competency-Based Teacher Education Program[1]
(with Linda Spatig)

We here, sort of a side-light, got the notion that, well, if you could develop instructional modules, then you ought to be able to develop an instructional module on how to develop an instructional module. And we put that package together ... and used it as part of the training for Teacher Corps and some other institutions ... all over the US ... and in Israel. (Interviewee #22)

Introduction

In this chapter, we examine the process of production, not in the heavy or light industrial sector but in the context of a university. The production process consisted of the development and implementation of a competency-based teacher education (CBTE) program, including the organization, curriculum, instructional materials or modules, and pedagogical activities. The goal of this production process can be viewed to be not only concerned with improving educational practice and enhancing the 'profession' of teaching. It can also be seen, metaphorically at least, as focused on the accumulation of 'academic capital', that is, the coin of the realm in universities which enables those possessing substantial amounts of it to 'live a good life' and exercise considerable power in the local, national and global political economy of (at least) university life. There is no question that during this period the College of Education moved from one that was almost unknown outside the local setting to one with a well established national and international reputation.

Our focus on how a CBTE program at the University of Houston was developed and implemented during approximately a decade from the late 1960s to the late 1970s (just prior to the period of ethnographic research reported in chapters 4–6) provides an excellent opportunity to examine the experience of workers, namely, university faculty. Of concern is how this segment of what Larson[2] terms 'educated labor' deals with attempts to shift the labor process and the relations of production from that characterized by relatively autonomous 'craft workers' operating in almost total isolation to that characterized by a factory-like, hierarchical system. The dynamics of this change in relations of production — both its technical and its political or governance aspects — are investigated for insights into the functioning of one of the major contradictions in (at least) capitalist social formations, that of proletarianization and professionalization. Although this contradiction is seen to be determined 'in the last instance' by the economic base in a society (or the world system, more generally) the details are socially constructed by real people often with sincere commitments to laudable goals.

The purpose of the discussion here, therefore, is to illuminate, in this particular case, to what extent and in what ways the professoriate was proletarianized, thus providing an opportunity to understand further the contradictory class position of a segment of the middle class(es) and the potential for their political alliance with the major conflicting classes under capitalism: bourgeoisie and proletariat. We also seek to describe how, if at all, resistance to the process of proletarianization occurred, and what blocks to this resistance emerged.

The Concept of Proletarianization

Before presenting the case study material, we shall outline some of the major theoretical issues connected with the concept of proletarianization. From both Weberian and Marxian perspectives, proletarianization is a process which historically has affected and continues to affect skilled workers, whether they be highly formally educated or not. The process, which is exaggerated during periods of economic crisis, involves an increased and rigidified division of labor, routinization of work tasks, the attendant separation of conception from execution, and an intensification of the labor process.[3]

Derber makes a useful distinction between technical and ideological proletarianization. The former is defined as the 'loss of control over the process of the work itself (the means), ... [the] technical plan of production and/or the rhythm or pace of work', while the latter is described as the 'loss of control over the goals and social purposes to which one's work is put.'[4] Derber argues, furthermore, that the process of ideological proletarianization historically preceded technical proletarianization among craft workers in manufacturing industry, and that to date, salaried 'professionals' have primarily experienced aspects of the ideological, but not the technical, form of proletarianization.[5]

The 'logic' of proletarianization and one of its major components, deskilling, in the capitalist mode of production, is explained by Braverman: 'The labor power capable of performing a process may be purchased (and reproduced) more cheaply as disassociated elements than as a capacity integrated into a single worker'.[6] This same logic of routinizing and simplifying work tasks to enable lower paid, less skilled workers to perform them, can be seen to be applied in the public or state sector — e.g., public schooling — at least in societies in which capitalist relations dominate the economy.[7]

Proletarianization must be viewed, therefore, not as an isolated process but as part of a contradiction dialectically related to other contradictions extant in (at least) capitalist political economies.[8] The other aspect of this contradiction is professionalization or reskilling, which involves the process of creating new techniques and new jobs, thus necessitating workers (usually a smaller number) to acquire or make use of 'new' skills. This may include increased capacity to supervise, control and conceptualize for other workers. This proletarianization/professionalization contradiction, moreover, may operate to mediate and thus help reproduce or expose and thus provide a basis for challenging other contradictions in the economy and the state — e.g., that production is a social activity, but ownership and control of the means of production is privately concentrated and that production takes place for profit accumulation rather than to satisfy workers' needs.[9]

Of interest here, however, is not just the contradictory dynamics, which in the 'last instance' are determined by the economic base. There is also a concern with human action and consciousness, which are conceived of as being constituted (constrained and enabled) by social structure, but also constitutive of that structure.[10] Thus, we would ask how practitioners would perceive and respond to the process of proletarianization, while at the same time helping to socially construct the details of that process.[11] One possibility involves passive acceptance of and adjustment to the changing nature of work and the attendant forms of alienation. Acceptance may result because practitioners' 'career aspirations ... encompass a future move into management'.[12] Practitioners might also not actively resist reductions in their autonomy, etc., if the direction taken by those in control is viewed as compatible with their own goals or beliefs. In this case, they do not experience any restraint; only their 'aberrant' colleagues are seen to be constrained to work appropriately.[13] In a sense, these practitioners opt to bargain for a share of the capital accumulated rather than seek to wrest control from those in power.[14] Practitioners may also appear to passively accept the changes but, in fact, secretly resist implementing them. This constitutes an example of 'strategic compliance'[15] — an individual strategy available to those without the power and resources (human, financial or ideological) to mount a public or sustained collective challenge to the change efforts.

Individual practitioners or groups of them might alternatively respond more actively by resisting, challenging, and even mobilizing themselves and the public against increased control and other aspects of the proletarianization process. These effects might entail party politics and lobbying,[16] collective bargaining and other forms of 'unionism',[17] or collective and individual action under the banner of 'professionalism'.[18] The effectiveness of each of these not unrelated strategies depends to varying degrees on availability of human, financial, and ideological resources. Given that most practitioners and occupational groups lack sufficient human and financial resources, they must often rely on ideology to mobilize themselves, to attract other sources of support from large, wealthy or powerful segments of society, or to convince the state of the legitimacy of their automony, etc.

One aspect of this ideological work consists of the occupational group seeking to manipulate the perception of the indeterminancy/technicality (I/T) ratio of their work. Jamous and Peloille distinguish *technicality* — the ' "means" that can be mastered in the form of rules' and can be codified — from *indeterminancy* — the ' "means" that escape rules and, at a given historical moment, are attributed to virtualities of producers'.[19] The higher the perceived I/T ratio of their work, the more likely the occupational group is to attain autonomy. In effect, occupational groups or individual practitioners adopt elements of the ideology of professionalism in arguing for automony, claiming that the non-routine nature of their work 'can only be handled by extraordinary expertise and judgment. Moreover, (it is claimed) even when these conditions are fulfilled, the professional is liable to fail in his [or her] endeavor since the outcomes of the activity are largely uncertain'.[20] But Johnson emphasizes that, to have any influence, professionals must seek to counter ideologies promulgated by others which undermine their claims to autonomy. He comments that 'the extent to which the state [or some other locus of power] captures through its own definition ... occupational services to principles of technicality, the ideological bases of indetermination are not available for purposes of occupational exploitation'.[21]

The Context of Development[22]

In 1963, the University of Houston was incorporated into the state system of higher education, having started as a private junior college in the 1920s and in the interim developed as a private university. One respondent described the era as follows:

> The University ... in 1963 ... entered into the state system ...
> The University was just at that time beginning to come on the
> pipeline for resources. ... It had a whole lot of money now; it
> was like having somebody die and leave you a fortune. (23)

The dramatic increase in resources from the state was amplified by a tremendous increase in enrollment. Thus, when a new Dean of the College of Education, Robert Howsam, was hired in 1966, he was in a position to recruit a sizeable number of new faculty; three of whom had established or burgeoning national reputations (see subsequent discussion). It also meant that within a couple of years of the Dean's arrival, the College was granted the resources to build a new building. One of the people, who participated in a University-funded tour of innovative buildings in the United States as part of the planning process, commented that the Dean:

> took the opportunity for the design of this building, the
> construction of this building, as a way of mobilizing the faculty,
> to cause them to begin to think about what kind of educational
> program they wanted to deliver and what kind of a professional
> product they wanted to turn out. (9)

During the same period, the national context was also very conducive to efforts to produce a competency-based teacher education program.[23] As one of the leaders of the program development process recalled:

> In this country there was a major emphasis on education and there was a major emphasis on multicultural education in the mid-late 1960s, and the improvement of cultures, minorities through education. And so there was a lot of money being put into education and a lot of emphasis being placed on it. ... The cultural milieu that brought about the 1960s also contributed to education as a way to solve those problems. (11)

The substantial federal funding for educational and social programs associated with the 'Great Society', operationalized during the administration of a former Texas school teacher, Lyndon Johnson, provided entrepreneurial opportunities for those in colleges of education. One interviewee recounted the experience at the University of Houston in this way:

> Also, at that time when the federal government was pumping a lot of money into higher education; and the overall thrust nationally was towards an attempt to find new and better ways of educating teachers; we went after the planning grant for one of those programs, unsuccessfully. And then, since we didn't get the planning grant, we decided to go after the proposal to be one of the schools that would develop the Models. ... Through that we sort of formalized, and got our thinking together, in terms of teacher preparation programs. We were unsuccessful in getting the grants [for either the planning or feasibility testing phases of the Models project] ... About the same time there was another grant possibility that came up called the Triple T Project, it was the Trainers of Teachers of Teachers, and a new funding effort in that was pursued by a conglomerate of Texas institutions. ... And then the state department [of education] [TEA] was also party to that whole group. ... And our thrust was toward a competency-based program. ... And those monies then went toward the putting together of our program ... in the early 1970s. (22)

The government, however, was not a neutral, passive benefactor. One of the three Models Project directors, who eventually was recruited and hired by the University of Houston, indicated that the federal agencies involved began, over time, to narrow the specification of fundable projects to the point of mandating 'competency-based' efforts. He noted that the US Office of Education Models Project was designed around the question:

> ... if you had all the resources in the world, what kind of an elementary teacher would you develop? And, lo and behold, even though these projects were spread throughout the country ... essentially all of them came up with competency-based teacher education programs, instructional modules, systems design and development. (21)

He went on to explain that a key person in the Bureau of Research within the Office of Education, which had funded the Models Projects, later:

> became involved in Teacher Corps. So when the RFPs [Requests for Proposals] came out for 6th Cycle Teacher Corps projects, they were to be competency-based. ... We're talking about the same people ... doing a lot of missionary work around the country. ... [There was] a project ... which was a developmental effort, where ... technical assistance [was provided] to some experimental 5th Cycle Teacher Corps projects, who before the specs actually called for it and required it, adopted a posture that they were going to use competency-based programs. And these were all minority institutions ... minority programs. (21)

The University of Houston was funded as one of the 6th Cycle Teacher Corps projects and it also was the recipient of:

> two or three other smaller grants, [including] a media grant. ... We were moving toward mediation of instruction. The notion was that anything you could lecture, you could mediate. And when you mediate it, then you can free yourself as well as the students. Then ... they can get it ... any time they want as opposed to when you're ready to lecture. ... That was sort of the forerunner to modularization, instruction modules, because that then became the jargon, the name for the packages. (22)

It is important to note, however, that the grant seeking activity was by no means random, and thus it would be inaccurate to view the nature of the grants obtained and related program development efforts as solely determined externally.[24] This point is explained below with reference to internal coordination of grant proposal efforts and to the informal, potentially mutually influential relationships between some key University of Houston faculty members and government sub-elites.

> Another part of that strategy was an effort on [the Dean's] part
> to make sure that all funded projects ... particularly training
> projects, and there were lots of them in those days, make some
> contribution in some way to the central thrust of the develop-
> ment of a professional teacher preparation program. Now, that
> does not mean that there was interference in terms of the
> direction of those projects. It just simply means there that most
> of those projects were fashioned from the outset, for example,
> Teacher Corps, in some way that was compatible with
> competency-based, instructional systems, that sort of thing. ...
> This College was moving in some of the same directions that
> funding agencies were moving in terms of their concepts of
> what should happen to teacher education. And [key faculty
> members] were very well connected and linked with the people
> who were in policy-making and fund-allocation positions in the
> federal government. (9)

To emphasize further that 'internal initiation' must be considered in
this case along with 'external transactions'[25] coming from federal and
state government, former Dean Howsam related that while interviewing for the position at the University of Houston:

> I made it perfectly clear to everyone from the president down
> that I intended to do things that nobody had thought about, that
> wasn't on the University's agenda, that if I came, it was because
> I saw the opportunity to do what you couldn't do elsewhere. ...
> Also that was communicated to the faculty, that
> I ... intended to operate in a change mode rather than a
> continuous mode, and I saw this as a great place to try some of
> these kinds of things ... and they seemed to respond ...

This theme of innovation, which was received enthusiastically by many
in the College and University at that time, was also emphasized in the
'College of Education Mission Self-Study Report', which read, in part:

> To be different and to make a difference. This is the continuing
> mission of the College of Education. Stated first in 1966, this
> commitment has continued unabated. Ten years later it is
> vigorously reaffirmed.[26]

During the interview, Dean Howsam went on to indicate some of the
things he had planned to do. In the following quote note not only his
reference to professionalism — another recurring theme — but also his

early concern that teacher education programs be oriented toward developing teacher competencies.

> I made it perfectly clear to the faculty that I was professional first, I saw teacher education as the training arm of the teaching profession. And that I thought that we were in desperate straits as a profession, and probably ... the most desperate thing of all was teacher education. ... I have worked with the profession as a profession all of my life. ... I said, 'We've got to get serious about making sure that we teach teachers the things that teachers are supposed to be able to do'.

That the move toward CBTE was at least in part a result of 'internal initiation' is also evidenced by the fact that the Dean devoted a significant proportion of his available new faculty salary monies to hiring three (of the eight) directors from the Models Project — people whom he had come to know and, of greater relevance here, whom he had come to know as proponents of competency-based teacher education. One of the former Models Project directors said that he understood that he had been recruited by the University of Houston because of the College's and his shared commitment to CBTE.

There is nevertheless no simple answer to the questions one of the interviewees said he had 'always asked' himself:

> 'Was Dean Howsam involved in it because he really believed in it or was it the thing to do? Was he searching out something that would put the College in the national limelight?' ... I used to ask myself: 'As soon as this passes on, are we going to leap onto something else? Will there be a new thrust?' (18)

There was a clear connection between the CBTE movement and the College — a connection initiated by the Dean and a small number of faculty in the late 1960s and strengthened by the arrival of the three Models Project directors and other sympathetic, newly hired faculty in the early 1970s. However, it is also clear that Howsam was 'a Dean who was ready to make his mark somewhere' (11), as one of the former Models Project directors put it.

Several of those interviewed recounted Howsam's 'end run to fame' speeches. According to one interviewee who was hired in the 1960s, Howsam said:

> 'We could not become a Harvard, we could not become a University of Chicago ... through the standard procedures. But

in order to put Houston on the map, we needed an end run to fame'. And it looked to him as if competency-based education was our avenue. (29)

And one of the former Models Project directors reported on what the Dean was saying in national forums outside the College prior to the interviewee coming to Houston:

> About that same time ... I heard Howsam say this: ... the University of Houston had decided that there were two ways a College of Education could achieve eminence. Way number one is through research. Way number two is by having outstanding programs. He did not think that, given the personnel that he had on board and given the resources that were likely to come to the University, that the research institution was going to cut it. He didn't see us becoming Stanford of the South. So he felt that the College could achieve excellence through innovation in teacher preparation. And began then, at that same time, to talk about a critical mass ... of people. (21)[27]

That the college and some of its 'stars' achieved national and international 'eminence', 'prominence', 'reputation', 'recognition', and 'publicity', was agreed to by both the supporters and the critics or 'loyal opposition' who were interviewed. One of the leaders of the College at that time remembered:

> And the story began to spread around the nation. ... And then we started to have people come to visit the ... building before it was even finished. ... We had hardly got it open when the first [national] conference on competency-based education was held here in 1971 in the KIVA [a large multi-levelled, circular shaped instructional and meeting space on the first floor of the College of Education building]. ... We had literally thousands of visitors from all over the nation and many parts of the world. ... Now here's a little old institution with a faculty never been, you know, what kind of a faculty it would have been. ... They developed one of the first competency-based programs, they developed a new building that nobody has ever seen the likes of, and the two fit together. And this is literally one of the leading programs of teacher education in the nation. All accomplished in a period of three or four years. (23)

A similar point had been made in the 1976 'Evaluation Study Report' prepared by the College for the Texas Education Agency in the Spring of 1976:

> To the nation the College is known for its developmental and promotional work in CBTE. It is sometimes referred to as 'The Mecca' of CBTE. ... The College is widely perceived across the nation as a leading innovative school of education.[28]

The questions that need to be addressed, however, are: how was this fame (or what we would term 'academic capital') accumulated so quickly and what impact did this program production process have on various members of the professoriate?

Producing the CBTE Program

Major elements of the program development process have been referenced in the above discussion. A University, which received a significant infusion of financial resources for building construction and faculty recruitment when it was incorporated into the State system, appointed a Dean, who had a strong commitment to professionalizing teaching and to improving teacher education and who shortly thereafter became a proponent of the CBTE approach. An innovative building, designed with a new teacher education program in mind, was built and attracted considerable, favorable attention. At the same time, funding opportunities from federal government sources were pursued, at first unsuccessfully. The large grants — 'Trainers of Teachers of Teachers' (1970) and 'Teacher Corps Sixth Cycle' (1971) — were obtained coincidentally with the arrival of the three Models Project directors. These new faculty members (and others recruited during this period) joined with some faculty already at the institution to undertake these funded projects. A tremendous amount of energy was directed toward conceptualizing and implementing a competency-based teacher education program at the University of Houston, as well as toward exporting the concept and promoting the College's reputation nationally and internationally. As the drafters of the College's 1972–73 Institutional Report prepared for the National Council for the Accreditation of Teacher Education (NCATE) explained it: 'a choice of strategy was adopted to make the College one of the leading innovative teacher education institutions'.[29]

In Fall 1971, an 'experimental' or 'pilot' program was started with sixty-four 'self-selected, highly [pro] biased students' (15) — 'a very small, hand-picked volunteer group ... a cut above your average student' (21). The following year, a second pilot program group of 134 students was launched. Parallel to these efforts, Teacher Corps interns, a 'bright and very committed', 'radical bunch of kids, ... missionary zealots who felt that the way to change the world was to help poor black kids in the inner city' (21), were being taken through a competency-based teacher education program, using similar modules and other elements as were included in the experimental undergraduate preservice programs.

Then in the Spring of 1973, the:

> ... faculty voted, 'We're *not* going to go into a third experi-mental group, we're going to go, we're gonna do it'. ... The faculty said ... 'We're convinced this is the way to go. We don't feel comfortable with there being a "traditional" program and an experimental program. Let's go for it'. (21)

Or as another colleague expressed it:

> ... In the Spring of 1973, the faculty said, 'Let's go full speed ahead with this and replace our current [preservice teacher education] program with a new program'. ... I think ... 1973–4 was a hellacious year because you go from 200 to 1,100 students. And everybody was pretty well swamped with paper work. And so that was a survival stage. Growing out of the survival stage was a less costly and less dynamic kind of program. ... So things became more formalized, more routinized. (11)

This 'less costly and less dynamic kind of a program' was produced because there was suddenly a much larger, 'less motivated' group of students to be served with proportionately less funding and by a larger, potentially less committed (to CBTE) faculty group.[30] We should also note that the period of full scale implementation happened to coincide with a growing world economic crisis and the attendant 'fiscal crisis of the state', evidenced in reduced revenues available for government funded projects.[31] All of these points are at least alluded to by one of the interviewees:

> ... Then it comes the day when you have to put up or shut up. You've [come to the end of an] experimental, specially funded program; you've got resources from the University tapering off ... so your ability to infuse it with new blood goes down except

as you get turnover.... And now we had to put it in, all the students had to be in it, every program we had, and we had to sustain it with regular university funds. Now that's a recipe for disaster, and everybody recognized it. ... Unless you have somehow changed the resource flow, you'll have to cut the pattern to fit the cloth. (23)

Another faculty member discussed how he experienced the transition to the full program implementation phase after having participated in a pilot program which was 'fairly idealistic [and] heavily loaded with sensitivity training and a lot of interaction ... a peak education experience'. He stressed that a model developed earlier was 'too expensive'.

> We found very quickly that the things that had been done in the other program, the one with 60 people, that had volunteers, highly motivated faculty, just would not work with the population of students and faculty that were in this program. Not to say they weren't motivated, they weren't as highly motivated. ... For example, the one-week retreat was just not possible. ... We didn't have money in the budget ... so we did some afternoon things ... that turned out to be less effective. ... Also, the involvement of the counselors, there weren't enough of them to spread across these programs. So, we had to look at instructional modules that were done that was not as expensive. (22)

The individual quoted above went on to describe how the Counselor Education faculty members, who had been organizing interpersonal skills and sensitivity training experiences during the pilot program phase, 'ultimately put together a series of instructional modules for the effective part of the program' (22).

Modules: Deskilling and Reskilling of the Professoriate

Modules, which were often slide-tape mediated instructional units accessible to students on an individual, self-paced basis, constituted a central feature of the CBTE program at the University of Houston and elsewhere. Modules became 'the big thing' and 'almost a magic word'.[32] As noted above, not only did modularization provide opportunities for individualized or self-paced learning by students, but modules also provided a less costly alternative to intensive (and expensive) face-to-face interaction between faculty and students. In addition, modularization served as a basis for systematizing the instructional program, in a sense as a form of social control. As one of the leaders of the College and of the CBTE movement nationally has written, an instructional module is 'a set of experiences intended to facilitate the learner's demonstration of objectives which were specified in the design phase of development' of the program.[33] The point was illuminated further during an interview with one of the people involved in organizing the full implementation of the program, who explained that:

> We worked on delivery systems. You know, ... given that you have this stuff and you have various people coming in each year to teach it, ... how do you assure that you get some coordination and some continuity without infringing on people's academic freedoms and creating superstructures that are too heavy for people. ... And we worked through the process of trying to deliver through instructional modules, you know, as a vehicle for that.(9)

This interviewee added that modularization efforts were 'the result of trying to find some way to deliver the program, given that those teaching it had not been involved in its design' (9).

The explicit allusion (above) to separating conception from execution makes the module thrust a clear example of the deskilling of some of the professoriate. Indeed, as one interviewee noted, this deskilling at the College level was linked ideologically to similar dynamics encountered by school teachers. When asked to explain the emphasis on modularization, this individual replied:

> In those days, see, we were coming out of that whole laboratory thing, where people all over the country were saying 'teacher proof stuff; make sure that it's all designed so it is teacher proof'. And so our orientation was to have every tit and tattle of this thing spelled out, so that if you ... came in to teach, there was no way you could mess it up. (9)

Modularization also seems to provide an opportunity for reskilling of the professoriate. And it is clear that some faculty or graduate student assistants were in a position to acquire and refine skills in curriculum or lesson content conceptualization and in designing audio-visual presentations for individual consumption. According to two of the leaders in the College, 'competency-based programs call for new skills, new knowledges, and new involvements on the part of teacher educators'.[34] They also identify some of the new skills and roles needed:

> The Learning Resource Director and the Clinic Professor are two examples of new faculty roles that might evolve in competency-based programs. Other possible specialist roles include module developers, audio-visual and communication specialists, and evaluators. These roles demand personnel who can and will work with other teacher educators in the development, implementation, and evaluation of student and program objectives and instructional activities.[35]

Note that the 'reskilling' was to involve primarily a small number of 'specialists', who would work with less skilled colleagues. Nevertheless, even among a subset of designated specialists, there is some question about how much reskilling occurred, in that the process of intensification — increased time and workload press — seems to have reduced the chance for developing skills or even producing quality work. As one interviewee described the situation:

> In operation it was really done very sloppily ... for a variety of reasons. There was a tremendous amount of work. And it was not at all atypical ... for a young graduate student [to be writing modules on sociology, but without having studied it]. But there was such confidence in the method of presenting objectives. ... And you had a bunch of stuff being mass-produced. You had secretaries over-worked. ...[Some of us tried to develop a module during an entire year], we really ... labored and struggled over it ... [and] we realized the immense amount of work to write [one] and we saw them being turned out every six weeks by other people and thought: 'that can't be very good'. And ... a lot of them were bad. (30)

Indeed, in some ways the emphasis may have been on producing something — over 800 modules were produced in the first five years of program development, according to Vogel[36] — that could be seen not only by the many visitors to the College, but also by college administrators and other members of the faculty. As one person active in promoting the CBTE program commented:

> [For the faculty ...] ... I think it may have had some positive benefits because it gave some people some things they could do

and accomplish. You can make a slide-tape and put it in the LRC, and you have accomplished something. [Now,] often you can get to the end of the day and look back and say: 'What have I accomplished?' (11)

Some of the leaders of the CBTE program development and implementation efforts stated in the interviews that they now think that stressing the modules, the delivery system, rather than emphasizing the need to achieve the competencies, was a mistake. However, there is a little question about whether modules were a 'central focus' of CBTE for the University of Houston and 'across the country'(11). One of these people articulated it this way:

I think we focused on the wrong thing, in part. We focused on the delivery system, the mediation of instruction, the modularization of instruction ... I think it was a mistake. And we may have done it because it was something we could show with a module ... We should have been about the business to see if competencies had been acquired ... by the students and not worried so much about how the competencies were acquired ... But we spent little or no time dealing with that aspect of it ...[Why ...?] ... So our initial, our opening guns were in that direction, and we just never did regroup and say: 'Okay, let's stop so much attention to this and go over to the other'. (22)

In one sense, then, modularization proceeded, even in the face of resistance (see subsequent discussion) by people who were not 'movers and shakers' and in the context of some questioning by the leadership of the CBTE movement, because it was a tangible and visible symbol associated with the academic capital that the College and some of its faculty had already been accumulating. Modules were 'something we could show' and 'our initial guns were in that direction'.

We should also re-emphasize, however, that modularization was integral to systematizing the program and, therefore, in controlling or making accountable faculty members who worked in the program. One of the leaders in the CBTE effort in Houston offered the following analysis:

The module issue, ... let me tell you about the 'catch-22' in that. You've got two ways to impose accountability in a program like this. One is to give people the curriculum and say: 'This is what you teach'. The other is to give people the objectives and to say: 'We expect your students to come out with this'. But if you do that, then you have to have a gate-keeping function at the exit end. The thing that was even less palatable to most people than modules was the notion of uniform testing. ... And what we were not willing to give up was the notion of accountability. We felt like that somehow we had to be sure that when we recommended a student for certification that student possessed a sufficient level of competence in terms of the behaviors we had assumed associated with effective teaching. (9) (9)

Modularization was complemented by other bureaucratic strategies for controlling and making accountable faculty teaching in the program. It may not be surprising, therefore, that some of:

The people who were not really in favor of the whole thing were a little bit upset about the press and the emphasis on it from the people who were running it, and that means the administration, you see, all the people in power were all for it. You see, on [the administration's] side, you know, they were very frustrated as well, that a significant proportion of the College was not going along with it. (30)

Insiders and Outsiders: Professionalism and Internal Stratification of the Professoriate

The interviewees' comments were replete with references to divisions within the College: between the 'go-getting young professionals who were going to design the new world' and the 'solid professionals who were delivering in the trenches' (9); 'insiders and outsiders' (22); 'the white hats, [who were] doing the work of the competency-based movement, and the black hats, [who] were those who resisted' (29); and 'first and second class citizenship' (15).

Comments about internal stratification of faculty in the College were offered by both those who were toward the top and those who were toward the bottom of the hierarchy. Interviewees mentioned financial differentials deriving from differences in salaries negotiated when people were initially employed. They also mentioned salary inequalities stemming from the differential rewards received by people perceived to be versus those perceived not to be productive contributors to the CBTE effort:

[The Dean] took a very active interest in the program. He

wanted it to succeed. ... And he made sure that those people who were involved in the process were rewarded for program development activities. ... He made a case for modules carrying the same sort of weight as other publications, especially modules that were picked up by other institutions and used. ... So the reward system reflected where [the Dean] expected this College to be going in terms of program. ... Here are the things that are going to count. (21)

In addition to the inequalities in salary, promotion prospects, and other 'perks and goodies', differences in status and recognition were also noted:

Another form of resentment came from the fact that there were few at the top that were getting recognized and rewarded and were going here, there and yon to do things while the others were staying at home and doing all the work. And so they [at the top] were getting their name in print, they were making some consultant money ... [Others] weren't getting any of the benefits, but in their view, and probably rightly so, they were doing most of the work, the hard work, and getting none of the glory. (22)

This status and economic benefit stratification, it should be remembered, was fused to some degree with inequalities in power. As one of the leaders of the CBTE effort confided:

I could readily understand how there were people who could have felt left out of this process or that it was somehow imposing something on them that they weren't comfortable with, and it was even more the case when you add that to the salary reward business. (21)

During this period the College, especially the administration of the CBTE program, was perceived by some as 'highly centralized' (30). When one of the critics of the program was asked about how the debates were framed during College faculty meetings, he responded:

[College meetings ... ?] No, there were very few democratic procedures at that time. A phrase [was coined] at that time, sequential democracy, which meant voting until you got it right. And, generally it was forced, it was forced on the faculty; not that a lot of the faculty didn't mind being forced, ... but it was top-down administration. ... You were either with us or you weren't. (29)

One of the leaders of the College and the CBTE movement paints a similar picture, when asked about debates in the college:

> It was not easy to debate, and I feel badly about that as I look back on it, ... because the power was all stacked up on one side. Bringing these people in, and bringing them in on a basis of commitment to this, left the people at home in a very shadowed position. They really couldn't, they weren't able to offer any alternatives, except to say 'we'll continue what we have been doing'. And they were up against, you know, it was sling shots against cannons. And the Dean was on the side of the cannons. ... The debates weren't debates. ... And there were always people who wanted to fight it ... but didn't really dare. (23)

It is salient to note that for some members of the 'brain trust' or leadership in the CBTE movement, programmatic decision-making 'was a very democratic process ... decisions were very democratically arrived at. ... We tried to move forward with consensus, you know, ... after we had thrashed out the options' (21). This interviewee, who agreed to come to the University of Houston 'with the understanding that I would have nothing to do with the administration' (21), noted how the College 'really matured' by the mid-1970s in terms of developing a structure of collegial (as opposed to administrative or managerial) authority.

> The College really matured. In the Spring of 1972 the faculty members of C & I and the Department Chair passed out 3 by 5 cards that had written on them what our salary was going to be for the following year. ... There was nothing. It was the arbitrary, I thought, and capricious, and clearly, sexually biased viewpoint of the Department Chair. ... When I walked in ... there was a notice on my desk telling me what courses I would be teaching in the Fall, and when I would be teaching them. I wasn't used to that. I always had a conference with my Chair. ... I went storming down to [the Chair] and said: 'Wait a minute; let's talk about this!' There were an awful lot of changes that took place during that period that accommodated the shift in program emphasis to competency-based. (21)

So when the decision was made by the faculty to make the transition from the smaller-scale, experimental pilot efforts to a full-program implementation of CBTE, in this interviewee's eyes, collegial authority had become the dominant mode for the College.

In a sense, this individual is correct; many decisions were taken by a vote of the faculty, and the program was not directly 'imposed by administration' (21). However, it should be clear from the discussion to this point that all faculty were not in a position to shape the issues that were voted on, nor was the faculty, particularly the newer recruits, a randomly selected group. One needs only to recall the salary and status differentials and to recognize the significant infusion of CBTE supporters into the faculty, generally, and into administrative positions and significant committee assignments, more specifically. A collegial form of governance, we would argue, involves a more equal distribution of power among the participants; colleagues may have exercised their franchise rights, but as was noted above, this was not in conjunction with any 'real debate' among equals. A researcher from Germany who studied the CBTE program in the mid-1970s reached a similar conclusion, stating that although:

> official statements stress that all departments participate in the decision making process, some College members insinuated that the implementation order had been pushed through by pressure groups with the support of the Dean.[37]

Nevertheless, this notion of collegial authority — a hallmark of professionalism — operated ideologically, at least for some of the leadership of the CBTE effort, to deflect consideration and possibly criticism of the hierarchically imposed mission for the College. And certainly the ideology of professionalism was a dominant force within the program, buttressing at another level the legitimacy of the program development and module production effort. In the following remarks by former Dean Howsam, stimulated by a question about the connection between the notion of academic freedom and the module development/implementation process, we also see that professionalism provided a basis for justifying the inequalities in salary, status and power in the College.

> Well, I'm very sensitive to the issues that are involved there. ... When you decide to implement [the CBTE program] with a group of people who didn't develop it, then you get into the controversy that arises between a profession and an academic enterprise. And I was committed always to the profession. I think that a person who teaches in a professional preparation program has to teach the best that a profession knows. ... A professor in the medical school wouldn't be allowed to do some

cockeyed [thing], and take over a privilege of a class and train doctors in witch-doctoring, for example. ... So, I have always felt that teaching is a profession, and ... a college of education is the training and development arm of the teaching profession. ... Now, that's an imposition of [me] on somebody else, but that's an assumption ... translated into a professional school. Now some people never got the concept of professional school and never saw themselves as implementors of the profession's purpose. And so that's always present in teacher education, because we still look at ourselves primarily as an academic enterprise rather than a professional enterprise.

He continued in response to probes for clarification about the modules:

And that's what the module was to lay out what the professor was to do, and the professor who was assigned to teach was ... to be committed to that as part of his profession.

Note how the ideology of professionalism, given its fundamentally contradictory nature,[38] functions to legitimate inequalities more generally in society and to support subordination of educated workers in organizations more specifically.[39] Efforts to incorporate representatives of the teaching profession into the decision-making apparatus, most notably through the Teacher Center concept, should be noted. The point, however, is that the framework and some, if not many, of the details of the CBTE program did not derive directly from collegial discussions among rank and file members of university-based, or school-based, educational workers, let alone the masses of 'lay' citizens. The program assumptions and components were constructed primarily by a segment of university-based teacher educators, whose ideas, for a variety of reasons besides their possible validity, were being promoted or reinforced by state and federal level governments. Recall that many of the elements of CBTE in Houston were developed by some of the 'stars' before they arrived on the scene in Houston. Remember also that this was a thrust that was boosted tremendously by a substantial infusion of federal monies. Both locally in Houston and nationally those driving the CBTE vehicle constituted an 'elite' segment of the 'profession', but only one of several elite groups who were willing to speak for the 'profession'.[40] This conflict in assumptions and proposed practice was certainly apparent at the national level and, as has been suggested above and will be delineated below, the dynamics within the University of Houston were no exception to this national picture.

Nature of the Critique: Reasons for Resistance

One interviewee recalled that the CBTE program was being developed by a:

> vanguard, a chosen few ... with the money and force behind them. ... [And it] was thrust upon a lot of people who had been here a lot of years. [The leadership] emphasized getting it off the ground [versus] studying it. The program frightened [those who had been here] a lot; some resisted for academic reasons: the validity of the way the idea was being put into operation. (15)

The academic or philosophical reasons centered around issues such as, 'there was no theoretical base ... [and] they really didn't want anybody hard-nosed evaluating' (30) the program. Another critic of the CBTE movement amplified these points when discussing the initial efforts in conjunction with the 'Triple T' project.

> We thought we were going to hash out pros and cons and finally to develop a group experimental program. ... The argument was over logic and philosophy versus practicality and product. ... [It was a] bastardized Skinnerian model. ... But the pressure was on to produce something, to create a project ... and worry about how they came together later. (29)

Another interviewee, who 'early in the game ... rejected ... the idea of CBTE', explained, in part, that:

> I don't like it, I guess I'm saying in a different form what I've already said, ... it's reductionistic in terms of education, we're pinning down, there's so much that ... we're not really capable of measuring; there's so much affective ... I'm not sure we can contain it down to a list of proficiencies. (18)

Some reasons for resistance could be understood in terms of not wanting 'to be part of the innovation' (15). One of the leaders of the CBTE effort discussed it this way:

> I think you could even go as far as to say it was resistance. ... There was a lot of: 'Why should I change what I've been doing? It's been working fine'. There was a lot of: 'What do you mean I've got to'. You know. (9)

The remarks quoted above, however, indicate that the resistance was stimulated not just by a proposal for change but by change being implemented in a way that was perceived to undermine their authority and challenge whether they had any skills to contribute. Another one of the leaders described the position of:

> the other camp that was saying, 'This is a matter of academic freedom. I'm the person solely responsible for the content of my course. Just keep your nose out of my business. I'm very capable and very competent in what I'm doing, and I don't need you to tell me what I [should] be doing'. (21)

The issue of academic freedom was raised at various levels. As the individual quoted below noted, academic freedom issues were broached in the College and in the University:

> This whole thing about academic freedom on this campus; I know that there were some people in other colleges concerned that we were being 'forced to teach one way', that we all had to be competency-based. This was a strike against academic freedom. ... I can remember talking over a cup of coffee [with a colleague] about: 'Was our academic freedom being challenged?' If somebody was going to come around and say, 'It's going to be modularized, and you better get your modules together'. (18)

The academic freedom issue was also part of the discussion at the state level when on June 10, 1972, the Texas State Board of Education approved a policy standard — lobbied for by some of the leaders in the CBTE movement at the University of Houston — which in effect mandated that only institutions using a performance or competency-based model would have their teacher education programs approved.[41] One interviewee, referring to a file of newspaper clippings, reported that after the intervention of a variety of groups, including the American Association of University Professors:

> On January 4, 1974, Attorney General John Hill said that neither the Texas State Commissioner of Education nor the Texas State Board of Education has the authority to require that teacher education programs presented for approval be performance-based. ... [This was] unconstitutional, that you can't mandate one best way to prepare teachers.

Although academic freedom claims seemed to be effective in the state level debates, they were not at the level of the College. Part of the reason for this involves the apparent strength of the former Dean's and others' professionalist argument that professorial 'prerogatives' had to be restricted for the good of the profession in 'professional schools' (see previous discussion). What is intriguing to speculate about in this regard, though, is whether challenging CBTE's systemizing thrust by unfurling the academic freedom banner may, in fact, have deflected attention away from what could have been seen as a more general process of proletarianizing the professoriate.

Many of those interviewees, who termed themselves opponents of CBTE, offered critiques in line with a notion of deskilling and drew upon issues associated with the indeterminacy/technicality ratio.[42] One person interviewed discussed the modularization efforts, positing that:

> The problem was the assumption ... that how you taught, what you taught and who[m] you taught were not related, that there was an ideal teaching way that was content free or student body free ... and instructor free. ... 'What is [the ideal way to teach]?' The answer starts to come down to some sort of personal contact, a physical presence, a personality, an eye contact, an ability of good teachers to read their audience, to decide when they're losing people, to modify. ... Then to the extent that that is true, then you really can't capture it; a good teacher would probably never do it that way again. (29)

Another interviewee communicated similar themes when discussing modularization and CBTE more generally:

> I began to see that with competency-based teacher education, that it was a kind of an organization kind of a thing that really wasn't getting at the heart of learning or the heart of teaching. If it was happening in any classes, it was the individual that was doing it and not the system so to speak. ... And sometimes that individual instructor thought it was the system that was doing it, when as far as I'm concerned, it was the individual personality and the dedication of that individual. ... If there's a negative part to the modules coming out: ... *The skill would be in the module* that perhaps [you] created, but still ... sometimes I feel that that is all [an instructor has] to offer is the experience that [he/she has]. (18)

However, in labelling CBTE's thrust as an attack on academic freedom — a narrower and a more occupational group specific notion than proletarianization — the faculty members may have limited their chances for seeing the parallels between what they and other workers were experiencing.

Types of Resistance

One might assume that this explicit reference to the deskilling process associated with modularization — 'the skill would be in the module' — would be articulated by a faculty member who actively criticized and resisted the proletarianization dynamic associated with the CBTE program efforts. But instead, this individual commented in response to the question, 'Were you totally alone in these reservations?':

> No, I'm sure there were other people. The, uh, we were pretty quiet, I think, as a group. ... I don't recall that anyone in any faculty meeting ever got up and screamed and shouted. If there was opposition, it was kind of we talked outside of any faculty meeting. ... I never felt that they could fire me, or I never felt really threatened. And maybe that's one reason why I was quiet and why everyone was quiet. I just went ahead and taught my classes the way I thought I should teach them. I even produced a couple of modules. ... One of mine was very well accepted by the people [at UH] who picked it up and used it. I used it in my own class but in my own context; I never distributed it as a module to my students. (18)

And later in the interview this faculty member clarified the nature of his passive resistance or 'strategic compliance', indicating that even one of his close friends, who was an active proponent of CBTE in the College, may not have known about his critique. Talking initially about his fear and dislike of one of the leaders of the CBTE effort, he stated:

> I was always cordial to him, but I always just felt that he and I operated on different wave-lengths and I didn't want to have to spend a lot of my time defending myself. And so ... there were individuals I avoided. ... [Another leader] and I have always been friends. ... I don't know if he ever knew all my reservations or not, because I did keep pretty quiet. (18)

An interviewee alluded to another form of resistance — similar to a 'slow down' or 'work-to-rule' — in discussing the modularization effort.

> And, of course, that's partly a function of a lack of trust in the teaching profession. ... What they don't realize is that you can't force teachers to do anything. ... [I expended some effort to develop a module] in response to that mandate that we needed

to have this in place by that given date. And I think it was over that year because we thought that the guillotine might fall. ... Okay, if we're going to be forced to do it, then let's do it on our own terms, and let's do it slowly ... let's try to do it right. (30)

There is additional evidence of more active criticism and resistance, primarily by members of the Foundations of Education Department (FED), but also from members of the Administration and Supervision Department (AED). As Vogel has reported, FED offered:

the strongest resistance to competency-orientation ... in general, and to the compulsory development and use of modules. ... [T]he department claimed more academic freedom in the design of its teaching activities.[43]

Similarly, in our more recently conducted interviews, the comment was made that: 'The major resistance came from the folks in Foundations' (21). But much of this public critique was generally isolated and apparently ephemeral. According to one of the leaders of the CBTE effort:

In the early phases [he, #29] raised questions about it, but ... I think he just backed away from it rather than continuing. He raised really good conceptual questions that caused a lot of good interaction, but because the group was going one way and he was going another, I think he just backed out of it pretty quickly.

The member of the 'loyal opposition' indicated, moreover, that the forms of resistance never really went beyond public debate and isolated, individualistic forms of non-compliance. When he was asked, 'What were the resisters doing?', he replied:

They were teaching in a classical way ... loyal opposition ... It was a common theme in the Foundations Department: 'Do your job and do it well; meet your students, teach the best you can'. (29)

Another vocal critic during the early phases of the program conceptualization and implementation process reported a similar experience of backing out.

I was involved from early on, developed modules, [but I was the only person who ever used parts of them, and then only in a group instructional setting]. After some time I wore out my welcome, partly because of the critical way I asked questions. Also, it was all I could take. (15)

There was also mention of forms of public critique and resistance. For example, one faculty member in the Foundations Department was reported to have introduced his course to students, some of whom worked closely with key faculty in the CBTE movement, by placing with considerable ceremony a cardboard box on the desk in front of the classroom. He is alleged to have announced that, 'Here is the module for this course', and then opened the box and in a magician-like way pulled out copies of his course syllabus, which he then proceeded to distribute.

Why the Limited, Ephemeral and Isolated Resistance?

Active resistance and non-compliance occurred, but apparently more often the negative appraisal of CBTE efforts was connected with passive and 'quiet' forms of resistance or 'strategic compliance'. What might account for this? First, it may be true that the resisters were so few in number that anything approaching a mass rebellion or struggle would have been out of the question. Certainly, this was the view of some of the leaders of the CBTE program development process. This was a period of incredible excitement and activity in the College — a time when being a member of the College 'community' was a source of considerable pride for many faculty. As one noted: 'I would be hard pressed to name one faculty member [in either the Curriculum and Instruction Department or the Health and Physical Education Department] who actively opposed it' (21). In a sense, though, this may merely be reiterating that passive and 'quiet' forms of resistance predominated.

We should also call attention again to the tremendous inequalities in organizational power between the proponents and the opponents, the 'cannons' and the 'sling-shots'. And as one interviewee emphasized, this differential in organization power was fused with a professionalist-type stratification of 'credentials' and 'reputations'.

Some faculty experienced cultural conflict in that they were told that the College is going one way and you're going another. Some people felt they would get punished if they didn't go along with the CBTE thrust. There were also more subtle ways of punishing such faculty: they were frozen out, not invited to various things, not being part of the group. Other faculty had no choice, because they didn't have the academic credentials to refute the people who were brought in and who had more publications, though not necessarily research. The leaders of CBTE were full professors with national reputations. [An opponent] would stand up and say things, but he was vulnerable because he didn't have the academic publications. So when [a proponent] made his point, others were forced into it; they had no choice. (18)

Inequalities in power and status, not to mention wealth, though, do not seem sufficient to account for the limited and private nature of the struggle against CBTE's proletarianization thrust — the deskilling of the professoriate, buttressed ideologically via claims both of an increase in the technicality/indeterminacy ratio and of the special requirements of programs in 'professional' schools. We must also consider strategies and ideologies which functioned to divide the group which might otherwise have actively and collectively resisted. Of relevance here is the fact that the major concerted effort to modularize the instructional system was focused on the undergraduate program. This meant that faculty, including some of the most vocal critics in the Foundations Department and the Administration and Supervision Department, could personally avoid the brunt of the proletarianization process because they could and did primarily teach graduate level courses. This avenue of escape seems to partly explain the tapering off of public criticisms and resistance.[44]

In addition, even within the undergraduate program, there seems to have been more focus on some of the courses than others. One of the leaders explained:

Competency-based, you see, was applied in this College ... to generic teaching. Competency-based was applied by some faculty members to content teaching, but the fundamental thrust was in the generic teaching realm. ... [To extend competency-based to content methods classes] would have alienated a lot of people. And they would have had a perfect right to say, 'You're meddling. ... What the hell do you know about [another curriculum content area]?' (23)

So faculty members who taught in the undergraduate program, but who taught content-specific methods courses rather than the generic methods courses for education students preparing to teach various subjects at various levels of the school system, were in a similar position to their colleagues, who taught graduate courses, to escape individually to some extent the impact of the proletarianization process.

However, we should note that there were efforts, albeit less intensive, to modularize all the courses in the undergraduate as well as at least some in the masters degree programs. Thus, we are not talking about havens from conflict, but somewhat safer shelters. This point is also supported by the fact that some form of shelters were available to most faculty in the College, because despite the open-design building, 'none of this was monitored' (30). As one of the leaders indicated:

> So we couldn't accept those bugouts, in principle you can't accept them; in practice you have to ... because we don't have any screws to turn. We never ... went in and based their evaluation on that; we never intruded into that; we should, but we never did. ... We never went in to see if they exemplified what ... the program explicated. We let them teach. We let their students evaluate them, but we never sent observers in; we never reached the stage where we began to turn the screws on the professor. But it's as logical as night following day that you will. ... We never went the distance that would have allowed them to complain. (23)

This individual went on to state that: 'The students would be the first ones to recognize that the professor wasn't doing it, and then it might turn up in the evaluation of the professor' (23). The irony of this faith — not only that students had sufficiently understood and agreed with the assumptions and program characteristics to evaluate instructors' performance on those criteria, but also that the student evaluation forms assessed validly the relevant dimensions — is given by the observation made by one of the vocal critics: 'The operation people were some of the strongest teachers; so, therefore, they could survive, you know, their classes made' (29). Other 'resisters' also discussed how they were able to deflect the impact of CBTE because their personal qualities as an instructor normally resulted in positive student ratings. Here again, space was created for at least some individuals to survive and, hence, there would be less motivation for them to join other colleagues in more active and collective forms of resistance.

Cultural Division and Collective Resistance

An important development in the College during the era preceding the full implementation of the CBTE program involved the emergence of the Foundations of Education (FED) Department. Soon after becoming Dean, Robert Howsam set in motion a departmental reorganization of the College, which among other things established the FED Department.[45] This Department was comprised of educational psychologists, educational technologists, research methods/statistics specialists, and social foundations faculty.

As noted above, it is this Department which proponents and opponents of CBTE alike viewed to be 'the main department that actually fought it, I mean actually questioned the validity of' CBTE (30) and 'the seat of the dissent to the movement' (29). The strength of this Department's opposition to CBTE appears to have been associated with the presence or absence of its first department chairperson, an individual described as 'very influential' and powerful, not only within the University, but within the State of Texas. Her presence provided protection for those in the Department who shared her critical views but who were not on a career track heading soon to another institution. When this person departed to become a high level administrator of a new campus of the University, FED was in a weaker position to organize opposition to the CBTE program development and modularization efforts.

Although the loss of their power base reduced the potency of their offensive and defensive strategies, in another sense it helped form a consolidated oppositional effort on the part of the remaining faculty. That is, opposition to CBTE provided a vehicle for 'finding itself', for developing its 'cultural' group identity. It brought the group closer together. One faculty member in FED offered the following rejoinder after commenting that the unequal rewards and power struggle 'just kind of hurt the morale' overall in the College:

> Specifically and interestingly enough, for the Department I was in, it probably helped the morale. It gave us ... an external force to fight, gave us a kind of internal cohesiveness. (29)

But it was more than just social integration; FED also developed more fully into a 'cultural' group, with its own worldview, value system and linguistic markers. Another FED member interviewed posited:

> Foundations people have a different kind of a mind-set, really. It's really more academic, it's more cautious, you know; we don't really believe in gimmicks. ... In our Department, if people would come in and say that they're interested in

sequencing instruction and all that stuff, you know, our informal discussion would be, 'sounds like a C & I-type'. (30)

It was these cultural differences from the Curriculum and Instruction (C & I) Department which were partly reflected in the previously quoted remarks about the distinction between an 'academic enterprise' and a 'professional enterprise', or as another interviewee termed it, the 'profession (C & I going full force) versus disciplines (statistics and FED)' (15). Such cultural distinctions are, of course, familiar to anyone who has 'lived' in a college of education. It is not that the cultural differences were created in this time and place, but that the cultural differences took on a greater salience.

In practice, then, this notion of the cultural divide between FED and C & I — a notion which was taken up by leaders and followers in both of these departments as well as other departments in the College — helped to consolidate opposition to CBTE among FED faculty members. FED, 'the black hats', were the minority group that from one perspective would not assimilate into the dominant culture, and thus prevented the College from making a greater contribution to the 'profession'. From another perspective FED was being persecuted because of cultural differences, which needed to be preserved at least as part of some pluralist social structure in the College.

At the same time, however, this cultural conflict conception of the struggle in the College may have prevented undertaking an analysis based on 'class' struggle: the workers versus the owners/managers of the means of academic production. Ideologically it functioned to restrict alliances between FED faculty members and those in C & I (as well as AED and HPE) who, as we have seen, shared many of the criticisms of CBTE and its proletarianizing impact on the professoriate. The cultural division hampered FED's communication even with C & I faculty members who were suspected to share a critique of CBTE. According to an informant from FED:

We felt we had some people of like mind in C & I. ... [However,] you were always a little more guarded in your discussions with C & I people because just from an interpersonal point of view, you didn't want to hurt anybody's feelings who was really committed to it. (30)

Moreover, for another individual in FED, the perceived, almost stereotyped cultural distinctions provided a rationale for why the

89

professoriate in C & I (but not FED faculty) could or should be proletarianized, thus limiting the possibility for 'class' solidarity.

> In a College of Education part of your function is training. ... And if you are, in fact, in that training role, ... then you ought to use the techniques that are best at training. ... And techniques, common modules ... are all good training techniques. But when you get into certain courses, like philosophies of education, theories of learning, [or statistics] ... then I think you're into the education mode. And, then, I would argue that the academic freedom issue [arises]. ... To divide things into modules you really had to buy into the concept of the linear model. ... I didn't think my courses were very amenable to it. But there might be some training courses, I don't know what they would be, I would think they'd be in C & I ... book-keeping functions of the teacher, the kind of redundant functions. (29)

Conclusions

We have presented part of the story of dynamics associated with efforts to produce the CBTE program at the University of Houston.[46] In the mid- to late-1960s, there was a thrust by the Dean and some other faculty to better serve the teaching 'profession' and, in so doing, to accumulate what we would term 'academic capital', a thrust that was initially supported by university administrators because of their own project for obtaining such 'capital' for the institution more generally. The efforts were made possible because of the financial support of the state — both Texas and the federal government.[47]

Ironically, although those acting as catalysts for the CBTE program development effort were oriented to professionalizing teaching as an occupation, the production of CBTE resulted in the partial proletarianization of some of the professoriate. The press for rapid accumulation of 'academic capital' did enhance the status, wealth and power of some faculty, but there was also evidence of many faculty becoming the target of processes Larson[48] identifies as associated with proletarianization: intensification of work pace, rigidification of the division labor, and routinization of work tasks. And, in Derber's[49] terms, some faculty experienced aspects of both ideological and technical forms of proletarianization.

It should be emphasized that we are not criticizing all aspects of CBTE; we certainly share a concern (as did critics/resisters) for competence among teachers and other groups. What we are attempting to illustrate are some of the (unintended) implications of the process of trying to produce such a program when part of the emphasis is on the rapid accumulation of 'academic capital'.[50] Furthermore, we want to clarify that we are not celebrating the individualistic, or even the (FED) cultural group, professionalist-type claims for complete autonomy. Such autonomy claims, indeed, often help support a system which functions in the interest of the few and not of the many.[51] As Derber posits: 'individualistic values of professionals discourage collectivist ideology and inhibit cooperative organization at the work place'.[52] Liberal notions of individualism and autonomy must be challenged if the needs of people generally are to become the focus of local and global political and economic policies and actions. The point of our discussion herein, however, is that the autonomy of the professoriate was challenged not by the collective interests of all people or even of all educators, but by a particular subgroup who had a particular conception of what was best and had the local and extra-local resources to try to implement their view. It may be that the CBTE thrust was in the best interest of all people, even though few of them had a direct voice in the discourse either in Houston or nationally. Nevertheless, just as Davis[53] argues that for centuries people have justified enslaving other people in the name of progress, we need to critically examine who is involved in designing the image of progress and whose interests are served by 'progressing' in this fashion.

Some readers may ask why we engaged in macro-level political economic theorizing about what, some would argue, is merely an example understandable at the organizational level as the rise and fall of an innovation — this CBTE program. Certainly, it is *not* to demonstrate the validity of a simple economically deterministic correspondence theory, that educational institutions automatically and necessarily reproduce capitalist relations of production because of their parallel structures.[54] Indeed, what we have shown is that any degree of correspondence between the social and technical relations of producing the CBTE program in a university setting *and* the social and technical relations of production in capitalist firms is the result of real people drawing on ideologies and constructing organizational forms in the context of struggle and contestation.

The leaders of the CBTE thrust were certainly not 'dupes', enacting a structurally determined and required set of behaviors. Although operating under recognized and unrecognized structural and ideological constraints, they acted creatively to construct what they believed was the best solution to problems they perceived to exist in teacher education, schooling and society. Similarly, those opposed to CBTE's proletarianization tendencies were not performing roles determined by the 'need' of capitalist political economies to reproduce themselves. Some joined the CBTE movement because they agreed with its philosophical tenets, because they perceived an opportunity for personal growth and professional advancement, and/or they sought to avoid the negative consequence of resistance. Others resisted the implementation of CBTE, either covertly or overtly, because of concerns about its assumptions or its proletarianizing impact — discussed in terms of threats to academic freedom. These faculty members were partly constrained (and sometimes enabled) by structure and ideology, but they approached their reality with a creative capacity.

Thus, compared to an economically deterministic conception, ours is a much more complex and dialectical perspective. We posit an important role for human consciousness and action, although shaped by ideas, opportunities and resources available at the time. We assert the importance of what people think and do, but also what they draw on or take for granted about the world in constructing their strategies. Of particular importance here is the action and consciousness of a key segment of the class structure, the professoriate, who as intellectuals and members of the middle class(es) occupy an ambiguous and con- tradictory economic position *vis-à-vis* the two major classes: prolet- ariate/workers and capitalist/owners.[55] Here we have seen some members of this group — *viz.*, university teachers — experience a process, which although not identical to that experienced historically and contemporarily by industrial (and other) workers, can be seen as an example of (partial) proletarianization.[56] That their critique and resis- tance got deflected and divided, partly by their own cultural construc- tions, is useful not only as a source of insight into the dynamics in which other workers are involved, but also as a basis for understanding the professoriate's class consciousness and its potential for alliance with other groups. Does the fact, for example, that in this case professors did not overcome the isolating tendencies and establish a form of 'class' solidarity in their struggles to counter a process of (partial) pro- letarianization, mean that at the same time the professoriate has deflected an opportunity for alliances with other workers in their struggle against similar processes? Did the resisters' actions and their (and others') understanding of the dynamic in which they were involved help to mediate the proletarianization/professionalization con- tradiction, even as the experience provided an opportunity close at hand to expose and challenge such contradictory social relations? Answers to questions such as this one are crucial as we seek to understand, and then intervene in, processes which in part help to maintain and legitimate (sometimes in contradictory ways) a social structure, which is oriented toward profit accumulation by a few rather than toward the needs of the many and which also, therefore, is inherently characterized by inequalities in wealth, status and power.

In the following chapter, we begin the ethnographic analysis of the teacher education program at the University of Houston as it was encountered during the early 1980s. Issues of deskilling of teachers — separating conception from execution of curriculum — will be explored again, though this time in relation to people being prepared to deliver the 'given' curriculum in school settings.

Notes

1 Revised and abridged version of paper presented at the annual meeting of the American Educational Research Association, Chicago, March 31–April 4, 1985. Sincere appreciation is expressed to colleagues who made this study possible by consenting to be interviewed and making available for analysis material in their files. Insightful comments on an earlier draft of this paper were gratefully received from Linda Bain, Robert Howsam, Henry Miller, Sheila Slaughter, and Philip Wexler. We would like to thank Beatriz Arias-Godinez for her assistance in documentary analyses and Rose Kassamali for typing many of the interview transcripts. As always, 'Dr' Tessa Jo Shokri is gratefully acknowledged for word processing this manuscript.
2 See LARSON, M., 'Proletarianization of educated labor', *Theory and Society*, 9(1980), pp. 131–75.
3 See HAUG, M., 'Deprofessionalization: An alternate hypothesis for the future', *Sociological Review*, 20(1973), pp. 195–211; JOHNSON, T., 'The professions in the class structure', in SCACE, R. (Ed.) *Industrial Society: Class, Cleavage and Control*, (London, Allen and Unwin, 1977), pp. 93–110; Larson, 'Proletarianization of educated labor,' pp. 139–40; OPPENHEIMER, M., 'Proletarianization of the professional', *Sociological Review*, 20(1973), pp. 213–27.
4 DERBER, C., *Professionals as Workers: Mental Labor in Advanced Capitalism* (Boston, G. K. Hall, 1983), p. 169.
5 See also Larson, 'Proletarianization of educated labor'.
6 BRAVERMAN, H., *Labor and Monopoly Capital* (New York: Monthly Review Press, 1974), p. 8.
7 See APPLE, M., 'Curricular form and the logic of technical control', in APPLE, M. and WEIS, L., (Eds.) *Ideology and Practice in Schooling*, (Philadelphia, Temple University Press, 1983), pp. 143–66; APPLE, M. 'Work,

class and gender', in WALKER, S. and BARTON, L., (Eds.) *Gender, Class and Education*, (Lewes, Falmer Press, 1983), pp. 53–67; APPLE, M., 'Teaching and "women's work": A comparative historical and ideological analysis', in GUMBERT, E. (Ed.) *Expressions of Power in Education*, (Atlanta, Center for Cross-Cultural Education, Georgia State University, 1984), pp. 22–49; BEYER, L., 'Aesthetic curriculum and cultural reproduction', in APPLE, M., and WEIS, L., (Eds.) *Ideology and Practice in Schooling*, (Philadelphia, Temple University Press, 1983), pp. 89–113; GINSBURG, M., WALLACE, G., and MILLER, H., 'Teachers, Economy and the State', revised version of paper presented at the 10th World Congress of the International Sociological Association, Mexico City, August 15–21, 1982; GITLIN, A., 'School structure and teachers' work', in APPLE, M. and WEIS, L. (Eds.) *Ideology and Practice in Schooling* (Philadelphia, Temple University Press, 1983), pp. 193–212; MCNEIL, L., 'Defensive teaching and classroom control', in APPLE, M. and WEIS, L. (Eds.) *Ideology and Practice in Schooling*, (Philadelphia, Temple University Press, 1983), pp. 114–142; SARUP, M., *Marxism/Structuralism/Education* (Lewes, Falmer Press, 1984).

8   See also discussion in Chapters 4 and 5.
9   For more details on this point, see Chapter 1.
10 See GIDDENS, A., *Central Problems in Social Theory: Action Structure and Contradiction in Social Analysis* (Berkeley, University of California Press, 1979) and related theoretical analysis in Chapter 1.
11 See Ginsburg *et al.*, 'Teachers, economy and the state'.
12 CHILD, J. and FALK, J., 'Maintenance of occupational control: The case of professions', *Work and Occupations* 9(1982), p. 164.
13 See GRACE, G., *Teachers, Ideology and Control* (London, Routledge and Kegan Paul, 1978), p. 216.
14 See Braverman, p. 10.
15 See LACEY, C., *The Socialization of Teachers* (London, Methuen, 1977).
16 See GYARMATI, G., 'Notes for a Political Theory of the Professions', paper presented at the 9th World Congress of Sociology, University of Uppsala, Sweden, August 1978; ORZACK, L., 'Professions in Different National Societies', paper presented at the 9th World Congress of Sociology, Uppsala, Sweden, August 1978.
17 See Oppenheimer.
18 See JOHNSON, T., 'What is to be known: The structural determinism of social class', *Economy and Society* 6(1977), pp. 194–233; Larson, 'Proletarianization of educated labor'.
19 JAMOUS, H. and PELOILLE, B., 'Changes in the French university–hospital system', in JACKSON, J. (Ed.) *Professions and Professionalization*, (Cambridge, MA, Cambridge University Press, 1970), p. 112.
20 TOREN, N., 'Deprofessionalization and its sources', *Sociology of Work and Occupations* 2(1973), p. 329.
21 Johnson, 'Professions in the class structure', p. 108.
22 The discussion presented below draws on interview and document sources of data, although interview data are most often used to illustrate the points. See Chapter 1 for methodological details. Each respondent was assigned a number corresponding to the date on which the interview took

place; these numbers are placed in parentheses after every quote so that the reader can assess the pattern of remarks by respondents.

23 See APPLE, M. 'Behaviorism and conservation: The educational views in four of the "systems" models of teacher education', in JOYCE, B. and WEIL, M. (Ed.) *Perspectives for Reform in Teacher Education* (Englewood Cliffs, NJ, Prentice Hall, 1972), pp. 237–62. Chapter 2 also provides relevant information on the political and ideological context of the emergence of the CBTE.

24 For related developments in the case of Harvard's Graduate School of Education, see POWELL, A., *The Uncertain Profession: Harvard and the Search for Educational Authority* (Cambridge, Harvard University Press, 1980), pp. 274–75.

25 See ARCHER, M., *Social Origins of Educational Systems* (Beverly Hills, Sage, 1979).

26 'College of Education Mission Self-Study Report', Texas Education Agency Evaluation Self-Study, University of Houston, Spring, 1976, p. 43.

27 For a more general discussion of the status-striving issues connected with the CBTE movement, see RAVITCH., D. *The Troubled Crusade* (New York, Basic Books, 1983).

28 'College of Education Mission Self-Study Report', p. 4.

29 College of Education, University of Houston, Institutional Report prepared for the National Council for the Accreditation of Teacher Education, 1972–73, p. 27.

30 It was not only a question of expanding the faculty group involved in program development/implementation efforts, it was also a question of gradually replacing the involvement of some of the 'critical mass' who had been recruited to 'catalyze' the College's effort. One interviewee described the situation this way:

> The job wasn't done [but] a lot of people were tired. ... They had been going way beyond the extra mile and they just had to cut back to the mile. ... And when they give it up and it devolves to some others in the organization, it's not likely to devolve at the same level of competency as it did before. ... I think that's what's happened to this College. ... [But I sometimes wonder what would have been accomplished] if the very top talents had been able to be kept harnessed to that wagon, and would continue to have taught and developed together. (23)

31 See O'CONNOR, J., *The Fiscal Crisis of the State* (New York, St. Martin's Press, 1973).

32 In a sense, modules became 'commodities' that were produced by faculty members, but often in a set of social relations in which others 'owned' or controlled the means of production. As one vocal critic of the CBTE movement explained, sometimes there were struggles over ownership of the commodity (i.e., the module) between what might be termed the producers and owners of the means of production. He mentioned that he had been asked to teach a modularized course for Teacher Corps interns.

He explained that he had agreed to develop some modules to be included in his instructional activities, but then noted that, 'When I got done, I had to fight to get my work back. They said: "No, the Teacher Corps paid for it". ... Finally, I managed to get one copy'(30).

33 HOUSTON, W. R., *Performance Education: Strategies and Resources for Developing a Competency-Based Teacher Education Program*, (Houston, University of Houston Publication, 1972), p. 72.

34 HOUSTON, W. R. and HOWSAM, R., *Competency-Based Teacher Education: Progress, Problems and Prospects* (Chicago, Science Research Associates, 1972), p. 120.

35 *Ibid.*, p. 116.

36 See VOGEL, D., *Professional Teacher Preparation Program of the College of Education* (Bielefeld, Germany, Institut fur Didaktik der Mathematik de Universjtat Bielefield, 1978).

37 *Ibid.*, p. 78.

38 See details provided in Chapter 5.

39 See GINSBURG, M., MEYENN, R., and MILLER, H., 'Professionalism and trades unionism: An ideological analysis', in WOODS, P. (Ed.) *Teacher Strategies* (London, Croom Helm, 1980); Ginsburg *et al.*, 'Teachers, economy and the state'; LARSON, M., *The Rise of Professionalism: A Sociological Analysis* (Berkeley, University of California Press, 1977).

40 For an indication of the range of views on the appropriateness of CBTE versus other models for designing teacher education programs, see Apple, 'Behaviorism and conservatism ...'; NATIONAL INSTITUTE OF EDUCATION, *Politics of Competence: A Review of Competency-Based Teacher Education* (Washington, DC, US Department of Health, Education and Welfare, 1975).

41 Vogel, p. 49.

42 Interestingly, one of the leaders of the CBTE effort in the College, although perceiving the situation that existed differently, appeared to indicate that he shared his opponents' concerns about pedagogical deskilling (if not about deskilling in the curriculum decision-making arena).

> I always felt ... that we were being asked to agree with the competencies and objective. ... But ... I always got the feeling that the delivery of those competencies, the delivery of instruction was at my option. ... No one ever walked in and said, ' ... in your course, you must use these modules'. (21)

43 Vogel, p. 173.

44 It is interesting to note that after the initial pilot efforts, many of the leaders of the CBTE also opted to teach graduate courses.

45 It is important to note that not only did Dean Howsam create the department which became a major source of opposition to his efforts to institutionalize CBTE, but he also continued to be a major proponent of the foundational disciplines' contribution to the 'profession of education'. For instance, he was FED's major ally in fending off attempts to delete foundational core course requirements in both the undergraduate and graduate level programs. Interestingly, when William Georgiades became

Dean in 1979, he also catalyzed a departmental reorganization of the College and one of the major changes this brought about was a breaking up of the FED Department, distributing its faculty in two newly configured departments.

46   For other aspects of and perspectives on the story of CBTE at the University of Houston, see FELDER, D., HOLLIS, L. and HOUSTON, R., 'Reflections on the evaluation of a teacher education program: The University of Houston experience', unpublished manuscript, 1981; HOLLIS, L., 'Competency-based teacher education: Past, present and future', in *Competency-Based Teacher Education: Professionalizing Social Studies Teaching* (Washington, DC, National Council for Social Studies Bulletin, No. 56, 1981); Houston; Houston and Howsam.

47   It is significant to note that, at least at the federal level, government participation was stimulated by an 'urban crisis', viewed in 'problem' or 'conflict' terms, but generated out of contradictions in the national and global capitalist political economy [see Chapter 2, and GRACE, G., 'Theorizing the urban', in GRACE, G. (Ed.) *Education and the City*, (London, Routledge and Kegan Paul, 1984), pp. 94–112]. Also noteworthy is the fact that as the economic crises deepened in the mid-seventies, spawning a 'fiscal crisis of the state' (O'Connor, 1973), program developers were forced into a position in which they could only continue the College's thrust by intensifying the proletarianizing processes which had been muted during the era of abundant resources.

48   See Larson, 'Proletarianization of educated labor'.

49   See Derber.

50   See MERTON, R., 'Manifest and latent functions', in *Social Theory and Social Structure* (New York, Free Press, 1968), pp. 73–138.

51   See discussion in Chapter 5.

52   Derber, p. 29.

53   DAVIS, D., *Slavery and Human Progress* (New York, Oxford University Press, 1985).

54   See discussion of these theoretical issues in Chapter 1.

55   See CARCHEDI, G., 'On the economic identification of the new middle class', *Economy and Society* 4(1975), pp. 1–86; Ginsburg *et al.*, 'Professionalism and trades unionism'; Johnson, 'The professions in the class structure'; POULANTZAS, N., *Classes in Contemporary Capitalism* (London, New Left Books, 1975); WRIGHT, E., 'Intellectuals and the class structure of capitalist society', in WALKER, P. (Ed.) *Between Labor and Capital*, (Boston, Southend Press, 1979).

56   See also ABEL, E., *Terminal Degrees: Job Crisis in Higher Education* (New York, Praeger, 1984); BEVERLY, J., 'Higher education and capitalist crisis', in DERBER, C (Ed.) *Professionals as Workers: Mental Labor in Advanced Capitalism*, (Boston, G. K. Hall, 1982), pp. 100–21; WENGER, M., 'The case of academic: Demythologization in a nonprofession', in GERSTL, J. and JACOBS, G., *Professions for People: The Politics of Skill*, (New York, Wiley, 1976), pp. 95–152.

Conceptions of Curriculum and the Anticipatory Deskilling of Preservice Teachers[1]

The half-educated [person] ... is likely to try (and fail) to understand the specialist[s] instead of obeying [them]. ... The educated [person] should know when not to think and where to buy the thinking he [or she] needs.[2]

Introduction

The research reported herein involved the use of ethnographic methods to examine a particular terrain — a 'competency-based' and 'field-based' preservice teacher preparation program — in order to describe contradictions in conceptions of the curriculum. The focus was on the messages in the formal and hidden curriculum of this program and on how prospective teachers' previously constructed conceptions of curriculum knowledge interacted with the messages they encountered. This 'micro' level description was then also interrogated for indications of how contradictions (and their resolution) in the organization and processes of teacher education can be seen to either expose or mediate contradictions within the economy. Of particular interest is the way the resolution of curriculum dilemmas or contradictions in the context of preservice teacher education relates to the deskilling/reskilling contradiction within the economy (and the state), which we dealt with in Chapter 3 as it implicated university faculty. As we shall see, the resolution of contradictions within the teacher education program under study operates to mediate the deskilling/ reskilling contradiction within education and the economy. Thus, teacher education may be conceived in this case as a process that encourages the development of half-educated persons into fully-educated persons, who 'know when not to think'.

This research is an example of the 'critical inquiries' which Berlak and Berlak call for, in that it starts with the assumption that:

> [N]o particular emphasis or pattern of resolution [of a dilemma or contradiction] can be defined in advance either as hegemonic or as supporting or supported by counter or alternative hegemonies. The relationship of particular patterns and particular contexts to social reproduction and change are problematic, that is, to be taken as hypotheses for critical inquiries.[3]

That is, the approach adopted here does not assume a simple or perfect deterministic process of reproduction. Rather, as more fully discussed in Chapter 1, by using the concept of contradictions, we attend to the relative autonomy of social structures, ideologies and human action. In this chapter, we will examine conceptions of curriculum as linked to extant class, race, and gender relations, with particular focus on the deskilling/reskilling contradiction in the economy as it implicates predominantly female jobs.

Deskilling/Reskilling Contradiction

As discussed in Chapter 1, one of the major contradictions within capitalist social formations is the social character of production and the private ownership and control of the means of production. Closely related to this contradiction is that 'production takes place for the purpose of profit [and] not for the satisfaction of consumption needs of workers or for the purpose of workers' job satisfaction'.[4] The economic contradiction of deskilling and reskilling is particularly relevant here.

Deskilling is part of a dynamic of proletarianization, which affects skilled workers — apparently females more so than males — through increased and rigidified division of labor, routinization of work tasks, the attendant separation of conception and execution, and the intensification of the labor process.[5] The 'logic' of proletarianization/deskilling in the capitalist mode of production as explained in Chapter 3 is based on the possibility of reducing labor costs by increasing the number and replaceability of potential workers who can perform the less skill-demanding tasks.[6] Reskilling, the other aspect of the contradiction, involves the process of creating new techniques and jobs, thus necessitating workers (usually a smaller number and not the same ones who have been deskilled) to acquire or make use of 'new' skills.

Recent analyses have discussed the proletarianization/deskilling as well as reskilling of educators.[7] Thus, our attention has to be directed not only to the private sector economy, but also to the public sector or the state. For instance, Apple describes both teachers' deskilling, which results from the introduction of prepackaged curricular forms:

> The skills teachers used to need, that were deemed essential to the craft of working with children — such as curricular deliberation and planning, and the ability to design teaching and specific curricular strategies for specific groups of individuals based on intimate knowledge of them — atrophy because they are less often required.[8]

and their reskilling in techniques for controlling students:

> The teacher is becoming something of a manager ... at the same time that the objective conditions are becoming increasingly proletarianized due to the curriculum logic of technical control.[9]

Contradictions in Conceptions of Curriculum

Just as the concept of contradictions assists us in analyzing economic relations, so too it provides a lens for making sense of how curriculum is conceived. Certainly, curriculum knowledge has been identified as one area in which dominant culture and an unequal social structure are reproduced,[10] in a sense elaborating from a critical theory standpoint the claim made over fifty years ago by Waller that the 'school is ... a gigantic agency of social control'.[11] Nevertheless, as Anyon explains, curriculum knowledge may be reproductive or non-reproductive, either contributing to or not contributing to 'the legitimation and perpetuation of ideologies, practices, and privileges constitutive of present economic and political structures'.[12] Moreover, even in situations where reproductive knowledge dominates the curriculum-in-use, contestation, resistance and struggle by students and others may help undermine social and cultural reproduction and produce social change.[13]

Our analysis of contradictions in conceptions of curriculum is grounded in Berlak and Berlak's 'dilemma language of schooling'.[14] In a more recent statement, Berlak and Berlak clarify that the dilemmas 'identify the contradictions and commonalities in teachers' consciousness, in a situations and in society that are manifest in the process of schooling'.[15] Of the sixteen dilemmas discussed by the Berlaks, three seem particularly germane for present purposes.

(a) knowledge as given — knowledge as problematical;
(b) public knowledge — personal knowledge;
(c) knowledge as molecular — knowledge as holistic.

Each of these will be discussed to clarify the content of the dilemmas and to relate the tensions identified by dilemmas to other work in the field.

Knowledge as given and knowledge as problematical identify contradictions between the extent to which one has an 'objectivist' conception of knowledge,[16] viewing knowledge as 'truth "out there"' versus a conception of 'knowledge as constructed, provisional, tentative, subject to political, cultural and social influences'.[17] This dilemma seems to capture the distinction Eggleston[18] makes between what he terms two ideological models of the curriculum: the 'received perspective' and the 'reflective perspective'. It also highlights the contradiction between, on one hand, 'socialization', 'achievement', and management models of the curriculum and critical and revisionist perspectives, on the other.[19]

Teachers live this contradiction in two respects. They do so, first, by the way they seek to orient students to conceive the curriculum. That is, do teachers encourage students to treat curriculum knowledge as given or as problematical? The second respect pertains to the way teachers think about the sources of curriculum knowledge they incorporate in their classes. In this respect, the distinctions Tabachnick *et al.*[20] discuss among bureaucratic, functional and independent teacher roles are relevant. To the extent that teachers take curriculum knowledge as given, they will be more likely to 'bureaucratically' implement the curriculum as formally defined and less likely to 'functionally' adapt or take an 'independent' role in defining the curriculum. There may be other constraints discouraging an independent role — e.g., district policy and administrator practice — but the conception of knowledge is seen to be important.

The second dilemma, or contradiction, is constructed on one pole by a view of knowledge as personal, in which worthwhile knowledge is that 'established through its relationship to the knower' and the other by a view that knowledge is based on 'public principles that stand as impersonal standards', in which 'accumulated traditions have value external to and independent of the knower'.[21] Bernstein's concept of frame, which 'refers to the strength of the boundary between what may and what may not be transmitted in a pedagogical relationship',[22] is implied in this dimension. The stronger the frame around curricular knowledge, the less likely it is that students' and teachers' personal knowledge will be incorporated in the curriculum.

The holistic-molecular dilemma 'represents contrasting ways of organizing and teaching school subjects'.[23] The foundation for this dilemma is Bernstein's concept of classification, which 'refers to the nature of differentiation between contents. Where classification is strong, contents are well insulated from each other by boundaries'.[24] The issues pertain not only to whether 'traditional' subject areas — mathematics, history, language, economics — are seen as separate, but also whether topics or units in one subject are viewed as isolated. A holistic conception of curriculum knowledge thus reflects an assumption of weak boundaries among contents, and a molecular or fragmented conception of curriculum knowledge reflects an assumption of strong classification of content areas.

Conceptions of Curriculum in Preservice Teacher Education

To investigate contradictions within the curriculum of a preservice teacher education program, how students experienced these contradictions, and what implications this has for contradictions of the economy, data were drawn from a longitudinal participant observation study conducted in the context of the secondary education certification program of the Professional Teacher Preparation Program at the University of Houston, Central Campus. Fieldnotes, documents as well as interview transcriptions were used to conduct as well as illustrate the analysis. (See a more detailed discussion in Chapter 1.) In the interviews with prospective teachers, I employed both retrospective and projective interview questions about curriculum decision-making. I initiated the discussion, if possible, by focusing attention on experiences during the semester — e.g., peer teaching lessons, practice lessons in schools, and student teaching — and asking interviewees to describe how they had 'gone about deciding what specific content you would teach?' I further probed:

> Who or what sources have you consulted in making these curriculum decisions? What did you take into consideration in deciding what specific content to teach?

I then encouraged interviewees to speculate about 'a situation in the near future when you will be employed as a teacher', using similar, though projective rather than retrospective, questions and probes.

Overall, relatively few components of the program's formal curriculum dealt explicitly with curriculum theory, curriculum decision-making, or the nature of knowledge. Generally, the readings and class discussions focused on instructional skills, methods and strategies. However, both the formal curriculum as well as the hidden curriculum of the program provided messages relevant to conceptions of curriculum.

Problematic Versus Given

Throughout the semesters of participant observation in the secondary education program, I encountered few comments indicating a need to treat the curriculum as problematic. In the first semester's multicultural education unit, the politics of textbook selection were mentioned, indicating that what was included in texts reflected cultural and political influences and thus was not primarily a compilation by neutral experts. One of the guest instructors in the multicultural education unit also discussed different conceptions of culture:

1 something out there which is acquired;
2 culture comes from mental/physical activities;
3 people create it — a philosophy particular to a group (fieldnotes).

This guest instructor went on to cite an example of how people use their own 'frame of reference' in approaching the educational experience, citing a black child who responds to a teacher's request to name a 'prominent' American by saying 'Malcolm X' rather than the expected, and 'acceptable', George Washington.

During the second semester in discussing the results of a test an instructor noted that it was possible to see more than one 'right' answer. This same instructor commented later in the semester that information about the contrasting functioning of the right and left hemispheres of the brain was only 'theoretical, not proven'. During an on-campus student-teaching seminar an instructor discussed the controversy between word-centered and meaning-centered perspectives for understanding the reading process. Students were also challenged to consider why they were teaching literature and why the particular works they focused upon were chosen.

There were also two occasions when instructors exhorted preservice teachers to adopt an independent stance toward curriculum decision-making, thus potentially encouraging them to treat existing curriculum knowledge as problematic. These occasions occurred during the 'multicultural education' unit conducted early in the first semester. In the second session of this unit, the narrator in the film, *Future Shock*, warned those present:

> Is technology always desirable? ... What we do today determines what tomorrow will be. ... The future need not be blindly accepted. ... Education should make people aware of the danger of technology. ... Don't accept everything. [It is important] that we make critical decisions about what we want and don't want (*Fieldnotes*).

These and similar remarks stimulated an animated discussion about teaching values in school — whether it can be avoided and which values should be included. Earlier in the class a guest instructor had opined: 'Your objectives, you decide upon by professional judgment as relates to your specific subject area' (*Fieldnotes*). This comment echoed one made by another guest instructor: 'You must realize you're the professional educator; you must decide about, determine the curriculum. A doctor or lawyer doesn't let others decide' (*Fieldnotes*). However, this latter comment was followed closely by the main instructor interjecting into the discussion: 'There comes a time when the system dictates, you must use your professional judgment in that context — you may lose you job' (*Fieldnotes*), thus providing some caution to those planning to do more than functionally adapt the curriculum.

These illustrations of a problematic, independence stance represented the exception in the program's curriculum. Generally, the readings and class discussions treated the content of the curriculum as given, not something about which one must make decisions. As is claimed for school classrooms,[25] controversies were rarely the focus of discussion in classes in the program — one of the second semester secondary education program courses being an exception — and a focus on controversies about the nature of curriculum knowledge was even rarer. In one of the assigned texts much of the commentary began with: 'Given a set of objectives'. Part of the givenness of the curriculum stemmed from the notion that content knowledge was acquired outside the required teacher education program courses. As students in the secondary education program were informed by their instructor on the first day of class in the first semester, 'In the College of Education the emphasis is on teaching people rather than teaching content. The college of your major is responsible for your content knowledge' (*Fieldnotes*).

Considerable emphasis was given to 'correctly' stating objectives, given curricular goals or topics, rather than on deciding what the topic or goal should be. The following lengthy excerpt from fieldnotes of a first semester class session, the only one that was nominally focused on curriculum issues, illustrates how class discussions (as well as assignments and examination questions) were devoted to 'competencies' in writing instructional objectives and preparing lesson plans, rather than on analyzing what knowledge or why certain knowledge should be included in the curriculum.

[The instructor] asks: 'How do teachers decide what to teach?' One student volunteers an answer relating to 'teacher's interests' but the contribution is not taken up by the instructor. A second student interjects a comment about the role of the 'State education agency and the district school board'. The instructor takes up this point, stating that the State has a definite role in determining curriculum content, time allocation to subject areas, and textbook selection. After a brief interruption due to [this class's instructor's] negotiation with [another instructor] regarding the placement of a screen/chalk board serving as a divider between the two open classroom spaces, [the instructor] emphasizes that it's better not only to make instructional objectives, but also to communicate them to one's students. Not much response to [instructor's] initial question, as discussion moves on toward instructional objectives. [The instructor] explains: 'Research and common sense support need for a relation between content (what), process — instructional strategies (how), and test (evaluation)'. [Instructor equates learner needs with level in the given curriculum.] ... [Instructor] explains 'Why you have to do intricate lesson plans even though most teachers don't use them'. ... [After answering student's question about course dropping/adding], the instructor continues: 'Goals are broad and vague. ... A teacher needs to know the school system's goals and objectives. Then one should assess the needs — performance capabilities — of the students. ... Next one selects instructional strategies and finally one analyzes instructional situation for future planning' ... [Instructor] places a transparency on the overhead projector which identifies the three components of an instructional objective: conditions, observable behavior/performance, and standards/criteria. ... [Instructor] goes through several examples of objectives ... and facilitates a discussion about the appropriateness of the objectives in terms of the following criteria: communicates clearly, focuses on outcomes, student-oriented, and specifies observable performance. ... [Instructor] suggests to class that they write one objective in their subject area for each 'domain of human behavior: cognitive, affective, psychomotor'. ... [Instructor] distributes 'suggested lesson plan format' and calls attention to two lesson plan assignments that will be due this semester. [The instructor] stresses: 'This format should be used now and through the end of student teaching' (*Edited Fieldnotes*).

In subsequent semesters, instructors commented favorably on these students' skills in writing instructional objectives and lesson plans, even while having students rehearse them periodically. The issues of curriculum theory or curriculum decision-making did not arise again in a focused way except once during a class session in the second semester. Part of this class session was devoted to discussing a 'curriculum development model'. The discussion, in fact, focused on writing instructional objectives and using different instructional strategies. The instructor helped make the transition from curricular to instructional level issues with the following remarks early in the discussion:

> Some things are given — societal level needs and philosophy; state, parish/district level general objectives, instructional objectives. Try teaching communism rather than democracy ... The teacher operates at the instructional level (*Fieldnotes*).

Note the contradiction to which preservice teachers are exposed: while the instructor indicates that curriculum knowledge — i.e., ideas about communism or democracy — is subject to social and political influences, she encourages the future teachers to act 'as if' it is unproblematic and a 'given' to be delivered to students in schools.

As they commenced their student-teaching experience the preservice teachers again had their instructional (versus curricular) role highlighted. As one supervisor explained to an assembled group of student teachers and cooperating teachers: 'We like student-teachers to experiment a little bit ... experiment in method. ... Use your own judgment. ... A student-teacher may come up with something radical; it might have to be toned down' (*Fieldnotes*). The instructor for the first semester's course had made a similar point, commenting during a conversation with the researcher, that student-teachers are told not to swerve from the cooperating teachers' content and sequence, although different instructional strategies are encouraged. She expressed the view that experiences during the second semester of the program would introduce more explicitly to students issues of curriculum decision-making, although the instructor of one of two required courses in the second semester told the researcher that she felt 'students might be ready for this topic as graduate students in a few years, after settling in' (*Fieldnotes*). On the assumption that not all teachers will pursue graduate studies, such waiting until the students are ready to understand the broader issues of their work has the implication of stratifying the educational work force in terms of those who should deliver the curriculum and those who should participate in or even systematically confront the issues of curriculum decision-making.

It is important to note that to varying extents the instructors in the program also defined their role as devising ways of presenting the given curriculum of the teacher education program. A set of nineteen competencies for the program and course specific objectives and modules, devised by some of the faculty in 'negotiation' with the state, formed the structure of the curriculum in which instructors then sought to involve students. As discussed more fully in Chapter 3, the program was conceptualized and developed by a small group of faculty, who then turned it over to other faculty members to deliver often in prescribed ways and in the context of a management system created to secure compliance.

Interestingly, when students in the program were given assignments to prepare and present lessons, they were often told that the topic or content was up to them to define. However, they were also referred to textbooks and various school districts' curriculum guides. Although not all students consulted these, there was a clear message that these were important resources. In one case during the second semester in the secondary education program students were given a topic, 'values clarification'. This was given to them, they were told, 'so you don't have to argue about what to teach, just how to teach' (*Fieldnotes*). This statement, ironically, both points to the problematic nature of curriculum and encourages students to avoid such issues and focus on instructional methods. Moreover, students encounter the contradiction of being told to devise instructional strategies, in a sense treating the choice of content as unproblematic, when the topic, values clarification, can be and, in this case, was one which problematizes knowledge, highlighting its constructed and provisional nature and emphasizing that it is subject to social and cultural influences.

In many ways, both the state and district curriculum prescriptions were given credence. Recall the comments noted above by the second semester instructor about what is given — 'state, parish/district level general objectives'. Similar points were made during the major first semester course. In the student-teaching seminar preservice teachers were admonished by instructors to 'abide by school laws, you're a guest' and to 'follow district curriculum guides' (*Fieldnotes*). A career counselor who met with the student teachers was asked whether one should inquire during a job interview about 'how much latitude I would have in curriculum, choice of novel ...' He replied that it would be better to 'focus on their needs as a district, not just your needs' (*Fieldnotes*).

The taken-for-granted constraints of the state were also communicated in reference to the teacher education program. Early in the first semester an instructor informed students that the 'state has added multicultural education, mainstreaming, and reading in the content area requirements' to the program (*Fieldnotes*). During the student teaching seminar an instructor related that a competency in career education was required by the state, and that the State (Texas Education Agency) and a 'professional' body, NCATE (National Council for Accreditation of Teacher Education), had criticized the teacher education program for not fully satisfying the required emphasis in multicultural education and reading in the content areas. Another instructor, in discussing the curricular implications of proposed competency exams for screening entrants and graduates of teacher education programs, noted that 'the State of Texas will force us to change whether we like it or not' (*Fieldnotes*).

While the emphasis was on others defining the curriculum, preservice teachers were encouraged to act 'as if' this was unproblematic and acceptable and to focus attention on developing the competency to identify and specify 'instructional goals and objectives which are based on learners' needs' (program handout). Another competency they were supposed to develop involved identifying:

> learners' emotional, social, physical and intellectual needs:
> draws upon knowledge of human growth and development,
> learning theories, social/cultural foundations, assessment tech-
> niques, curriculum goals and content in order to gather
> information about the learner and to identify instructional
> needs. (*Program handout*).

Although this competency seemed to orient preservice teachers
potentially to political and ethical issues of curriculum, thus rendering
curriculum knowledge as problematic, the notion of needs was, in fact,
operationalized on a much narrower basis, as is evidenced in the
following clarification of the former competency: 'reconciles curricular
and educational goals with present *level* of learner needs' (program
handout; emphasis added). Learners' needs came to mean children's
level of achievement or attainment in a given curriculum area.[26] For
example, one instructor explained that taking learners' needs into
account would mean that one might not teach what is supposed to be
taught at a certain grade level; rather a teacher might have to move two
years back or two years forward in the curriculum[27]

Public Versus Personal

There appeared to be a mixture of messages in the formal and hidden
curriculum concerning the contradiction between curriculum knowledge as comprised of public knowledge, which is validated by public
principles and impersonal standards, and personal knowledge, which is
deemed worthwhile and adequate through its relationship with the
knower. The emphasis on the givenness of both school and college
curricula served to highlight the public end of this dimension. The
'Foundations of Education' course, perhaps more than others, stressed
the importance of the ideas of prominent philosophers, psychologists
and sociologists, regardless of whether such ideas enabled prospective
teachers to make sense of their experience. Also, in the first semester's
major course it was unusual for personal knowledge, even that derived
from assigned school observation experiences, to be incorporated in
formal class sessions, although students turned in brief descriptions of
and reactions to their observations of a prespecified feature of classroom
interaction or school organization.

In one of the few instances where personal knowledge was

indicated to be the primary source of content — during a class session on the topic of 'teaching as a profession' — the contradiction between an emphasis on personal versus public knowledge was strongly in evidence. The class session began with the instructor encouraging students to share the meanings they attached to the term, 'professionalism', and their view regarding whether or not teaching is a profession. Although the instructor appeared uncommitted about which criteria of 'professionalism' were relevant and did not take a stance on the issue of whether teaching is a profession, she stressed that a distinction (which had been highlighted in assigned readings) existed between 'trades' and 'professions'. After the discussion, moreover, the instructor had the students view a slide-tape presentation which drew on expert testimony to assert in an unequivocal manner that there were five criteria that distinguish 'professions' from other occupations. In introducing the slide-tape presentation the instructor communicated the message that it contained the generally accepted, 'scientific' answers to the questions previously posed. (See Chapter 5 for a more detailed discussion.) Thus, not only was there a stress on knowledge as given, but public knowledge was emphasized even in this case when student's personal knowledge on the topic was invited and available to be accorded worthwhile status.

The boundary or 'frame'[28] between personal and public knowledge was weakened considerably in the second semester (as will be discussed below), but this instructor explained to students:

> My philosophy is that you take five to six hours gearing up for your writing the two-hour quiz. ... In teacher education you need to learn and internalize a number of concepts. (*Fieldnotes*)

For the student-teaching seminar, the frame became stronger again, though not totally impervious. Indeed, the instructor seemed to indicate that personal knowledge should be restricted from the student-teaching experience when warning a group of secondary education students:

> The supervisor is the one who puts down the grade. ... I asked the SBTEs to allow a climate of experimentation [in methods]. ... But student teaching is hard because you may have to decide what parts of your personality to bury. (*Fieldnotes*)

In the second semester, the focus on communication and group dynamics served to break down the public/private knowledge boundary. Although a similar topical focus obtained in the first semester and (as noted above) the second semester instructor viewed public knowledge to have a legitimate and important place in the program's curriculum, students' and instructors' personal knowledge was much more prominent in this second semester course. On the first day of class the students and instructor shared the contents of the 'three chapters of their life'. This was the first of many exercises in which both students and the instructor were called upon to communicate in class about the meanings they attach to their lives both within and outside the program experience. Insight journals were not only assigned, collected and responded to individually by the instructor, but some of the entries were shared with the class as a whole. These journals were based on assigned and unassigned topics and drawn from school observations and other (family, etc.) experiences. Through these and other activities, the curriculum-in-use included a high proportion of ideas, issues, and topics that were of personal significance to students or the instructor, with thus less emphasis on material that was validated solely by tradition or public experts. In this case, contrary to the norm in the program and in the field of education more generally, there was some 'encouragement for teachers to view themselves as originators of knowledge'.[29]

Molecular Versus Holistic

In analyzing fieldnotes based on observation in the secondary education program, I discovered only one example of what appeared to be a call for a more holistic approach to curriculum knowledge. One of the career counselors at a meeting of student-teachers commented with regard to job searching that districts were looking for teachers with 'multidisciplinary background'. However, this actually connoted being able to teach two or more separate subjects.

More generally, the message from the formal and hidden curriculum of the program emphasized fragmented and molecular knowledge. Remember the boundary (discussed previously) separating the course content in the College of Education from subject area departments. And note that given the single discipline basis of these other departments, the classification of knowledge was further reinforced. Even within the College of Education, the molecular nature of curriculum knowledge was stressed. For instance, the following describes one of twelve 'characteristics of the instructional system' of the teacher education program:

> Modularized; that is, the delivery of instruction is accomplished through the utilization of instructional modules; instructional modules are sets of learning activities ... which are intended to facilitate the learners' acquisition and demonstration of a particular competency or set of competencies. (*Program handout*).

This modularization and related press toward a molecular conception of knowledge was evidenced both in looking within and between courses in the program. The knowledge in 'methods' courses was separated from the knowledge in the 'foundations' course. Within the 'foundations' course the philosophical, historical, sociological, psychological and measurement units were so nonintegrated that no curricular problems occurred when a subsequent reorganization of the department structure of the College 'necessitated' the course to be split into two courses. During the first semester's 'methods' course (as discussed above), there was a unit on multicultural education included. Students in the course were oriented to the unit, which was taught by guest instructors, with the following introductory comment by their regular instructor: 'Multicultural is required for certification, very interesting'; and their regular instructor reoriented them at the end of the unit: 'Back at it for real on Tuesday!' (*Fieldnotes*).

The molecular conception of knowledge was also bolstered by the practice of grouping students by subject area for various components of the program. Groups of students were identified as 'math people' or 'English majors', for example.[30] Some of the instructors also exhibited a strong identification with 'my subject'. While secondary education students could enroll in the same class for the 'foundations' course, the major courses in both the first and second semester, as well as the student-teaching seminar, they were divided formally in their second semester methods course, 'The Structure and Process of Teaching', along subject-matter lines.[31] For school observations in the first semester, the students were physically separated into subject areas by school secretaries before being assigned to classrooms. The first semester course instructor told a researcher at one point about plans to further separate students for observation assignments: sending all math and science majors to one school, social science majors to another, etc. During the orientation session for the student-teaching phase, students met with supervisors and cooperating teachers in subject area groups. And although some of the student-teaching seminars included all secondary students (and sometimes elementary and all level education students, too) others were subgrouped by subject area. One of the instructors expressed a concern that this subgrouping could not be more thorough because there were too few students to warrant totally separate classes for each subject area group.

Preservice Teachers' Conceptions of Curriculum

As a participant observer in this teacher education program, I encountered a strong message about the legitimacy of existing curriculum knowledge, which was developed or approved in the context of Texas where recently a high school course, 'Economics With Emphasis on the Free Enterprise System ... and its Benefits', was established as a requirement for graduation. And while there were contradictions to this dominant message, curriculum knowledge was often treated as an unproblematic given and emphasis was placed on developing preservice teachers' skills and strategies for delivering 'the curriculum'. This message may have been reinforced by the more general 'aura of factuality' which clothes many of the conceptions of physical and socio-cultural 'reality' in universities dominated by the 'religion of science'.[32] As Giroux states:

> Supported by claims of objectivity and impartial scientific research, students in teacher education find themselves operating out of predefined categories and styles of thought that make curriculum appear to take on a life of its own.[33]

Although articulated within a different class, societal and historical context, the content and goals of teacher education as I experienced them seem strikingly similar to those intended for the primarily working class students in nineteenth century English elementary schools. According to Tawney elementary education was:

> designed on its intellectual side to confer by means of mass instruction a minimum standard of proficiency, and on its social side to create an orderly, civil and not inconveniently restive population, with *sufficient education to understand an order, and not so much to question it.*[34]

Preservice teachers were, for the most part, educated in how to follow orders — i.e., to take a prescribed curriculum and deliver it with a variety of techniques. However, because they were also usually 'not given ... the conceptual tools they need in order to view knowledge as problematic, as historically conditioned, socially constructed phenomenon',[35] they were not helped to analyze, let alone question the orders, the pregiven curriculum.

The point is not that most preservice teachers had to be strongly influenced to treat curriculum as given or unproblematic. Indeed, as the interview data collected in September, 1980, indicate, most of them entered the program with such a conception of curriculum knowledge. When the preservice teachers interviewed were asked: 'What abilities and skills do you think a teacher needs to be successful?'; they sometimes mentioned 'knowing your subject' or 'competent in subject'; but they all stressed skills for delivering the curriculum. And like most of the responses, the excerpts below provide both a sense of curriculum knowledge as given and unproblematic and a description of the teacher's role as finding ways of delivering the curriculum in a stimulating manner.

> To communicate to everybody on every [ability] level; to make things interesting, not boring; to continually come up with new ideas; ... to know there were resources to use and not have a dull routine. (*Christine*)

> To make material interesting and useful; ... to know how to find which methods work. (*Jerry*)

> To know students ... and if I'm getting through to all of them; even if material is boring, to try to get all to learn. (*Rachel*)

> The ability to break the monotony of the subject matter; a sense of humor to ease the tension; not focus only on the textbook — use visual aids, media, experiments — to provide more incentive for students to learn. (*Richard*)

The point is that the program, by not drawing much attention to the issues and by treating school and college curriculum knowledge as given, reinforced preservice teachers' conceptions.[36] At least with respect to curriculum decision-making, the program seemed to sustain an intuitive and imitative (as opposed to an explicit and analytical) nature of learning the teacher's role, which Lortie[37] suggests is dominant prior to entering a formal preparation program.

This is not to suggest, however, that these preservice teachers were passive in their orientation to curricular and instructional tasks.[38] There were clear indications that they engaged in, and anticipated engaging in, functional adaptations[39] of the curriculum. Nevertheless, consonant with messages encountered in the program, the form of adaptation that many of those interviewed hinted at was not one involving restructuring content as much as devising novel ways of delivering the curriculum — to 'spice it up' and to make the classroom experience more enjoyable for the teacher as well as students.[40]

> *Carol*: I think I would try new things. .. I have a really good file already with things I want to try, of good ideas, of things that sound good ...
>
> *MG*: Are these different techniques of presenting the lessons or different content areas?
>
> *Carol*: No, it's basically the same thing. It's different ways of approaching literature and different ways of approaching grammar, because that's what I will be dealing with. ... Even it's just simple things like starting out with some kind of attention-getter ... capturing the right side of the brain at the beginning of the lesson.

Moreover, one respondent, Dana, who treated curriculum knowledge as problematic and evidenced a strong, independent stance toward the curriculum during the first semester of the program, continued to reflect this position as she moved through the program and into her first year as a teacher. For example, at the beginning of the program, Dana identified as goals she would have as a teacher: 'To make students aware of other things in the world besides what they are exposed to in their own culture and community; to expose students to a range of alternatives; and to not put emphasis on facts, but more on different explanations of why things happened'. Then, at the end of the second semester in the program, she commented:

> Basically, my orientation right now is to be able to teach more than what's in the textbook. And I found out something. I found out that college textbooks are just thicker than high school; they don't necessarily contain more different information. ... I found the same generalizations and basic orientation. I found the same neglect or omission of certain aspects of American life in both of them. ... The way I'd teach American history is to teach all of it. (*Dana*)

And she described her experience as a student teacher in the following manner:

> Here there ... was no curriculum guide. There were suggestions

116

that [my cooperating teacher] had made. ... Okay, so I had to go find some materials. ... I found more things than I ever expected I would: about ten different books, different perspectives. (*Dana*)

After one semester of employment as a teacher her problematic, independent orientation to curriculum knowledge remained. At that point, Dana discussed here plans for the following semester, in which she would emphasize 'citizen inputs into the system and problems of democracy'. The proposed unit would 'deal with government structures, different ways societies are organized'. She indicated, furthermore, that she wanted to stimulate critical thinking among her students by raising questions about whether the existence of electoral politics, voting, necessarily was associated with an effective and appropriate system of government. She illustrated the type of question she would ask: 'Well, just because the majority of people want it does that mean it's right?' Her proposed unit, thus, would encourage students to treat as problematic curriculum knowledge as well as knowledge obtained from other sources.

Another relevant case is Jane, who during the program had gradually moved from a position of taking for granted curriculum knowledge to one representing a more problematic, independent stance. Associated with this movement was her growing concern with relying on 'personal' as well as 'public' knowledge as a source for curriculum — a concern referred to at the end of the second semester of the program:

Maybe I'd try to seek some input from the students as to what they would, maybe, areas that aren't covered in the books that they would, maybe, you know, want to know about. (*Jane*)

This movement was accelerated during student teaching because of the input of a university supervisor and, even more so, of a cooperating teacher. Jane discussed why she gathered additional sources when developing units to be taught. She said she searched for:

Other viewpoints, I think. ... When we did Indians, I used a lot of things like that. The Indian battles and the massacres: I read two different views. Say, maybe, the viewpoint of the Indians and the viewpoint of the cavalry men. (*Jane*)

However, this movement seemed to undergo a reversal in the next six months. She commented after her first semester employed as a teacher

117

that:

> I did a couple of times ... at the beginning of the semester go to outside sources. [For example,] we talked about ... before the Civil War, we talked about the beginning of sectionalism in the South. And I wrote some of my own letters, like I pretended two brothers, one was living in the north and the other living in the south ... to give different viewpoints. (*Jane*)

However, her emergent, independent, problematic stance seemed to evaporate, or at least to be set aside. She more generally described her instructional activity during that semester by stating, 'I worked mainly from the text', the same one available during student-teaching. This reliance on the textbook occurred despite the fact that she had previously claimed her cooperating teacher 'didn't like the textbook [and], therefore, her viewpoints rubbed off on me'.

This educator's movement back toward what Tabachnick *et al.*[41] term a 'bureaucratic' or 'functional adaptationist' stance, thus less often acting in consonance with her previously developing view that curriculum knowledge is problematic, stems partly from the 'intensif-cation'[42] she experienced on the job (e.g., increases in paper work) and at home (as she made preparations for her first child). She was hard pressed to perform the various duties 'expected' of her, especially because of the drain on her energy resulting from a 'difficult' first trimester of her pregnancy, while also trying to develop and offer a critical, problematic view of the knowledge in her subject area. Her situation was further exacerbated because of the relatively limited content knowledge, especially about the controversies and the 'deep structure'[43] that she and many of her peers possessed. Under these circumstances a tremendous amount of (apparently unavailable) time and energy would have to be devoted to researching ideas and developing a critical, problematic approach to the curriculum. The material included in the textbook and curriculum guides provided a short-term solution to the intensification problem.

Despite these two cases, exemplifying a more and a less resilient tendency toward adopting a problematic, independent stance toward curriculum knowledge, we should recall that most of those interviewed were being prepared to deliver what was seen as given curriculum knowledge. Thus, for instance, a student in the program could relate that she encountered more 'latitude' as a student-teacher than she had expected, indicating, however, that she was comfortable when the curricular content was prescribed.

You got a lot more latitude with literature [— one can choose from a list of plays or novels —] than with writing. ... Now, they [the district curriculum guides and assigned textbook] are more specific about what they expect you to do in grammar and composition. They're teaching writing as a process there, which along with it comes five or six or seven different skills that they really want you to cover. How you cover it is left up to you. ... You can choose whatever way you want to attack those skills. (*Carol*)

It may be the competency-based and school-based emphasis in the program which help explain the technical (versus political and ethical) and utilitarian orientation to curriculum and instruction.[44] Regardless, the press to develop their skills as 'curriculum delivery service workers' seems to help prepare preservice teachers for the current nature of school teachers' work, which (as previously discussed) has been described in terms of being 'deskilled' and 'proletarianized'. These preservice teachers are in the process of becoming teachers, who for the most part will not have developed skills in curriculum decision-making. Thus, the teacher education program can be seen to help mediate the deskilling/reskilling contradiction, in that its 'trainees', who are in a sense being deskilled in anticipation of their work as teachers, will be less likely to experience personally the dynamics their occupation is undergoing.[45]

Moreover, there is evidence that some prospective teachers actually celebrate the deskilled teacher's role they encounter. Release from the responsibility of making curricular decisions is experienced as a form of liberation, a way to escape from or limit the process of intensification of work demands.[46] For example, Cindy, who after her second semester in the program had expressed concerns about the anticipated time demands of teaching and wanted to avoid 'getting into things that might be censored', discussed how a prescribed curriculum made her first several weeks of teaching less of a strain than expected.

MG: What about now since you've taken the job in [a school district], what are you working from in the curriculum? ...

Cindy: For one thing, well, I've received the curriculum guides. ... And we have guidelines, you know, which days to teach what. I guess you do not have to stick to it specifically, but, you know, as close as possible. ... The textbooks are great. They have at the beginning of the

> textbook, for each section you teach, teaching suggestions with specific examples to even use on the board. ... They even have objectives stated out.

MG: So, basically you are working from the curriculum guide [and the textbook]. And there is a lot of material already done for you. Do you feel comfortable with that?

Cindy: Oh yea! It makes it a lot easier. And I found [it] to be, well, maybe not easier to teach, but easier on the teacher.

Concluding Remarks

In conclusion, we have seen an example of the point made by Lynch and Plunkett that:

> Teacher education not only functions to produce teachers but, as a set of processes and institutions, reflects [and helps reproduce] a mass of cultural and structural features both of the educational system to which it is most immediately linked and of the wider society and economy to which it owes its existence.[47]

In this case the preservice teacher education program most often reinforced its trainees' conceptions of the curriculum as given and unproblematic, as something that needs only to be considered in relation to designing 'appropriate' strategies for delivering it to students of various ages and 'abilities'. In helping its graduates make a smoother transition into work in school settings, where teachers (and, for that matter, principals) are assigned the task of delivering curriculum that others have conceived, the program helps to mediate the deskilling/ reskilling contradiction in the economy and the state. Preservice teachers are *anticipatorily deskilled* — that is, never helped to develop curriculum decision-making skills nor oriented to viewing such skills as integral to the teacher's role — and, therefore, they may be less likely to resist the deskilling trend in teachers' work.

The implications of this 'anticipatory deskilling' process must be critically examined not only because of teachers' contradictory location within class relations,[48] but also because of the way in which patriarchal relations infuse the workings of teacher-administrator relations.[49] On one hand, many of these prospective teachers may not experience or recognize the deskilling of their occupation, and in part because of this they may be less apt to empathize with other groups of workers who are being deskilled within the 'logic' of capitalist social formations. As Bernstein notes, a 'strong classification between producers and reproducers of knowledge [between scholars/curriculum developers and teachers] parallels the strong classification between the dominating [capitalist and manager] and dominated [worker] categories of the mode of production'.[50] Hence, even while teachers as an occupational group find themselves becoming more like the dominated or worker category, some prospective teachers are being helped not to recognize or experience the struggle of this proletarianization process.

On the other hand, we should note that the predominantly female population of preservice teachers in the secondary program will enter school systems where a predominantly male group of educational administrators, school board members and legislators as well as university scholars will conceive the curriculum and oversee its execution by teachers. Hence, although evidence of resistance was noted, we observe a dynamic facilitating the reproduction of patriarchal relations both directly for teachers but also indirectly for those who witness the scene. Just as women may be more likely to be proletarianized than men,[51] it may not be coincidental that a predominantly female population is being 'anticipatorily deskilled'. Here, we observed some male, but mostly female preservice teachers not being provided with the skills to conceptualize curriculum knowledge nor being encouraged to challenge others, who will likely be males, about who should decide what to teach. In this sense, the contradictory gender relations in education are mediated — the possibility for such relations being reproduced is enhanced.

The situation described herein seems to illustrate one way 'a contradictory social order maintains its social hegemony ... by communicating methods through which individuals can form stable social identities in the face of social contradictions'.[52] Anticipatory deskilling is a means of enabling prospective teachers to more comfortably encounter the deskilling/reskilling and other contradictions as they are played out in state schools and perhaps also as it gets worked out in the economy.

We should recall, however, that some of those in this preservice teacher education program at least began to question the givenness of curriculum knowledge, and became oriented to exposing their own students to the problematic nature of curriculum knowledge. The fact that these instances were witnessed is important. While 'concrete curricular work ... cannot substitute for political and economic organization and action to alter the structural conditions we face, it is still

121

essential that certain things go on where they can in school'[53] as well as in universities. Certainly, there would have been more of a challenge to the existing social structure, with its inherent social contradictions, if preservice teachers had received more exposure to the deep structure of knowledge in their (and other) subject areas; if they had more frequently and systematically acquired the skills to treat curriculum knowledge as problematic; if they had been encouraged to examine the way the program and they as preservice teachers resolved the problematic-given, public-personal, and molecular-holistic dilemmas; if they had been alerted to conceiving the teacher's role as constituting and being constituted by social class as well as gender relations; and if those who exploited contradictions to bring to bear a more critical approach to teaching had sought more to work collectively.

Moreover, we should note that while the prospective teachers were being anticipatorily deskilled, they were not in any sustained fashion being anticipatorily reskilled in the area of classroom management and control.[54] This lack of correspondence between teacher education and schooling may lessen the reproductive effect of the teacher education–schooling correspondence with respect to curriculum decision-making. This is not to argue that this represents a serious challenge to existing social relations, nor that there will not be moves by well-intentioned actors to achieve correspondence in this regard. Indeed, more recent efforts at redesigning this program include a substantial emphasis on 'classroom management'. This is only to argue, echoing the point by Berlak and Berlak[55] quoted in the introduction, that human action and consciousness are relatively autonomous from the dynamics of the economy and the state. We must critically examine this relative autonomy, highlight contradictions, and seek to exploit these opportunities to promote progressive social changes in universities, schools, the family, the state, and the economy.

As we move, in the next chapter, to a focus on ideologically informed conceptions of professionalism, we should keep in mind these points and remember to treat curriculum knowledge in teacher education as problematic. We will discuss the issues more thoroughly in Chapter 7, but it should be noted that efforts at reforming teacher education may be oriented toward developing half educated persons, who try to 'understand the specialist[s] instead of obeying [them]';[56] educated persons, who 'know not to think and where to buy the thinking [they] need';[57] or liberationally educated persons, who through dialogue not only come to share with 'experts' what both previously have learned via different experiences, but also can 'recognize and unveil reality critically',[58] thus perceiving, for example, how professionals and other specialists/experts function in the context of broader political, economic and cultural relations.

Notes

1 This chapter is derived from GINSBURG, M., 'Reproduction, contradictions, and conceptions of curriculum in teacher education', *Curriculum Inquiry* 16 (1986), pp. 283–309. The manuscript was a third revision of a paper presented at the Annual Meeting of the American Educational Research Association, Montreal, 11–15 April 1983. Katherine Newman's contribution to the earlier draft is gratefully acknowledged. I wish to express my appreciation to Beatriz Arias-Godinez for transcribing some of the interviews on which this study was based. I would also like to thank Linda Bain, Ann Berlak, Michael Connelly, Joe Farrell, Sheila Slaughter and Philip Wexler, as well as several anonymous reviewers for their insightful comments and suggestions on earlier drafts of the article.

2 THORNDIKE, E., 'The psychology of the half-educated man', in KARIER, C. (Ed.) *Shaping the American Educational State, 1900 to the Present*, (New York, Free Press, 1975), pp. 238–244.

3 BERLAK, A. and BERLAK, H., 'Toward a nonhierarchical approach to school and leadership', *Curriculum Inquiry* 13 (1983), p. 273.

4 CARTER, M., 'Contradictions and correspondence: Analysis of relations of schooling to work', in CARNOY, M. and LEVIN, H. (Ed.) *The Limits of Educational Reform* (New York, Longman, 1976), p. 60.

5 On the general issue of deskilling and proletarianization, see Chapter 3; JOHNSON, T., 'What is to be known: The structural determinants of social class', *Economy and Society* 6 (1977), pp. 194–233; JOHNSON, T., 'Work and power', in ESLAND, G. and SALAMON, G. (Ed.) *The Politics of Work and Occupations*, (Milton Keynes, England, Open University Press, 1980), pp. 335–371; LARSON, M., 'Proletarianization of educated labor', *Theory and Society* 9 (1980), pp. 131–175; OPPENHEIMER, M., 'Proletarianization of the professional', *Sociological Review* 20 (1973), pp. 213–277. On the issue of 'women's work' being deskilled more so than men's, see ACKER, S., 'Women and teaching: A semi-detached sociology of a semi-profession', in WALKER, S. and BARTON, L. (Eds.) *Gender, Class and Education* (Lewes, Falmer Press, 1983), pp. 123–39; BUSWELL, C., 'Pedagogic change and social change', *British Journal of Sociology of Education*, 1 (1980), pp. 293–306.

6 BRAVERMAN, H., *Labor and Monopoly Capital* (New York, Monthly Review Press, 1974), p. 8.

7 See APPLE, M., 'Curricular form and the logic of technical control', in APPLE, M. and WEIS, L. (Eds.) *Ideology and Practice in Schooling*, (Philadelphia, Temple University Press, 1983), pp. 143–66; APPLE, M., 'Work, class and gender', in WALKER, S. and BARTON, L. (Eds.) *Gender, Class and Education*, (Lewes, Falmer Press, 1983), pp. 53–67; APPLE, M. 'Teaching

and "women's work". A comparative historical and ideological analysis',
in GUMBERT, E. (Ed.) *Expressions of Power in Education*, (Atlanta, Center for
Cross-Cultural Education, Georgia State University, 1984), pp. 22–49;
BEYER, L. 'Aesthetic curriculum and cultural reproduction', in APPLE, M.
and WEIS, L. (Eds.) *Ideology and Practice in Schooling*, (Philadelphia, Temple
Press, 1983), pp. 89–113; GINSBURG, M., WALLACE, G., and MILLER, H.,
'Teachers, economy and the state', revised version of paper presented at
the 10th World Congress of the International Sociological Association,
Mexico City, 15–21 August, 1982; GITLIN, A., 'School structure and
teachers' work', in APPLE, M. and WEIS, L. (Eds.) *Ideology and Practice in
Schooling*, (Philadelphia, Temple University Press, 1983), pp. 193–212;
MCNEIL, L., 'Defensive teaching and classroom control', in APPLE, M.
and WEIS, L. (Eds.) *Ideology and Practice in Schooling*, (Philadelphia, Temple
University Press, 1983), pp. 114–142; SARUP, M. *Marxism/Structuralism/
Education* (Lewes, Falmer Press, 1984).

8   Apple, 'Curricular form and the logic of technical control', pp. 151–52.
9   *Ibid*. Moreover, Apple has observed that the case of teachers is unusual
because members of the same occupational group and, indeed, the same
people are being both deskilled and reskilled. This point, coupled with the
fact that reskilling for them involves taking more of a managerial
function, is interesting in light of Johnson's contention that 'proletarianization is a process referring not merely to the devaluation of work or labor
power in terms of the further fragmentation and routinization of tasks
within the labor process but also the elimination of that element of work
associated with the *global function of capital*' (T. Johnson, 'What is to be
known: The structural determinants of social class', p. 184). This notion
of 'global function of capital', derived from Carchedi [CARCHEDI, G.,
'On the economic identification of the new middle class', *Economy and
Society* 4 (1975), pp. 1–86], refers to the performance of tasks — notably,
control and surveillance of workers — required to extract surplus value in
the production process being performed by others than capitalists. Thus,
although I would not want to argue that education is a surplus value
producing process [but, for a discussion of notion of academic labor, see
EVERHART, R., 'Classroom management, student opposition and the labor
process', in APPLE, M. and WEIS, L. (Eds.) *Ideology and Practice in Schooling*,
(Philadelphia, Temple University Press, 1983)], the dynamic of proletarianization does appear to take an unusual twist for educators.
Moreover, given this twist and some teachers' internalization of the
'ideology of professionalism', the proletarianization process may not be
experienced as such, at least initially (see Ginsburg, Wallace and Miller).
10   See APPLE, M., *Ideology and Curriculum* (Boston, Routledge and Kegan
Paul, 1979); BERNSTEIN, B., 'On the classification and framing of
educational knowledge', in BERNSTEIN, B. (Ed.) *Class, Codes and Control*,
Vol. 3, (London, Routledge and Kegan Paul, 1975b), pp. 174–200;
BOURDIEU, P. and PASSERON, J. C., *Reproduction in Education, Society and
Culture* (Beverly Hills, Sage, 1977); EGGLESTON, J., *The Sociology of the
School Curriculum* (London, Routledge and Kegan Paul, 1977); YOUNG,
M., 'An approach to the study of curricula as socially organized knowl-

edge', in YOUNG, M. (Ed.) *Knowledge and Control*, (London, Collier-Macmillan, 1977), pp. 19–46.

11 WALLER, W., *The Sociology of Teaching* (New York, Wiley, 1932), p. 293.

12 ANYON, J. 'Social class and school knowledge', *Curriculum Inquiry* 11 (1981), pp. 31–32.

13 See GIROUX, H. 'Teacher education and the ideology of social control', in GIROUX, H. (Ed.) *Ideology, Culture and the Process of Schooling*, (Philadelphia, Temple University Press, 1981), pp. 143–162.

14 BERLAK, A. and BERLAK, H., *Dilemmas of Schooling: Teaching and Social Change* (New York, Methuen, 1981); see also TABACHNICK, R., ZEICHNER, K., DENSMORE, K., ADLER, K., and EGAN, K., 'The Impact of the Student Teaching Experience on the Development of Teacher Perspectives', paper presented at the annual meeting of the American Educational Research Association, New York, March, 1982.

15 Berlak and Berlak, 'Toward a nonhierarchical approach to school and leadership', p. 273.

16 See BARTHOLOMEW, J., 'Schooling teachers: The myth of the liberal college', in WHITTY, G. and YOUNG, M. (Eds.) *Explorations in the Politics of School Knowledge*, (Nafferton, Driffield, England, Nafferton Books, 1976).

17 Berlak and Berlak, *Dilemmas of Schooling*, p. 147.

18 Eggleston, pp. 52–70.

19 See Anyon, 'Social class and school knowledge'; APPLE, M. 'Power and school knowledge', *Review of Education* 3 (1977), pp. 265–49; Apple, *Ideology and Curriculum*; BEYER, L. and ZEICHNER, K., 'Teacher Education in Cultural Context: Moving Beyond Reproduction', paper presented at the annual meeting of the American Educational Research Association, Los Angeles, April, 1981; KLIEBARD, H., 'Persistent curriculum issues in historical perspective', in PINAR, W. (Ed.) *Curriculum Theorizing: The Reconceptualists*, (Berkeley, McCutchan, 1975), pp. 39–69.

20 See Tabachnick, *et al.*

21 Berlak and Berlak, *Dilemmas of Schooling*, p. 144.

22 Bernstein, 'On the classification and framing of educational knowledge', p. 89.

23 Berlak and Berlak, 'Toward a nonhierarchical approach to school and leadership', p. 278; see also Tabachnick *et al.* and Hammersley [HAMMERSLEY, M., *Teacher Perspectives* (Milton Keynes, England, Open University Press, 1977)] on related distinctions, respectively, between 'holistic' and 'fragmented' and between 'integrated' and 'unrelated'.

24 Bernstein, 'On the classification and framing of educational knowledge', p. 88.

25 See Apple, *Ideology and Curriculum*; ZEIGLER, H. and PEAK, W., 'The political functions of the education systems', *Sociology of Education* 43 (1970), pp. 129–142.

26 See also HAES, J., 'Conceptions of the curriculum: Teachers and "truth,"' *British Journal of Sociology of Education* 3 (1982), pp. 57–76.

27 This reductionist notion of 'needs' as students' level of achievement is the 'given' curriculum also surfaced in interviews with some of the preservice

125

teachers. For example, Roberto explained how he planned to make curricular decisions as a teacher:

> Okay, first I would like to know my students: what kind of population I would have. ... I guess I would do a kind of preassessment and to make sure that I would zero in on their specific needs; and then fit their needs to the curriculum as the school mandates.

And Carol indicated her plans in a similar manner:

> I would start with the curriculum that's already outlined in the department. You know, depending on the grade level I'm teaching, if I'm teaching major works [advanced] or basic. ... Once in the classroom I would probably try to do some kind of evaluation of the classroom level to see who needs what.

28 See Bernstein, 'On the classification and framing ...'
29 ELBAZ, F., 'The teacher's practical knowledge: A report of a case study', *Curriculum Inquiry* 11 (1981), p. 45.
30 See also LACEY, C., *The Socialization of Teachers* (London, Methuen, 1977).
31 Interestingly, this course is the one that a first semester instructor suggested would help to orient preservice teachers to curriculum issues (see earlier discussion).
32 DOBBERT, M. 'Education, schools and cultural mapping', in SPINDLER, G. (Ed.) *Education and Cultural Process: Towards an Anthropology of Education,* (New York, Holt, 1974), p. 212.
33 Giroux, pp. 153–155.
34 Quoted in HARTNETT, A. and NAISH, M., 'Technicians or social bandits? Some moral and political issues in the education of teachers', in WOODS, P. (Ed.) *Teacher Strategies,* (London, Croom Helm, 1980), p. 270; emphasis added.
35 Giroux, p. 155.
36 Treating the curriculum as unproblematic may be easier for preservice teachers because of the extent to which their own identities and authority are tied to the authority of their subject [see HARGREAVES, D., 'The occupational culture of teachers', in WOODS, P. (Ed.) *Teacher Strategies,* (London, Croom Helm, 1980), pp. 125–48]. We noted, for example, how the program at times reinforced subject 'sub-cultures' [see Lacey; BALL, S. and LACEY, C., 'Subject disciplines as the opportunity for group action: A measured critique of subject sub-cultures', in WOODS, P. (Ed.) *Teacher Strategies,* (London, Croom Helm, 1980), pp. 149–77] and thus reified subject identities. We also noted some instructors whose own identities were linked to a subject area. Treating as problematic the basis of one's identity and authority — the curriculum knowledge of one's subject — may tend to threaten one's authority and to create problems for one's identity, whether you are a university professor, a preservice or an inservice teacher.
37 LORTIE, D., *School Teacher: A Sociological Analysis* (Chicago, University of Chicago Press, 1975), p. 62.

38 See also LECOMPTE, M. and GINSBURG, M., 'How students learn to become teachers', in NOBLIT, G. and PINK, W. (Eds.) *Schooling in Social Context: Qualitative Studies*, (New York, Ablex, 1987), pp. 3–22; SPATIG, L., GINSBURG, M., and LIBERMAN, D., 'Ego development as an explanation of passive and active models of teacher socialization', *College Student Journal* 16 (1982), pp. 315–25.

39 See Tabachnick *et al.*

40 See also comments quoted above from interviews conducted at the beginning of interviewees' program experience.

41 See Tabachnick *et al.*

42 See Larson.

43 Bernstein, 'On the classification and framing of educational knowledge', p. 94.

44 See APPLE, M. 'Behaviorism and conservatism: The educational views in four of the "systems" models of teacher education', in JOYCE, B. and WEIL, M. (Eds.) *Perspectives for Reform in Teacher Education*, (Englewood Cliffs, NJ, Prentice-Hall, 1972), pp. 237–62; Beyer and Zeichner.

45 Note, however, that there was also little attention in the program (except in student teaching) to preparing students in the secondary program for the 'reskilled' activity of classroom management/control. Thus, while the program helps to mediate the deskilling/reskilling contradiction (both directly for teachers and indirectly for students and perhaps other workers via teachers), there is not a perfect 'correspondence' between the program and the 'needs' of the school as a workplace.

46 Buswell (p. 304) notes that the deskilling of teachers may itself create a contradiction for them, in that while teachers' 'own knowledge, skill and expertise have been devalued ... they are expected to represent the embodiment of knowledge and expertise to pupils in schools and classrooms with hierarchical teaching relationships'. This contradiction may be resolved, interestingly, by teachers' greater reliance on curriculum knowledge conceived and made available to deliver by other 'experts' or authorities. But see Everhart (p. 187) and Braverman (p. 440) for the alienation this may cause among students.

47 LYNCH, J. and PLUNKETT, H., *Teacher Education and Cultural Change: England, France and West Germany* (London, Allen and Unwin, 1973), p. 53.

48 See Johnson, 'What is to be known'; JOHNSON, T., 'The professions in the class structure', in SCACE, R. (Ed.) *Industrial Society: Class, Cleavage and Control*, (London, Allen and Unwin, 1977); Sarup.

49 See Apple, 'Teaching and "women's work"'; M. Strober and D. Tyack, 'Why do women teach and men manage?', *Signs* 5 (1980), pp. 494–503.

50 BERNSTEIN, B., 'Aspects of the relations between education and production', in BERNSTEIN, B. (Ed.) *Class, Codes and Control*, Vol. 3, (London, Routledge and Kegan Paul, 1975), p. 186.

51 See Acker; Apple, 'Work, class and gender'; Apple, 'Teaching as "women's work"'; Buswell.

52 WEXLER, P. 'Educational change and social contradiction: An example', *Comparative Education Review* 23 (1979), p. 255.

53 APPLE, M. 'Reproduction, contestation and curriculum: An essay in self-criticism', *New Directions in Education: Critical Perspectives*, Occasional Paper No. 8 (Buffalo, Faculty of Educational Studies, State University of New York at Buffalo, 1981), p. 35.
54 See also Note 45.
55 Berlak and Berlak p. 273.
56 Thorndike, p. 239.
57 *Ibid.*, p. 244.
58 FREIRE, P., *The Politics of Education: Culture, Power and Liberation* (South Hadley, MA, Bergin and Garvey, 1985), p. 102.

Chapter 5

Ideologically Informed Conceptions of Professionalism[1]

A professional is a person allowed to affect the most priceless possession of a family — the attitudes of its children — but who is paid less than those who hammered the nails into the family's house. A professional is a person competent to determine the curriculum of a school, but who is given a list of novels he [or she] may or may not teach.[2]

Introduction

In this chapter we examine in detail one of the concepts that has surfaced in discussions in previous chapters, the concept of professionalism. This is not undertaken, however, to address the proverbial question: 'Is teaching a profession?' Too much has already been written on this question[3] informed by a 'trait theory' approach that has been convincingly criticized because of the variation among lists of traits employed, the static and ahistoric assumptions implied, and the overly positive, even apologist, tone exhibited.[4] Rather, our focus on conceptions of professionalism — evidenced in the messages of the formal and hidden curriculum of the program and in preservice teachers' discourse — is designed to illuminate the contribution of the ideology of professionalism[5] to the reproduction of inequalities in wealth and power characteristic of capitalist and patriarchal structures in (at least) the United States.

This is not to argue that class relations or gender relations are solely or primarily reproduced by the ideology of professionalism or even

129

more generally through dynamics at the ideological level.[6] This is only to claim that the ideology of professionalism, particularly its contradictory nature, warrants attention in its relationship with unequal and unjust social relations.[7] Therefore, as we examine the messages in the teacher education program curriculum and preservice teachers' conceptions of professionalism, we will want to keep in mind how the ideology of professionalism, which is drawn upon and reproduced, serves to mask/mediate or expose/challenge the contradictions associated with the class and gender relations operating at the school and broader societal levels.

Messages in the Teacher Education Program Curriculum[8]

As a participant-observer in (at least) this preservice teacher education program, I continuously encountered the terms, profession, professional, professionalization, and professionalism.[9] The program was officially labelled as the '*Professional* Teacher Preparation Program' and the name of the first required course was 'Introduction to the *Profession* of Teaching'. Moreover, at the first session of this course, the instructor oriented the students as follows:

> This is a *professional* training program. ... You are not expected to learn how to teach (solely by taking classes). ... Just as for a medical doctor ... (there are required) experiences in the field. ... We adopt a *professional* model. ... When you get a degree you don't stop learning. You need to keep up with new techniques ... and know how to evaluate your own *professional* competence. (*Fieldnotes: 9–2–80*)

Three weeks into this first semester course, an entire three-hour class session was devoted to 'Teaching as a Profession'. In preparing for this session, students were to read that competent, dedicated teachers may need the protection and powerbase of an organized occupation;[10] that according to professions' 'more-or-less recognizable set of characteristics that distinguish them from nonprofessions',[11] teaching does not fully measure up, especially in terms of salary level, and can only be considered to be a 'semi-profession';[12] and that professionalism is generally a positive phenomenon, something towards which teachers should strive: 'In reality, there is no choice but to change toward greater professionalization if schools are to meet their challenge'.[13] The class session included a discussion and a slide-tape presentation; each yielded a different set of criteria that could be used to distinguish 'trades' from 'professions' and then was applied with some qualifications and debate to render teaching as less than a full profession. Overall, preservice teachers were encouraged to prepare themselves for a profession or to *make* teaching into a profession.

The issues of professionalism and its relation to teaching continued to be a feature throughout the first semester and the remainder of the program sequence. For example, the instructor of a required course during the second semester explained to the class at its first meeting: 'Teaching is a very real profession. ... It's a great profession, but not without growing experiences, both painful and pleasurable'. During the student-teaching semester, one of the weekly 'seminars' was devoted to the topic of 'Teaching as a Profession'. And at the graduation ceremonies, the speaker giving the invocation offers the following prayer: 'Bless these graduates. ... Their years of preparation blessed by God. ... Help us to be good teachers, to think of our *profession*, our vocation' (*Fieldnotes: 12–31–81*).

Instead of continuing to simply chronicle the encounters with professionalism, I will discuss three themes related to professionalism which appear in the excerpts above and which were prominent throughout the program: professionalism and remuneration/service ideal, professionalism and power, and professionalism as individual attitudes/behavior in the social construction of competence. These themes will also frame our discussion later in the chapter of preservice teachers' conceptions of professionalism.

Professionalism and Remuneration/Service Ideal

The first theme revolves around financial issues and teaching's relationship to occupations which receive both higher and lower remuneration. There was frequent mention in class sessions by instructors, guest speakers and students about the (relatively) low salaries teachers receive and about the need or the actions taken by teacher organizations to increase the financial and related benefits of working as a member of the teaching 'profession'. The issue about the approximately 50 per cent of workers in the United States (and a much large percentage from a global perspective) who earn less pay than teachers was rarely raised. When it was, it was usually done to justify higher salaries for teachers because of differences in the (mental/'professional' *vs.* manual) nature of the work or the level of education of people who do the work. Attention was more often focused on the higher paid fields — notably, law and medicine; here the concern was that teachers already should be accorded such benefits or should strive to deserve them. Inter-occupational inequalities in financial rewards were not a concern in the context of discussions about teachers' professionalization efforts, although at other times, students did encounter messages in which concerns about inequalities were expressed.[14] No notions that teachers might share interests with other (lower paid) workers were available to students in the program.

The messages conveying the salience and legitimacy of seeking greater financial rewards, however, did not exist in an uncontested terrain. In fact, one of the contradictions in the ideology of professionalism surfaced as preservice teachers also encountered messages de-emphasizing remuneration issues and stressing what might be called the altruistic service ideal. For instance, at an orientation meeting for student-teachers, their cooperating teachers and their supervisors, a university instructor welcomed those assembled and commented: 'The excitement is rewarding. ... Every time you start this crazy kind of thing ... you recognize you're not in it for the money' (*Fieldnotes: 9–18–82*). This point was sometimes reinforced in the hidden curriculum, because although instructors at times discussed with students their concern about their own salaries, which they described as low relative to faculty in other colleges and to other professions, as a general rule, they continued to carry out their duties with considerable zeal. Students in the program did not encounter examples of faculty organizing to attain higher salaries. The students did, however, witness a collective effort by teaching assistants aimed at enhancing their pay — a strategy which was criticized by some key faculty in the college.

Moreover, during a graduation ceremony, a speaker addressed the students saying:

> You are entering a most important enterprise ... a profession called education. [I want to applaud] your commitment. ... You could not have chosen a more appropriate time. This is a most challenging period. ... There are no more important people than those who teach young people. (*Fieldnotes: 12–13–81*)

And another speaker later referred to the graduates and exclaimed to the audience:'What you are going to see is one of the most professional, dedicated groups' (*Fieldnotes: 12–13–81*). Then, minutes after these speakers appealed to and applauded the prospective teachers' commitment based on an ideal of service to the client and/or society, a choir entertained the audience with a rendition of the 'Tom Sawyer Medley'.

In this performance, Aunt Polly asked Tom to white-wash the fence, but he managed to talk other people into doing it for him. These people set to work singing: 'Ain't doing this for money' since it's 'pure enjoyment ... gratisfaction, pride from putting our shoulders to the wheel' (*Fieldnotes: 12–13–81*). While the parallel between the situation of Tom's workers and of teachers was not perceived by some preservice teachers and university instructors who were informally interviewed after the ceremony, others did comment on it.

Professionalism and Power

Issues of power (authority and autonomy) in relation to professionalism were highlighted to varying extents in the assigned readings for and discussions during the 'Teaching as a Profession' class session in the first semester (discussed above). Students periodically encountered these issues as they moved through the program. Sometimes, the messages were oriented toward encouraging or exemplifying teachers as professionals exercising power. One instructor in the first semester's special session on multicultural education stressed: 'You must realize you're the professional educator; you must decide about, determine the curriculum. A doctor or lawyer doesn't let others decide' (*Fieldnotes: 9–9–80*). Similarly, during the second semester of the program, the instructor urged students: 'Don't be afraid to abort a lesson and seize the moment. ... Use your professional judgment. ... Like a doctor, you might change directions' (*Fieldnotes: 3–26–81*). And during the student-teaching 'seminar' a guest speaker discussed what at least one teacher organization (Texas State Teachers Association, an affiliate of the National Education Association) can accomplish:

> Teacher organizations are important. ... We need unity ... we need autonomy, a decent salary. ... [TSTA] will be lobbying in Washington to get teaching recognized as a profession. ... Stand up for yourself and be proud. ... Don't say, 'I'm only a teacher'. ... Since we want to become autonomous, we need to require exams, to police our ranks. ... [We also successfully lobbied for a] due process, fair dismissal bill [in the state legislature] ... to protect you. (*Fieldnotes: 9–22–81*)

The last quote also indicates that a major force in teachers' (and other professions') quest for power is the State.[15] This point was clarified by a guest speaker, who was introduced as a 'real professional' and who

informed student teachers in response to a question about state prescribed teacher competency testing, that:

> You will have to take the test beginning May of 1984. ... We
> [TSTA] had a battle because they [the State] wanted to do it
> immediately. ... We hope to affect what that test will be. ... $1
> million dollars being spent to develop that test. ... We will fight
> hard to ensure that the test will not be used to evaluate teachers.
> ... There's a move across the US to use student test performance
> as a basis for teacher evaluation. We're going to fight that like
> mad! (*Fieldnotes: 2–9–82*)

During the period of the research in this preservice program,
instructors and guest speakers not infrequently referred to the state's
role in shaping education and the occupation of teaching. The extent of
commentary at this time may have been higher than previously in that
many of the remarks were directed toward current deliberations of the
Texas State Commission on Standards for the Teaching Profession.
This Commission, which was chaired by the superintendent of a nearby
school district in which some in the program did their student teaching,
was in the process of redefining the structure and prerequisites for
teaching certificates. On several occasions, students in the program
were informed about the status of these deliberations (e.g., plans to
require passing a 'basic skills' competency test prior to entering teacher
education and to further stage the process of acquiring a lifetime
certificate), while concomitantly they were advised to relax since the
changes would apply only to future cohorts of preservice teachers.
    Although there were also some references to teachers in schools or
universities 'negotiating' with the state about these and other changes
that would affect the occupation, the tone was more often in line with
the comments of one instructor: 'The State of Texas will be forcing us
to change whether we want to or not' (*Fieldnotes: 4–20–83*). This was
also evidenced in comments about the curriculum (see Chapter 4).
    The point is that, despite laughter during a discussion about the
'Rules of 1872' restrictions on teacher behavior (e.g., smoking,
marrying, or getting a shave in public) and comments on how much
further teaching had become professionalized since that time (*Fieldnotes:
9–23–80 and 2–9–82*), students in the program frequently encountered
messages indicating the limited powers teachers had *vis-à-vis* the state.
For example, when on several occasions the issue of teachers striking
arose, students were reminded that 'In Texas, it is illegal to strike'
(*Fieldnotes: 9–22–81*). Additionally, when orienting students to filling

out applications for certification, one instructor seemed to summarize his and, more generally, teachers' relationships to the state: 'You're dealing with the TEA [Texas Education Agency] and if they say white is black, then white is black' (*Fieldnotes: 11–7–81*).

Professionalism and Individual Attitudes/Behaviors in the Social Construction of Competence

It is perhaps not surprising in a program billed as 'Competency Based Teacher Education' that considerable attention was given to achieving 'competence'. Moreover, as an instructor oriented student teachers during the initial 'seminar' of the semester: 'The State wants us to make sure you are competent' (*Fieldnotes: 8–28–81*). Certainly, there were many components of the program designed to develop and evaluate the nineteen 'competencies' around which the program was ostensibly organized. Throughout the program, students were alerted to these competencies, provided with clarification of their meaning, and advised about activities they might engage in to acquire them.

What is somewhat surprising, however, is that students are coached in how to demonstrate, by exhibiting certain behaviors and attitudes, that they are competent with respect to these nineteen competencies. As one instructor told an assemblage of student teachers during an initial 'seminar' session for that semester: 'Look for unique ways of demonstrating the competencies' (*Fieldnotes: 8–29–81*). The coaching, it seems, stems from the focus on behavioral indicators of competencies and from the admittedly limited opportunities to observe students' performance of such. For example, after reminding student teachers of the nineteen competencies which formed the basis of the 'Final Evaluation Report', and providing examples of elements that could be included in a lesson to demonstrate competence with respect to one competency dealing with presenting career education concepts, an instructor discussed some of the other competencies, stating:

> I want you to apply your professional education. ... Indicators for these nineteen competencies are given on pages 15–18 [of the Secondary Student Teaching Handbook, 1981–82]. ... When I go to see a lesson I want to see a complete lesson plan. ... No [lesson plans don't have to be typed], but make them look professional, not something on the back cover of a checkbook. (*Fieldnotes: 1–15–82*)

In addition to the coaching, there appeared to be an element of collusion with students in insuring that they had every opportunity to demonstrate their competence. At an orientation meeting for instructors/supervisors, cooperating teachers (SBTEs) and student teachers, an instructor in the secondary education program explained that not only should supervisors observe at 'prearranged times', but that they should be informed by student-teachers regarding 'what should be observed', that is, which particular competencies were to be emphasized in the lesson. These instructions were followed by suggestions for demonstrating those competencies which were 'more difficult to deal with' (*Fieldnotes: 1–21–82*).

Furthermore, the idea that demonstrating competence may not be equivalent to being competent was communicated explicitly at other points of the program. For instance, during a 'seminar' session on resume preparation, student teachers were told by a guest speaker: 'Often the most qualified person doesn't get the job; it's the person who best communicates [his/her] qualifications' (*Fieldnotes: 2–23–82*).

More generally, preservice teachers encountered messages in the program which encouraged them to create and manage, through their manifest behavior and attitudes, an impression of themselves as professionals. During the first semester of the program a guest instructor stressed:

> Too often we apologize for being a teacher. We must feel good about ourselves and transmit this feeling to others. ... [There are] people who don't get well, clients who lose court cases [and thus] teachers should not feel incompetent because some kids are not learning enough. (*Fieldnotes: 9–9–80*)

Such encouragements coexisted with explicit instruction in how to socially construct such images of professionalism. Considerable emphasis was given to the form or style of presenting work, sometimes to the point of relegating substance or content, particularly with respect to writing behavioral objectives and lesson plans (see quote about checkbook above). During the student-teaching 'seminar,' moreover, those present were told by a school district personnel director, 'fill out job application forms at home [rather than at the personnel office] so you can do it more professionally' (*Fieldnotes: 2–30–82*).

The greatest stress with respect to socially constructing an image of professionalism was on the nature of personal attire. For instance, just prior to school observation visits during the first semester, students were advised by their instructor to 'conduct yourselves as professionals, which means — dressing as a professional' (*Fieldnotes*: 9–18–80). The advice was given more emphasis as students in the program prepared for student-teaching experiences and for job interviews. A guest speaker in the student teaching seminar opined:

> Sell yourself. ... Dress conservatively. Coat and tie for men and dresses for women. Be neat and well groomed. ... It's an employer's market. ... When teaching, you [women] can wear slacks, but when you meet with parents, dress like you would for an interview. (*Fieldnotes*: 9–22–81)

This advice to dress professionally — 'conservatively' or 'sensibly' — was also given nonverbally by instructors and (even more so by) guest speakers, who usually were attired in the fashion described above. By contrast, most students attended class sessions dressed in jeans or other 'unprofessional' attire, except when they came to class immediately after school observation or student-teaching stints in the schools.

To describe this is perhaps not only to note that students were being given good (and perhaps necessary) advice in getting and keeping the job they desired. However, it appeared that something else was being communicated — an issue very closely related to social class stratification. In a culture in which white collars and blue collars serve as symbols of a complexity of differences in lifestyle and life chances as well as economic and political power,[16] it would be difficult for references to clothing to be understood otherwise. The point is that students were not only being advised on how to get a job, but on how to symbolize their aspired to class position with clothing. No blue collars or bib overalls for these aspiring 'professionals'.

Preservice Teachers' Conceptions of Professionalism[17]

In the context of this teacher education program, containing the above noted messages about professionalism, how do prospective teachers come to conceive of professionalism? Do they view teaching to be a profession and how do they perceive and evaluate the hierarchy associated (implicitly or explicitly) with professions as a segment of the division of labor? After briefly examining the answers to these questions, we will discuss in more detail the preservice teachers' conceptions of professionalism with reference to the three themes identified in the program curricular messages: professionalism and remuneration/service ideal, professionalism and power, and professionalism and individual attitudes/behaviors in the social construction of competence. These themes were articulated by preservice teachers both to clarify their perspectives concerning whether or not teaching is a profession and to legitimate or critique social inequalities.

Of the preservice teachers interviewed at least once after the beginning of their first semester in the program only one ever responded negatively to the question, 'Do you think teaching is a profession?' This respondent, a masters degree student who became a part of the interview sample during her second semester in the program explained:

> Teachers themselves will not allow it to be considered a profession. Few of them join any organizations. They never want to be accountable for what they do, which is different from a professional. Um, they certainly don't have any advanced educational training that other professions do ... [I]t seems to be looked at as a temporary job. ... Then once you're in teaching ... in the system [the administration] gives you no automony and the pay really wouldn't draw you to teaching. ... [And yet] I think that teaching is something that's certainly as vital, in a lot of ways more vital, than doctors and CPAs because you have an opportunity for a year to infiltrate the minds of a lot of people. (*Mary: 5–13–84*).

And after completing student teaching she reasserts that teaching is not a profession, adding that 'they don't act professionally' and that 'they don't police themselves' (*Mary: 1–24–83*).

Interestingly, some of the same themes (to be discussed in more detail later) were raised by each of the other respondents who affirmed that teaching is a profession. One of these prospective teachers qualified his positive response by terming teaching as a 'younger profession' (*Roberto: 5–4–81*) and 'a very low status profession ... a very unappreciated profession ... [and] an unprofessional profession' (*Roberto: 5–28–82*). None of the other respondents wavered in their belief that teaching was a profession, although, as they progressed through the program, they began to question whether all teachers were professionals and whether others (e.g., the public) shared their view. This doubt about the 'public's' perception of teaching as a profession came partly from increasing criticisms in the media — this was the period proceeding the 'flood' of reports on the 'rising tide of mediocrity' (as the National Commission on Excellence in Education[18] termed it).

Many of the College of Education faculty were strongly committed to teaching as a profession[19] — a point commented upon by one student in the sample: 'The college here wants so much to impress upon us that teaching is a profession' (*Sonia: 5–28–81*). Ironically, however, students' doubts about teachers' status as a profession stemmed partly from the issues (noted above) that were raised in the formal curriculum of the program. As one respondent commented:

> I had never had to confront the issue of whether or not I thought a teacher was a professional until I started in the education classes. ... You know we spent an awful lot of time on it this semester, too. And I thought, well, there must be a question in somebody's mind somewhere, you know, or else we wouldn't be spending so much time on it. (*Donald: 5–15–81*)

Preservice teachers interviewed thus presented a strong, almost univocal, message — that teaching is and should be considered a profession, although not a consummate profession. They remained attached to this position, despite encountering questioning about and challenges to it by the 'public', educators in the field, and university faculty.

As these prospective teachers discussed issues of professionalism and teaching they also indicated how they perceived the hierarchy associated (implicitly or explicitly) with professions as a segment of the division of labor. Seven of the fifteen interviewed, including the respondent who did not see teaching as a profession, discussed professionalism and never questioned the system of occupational stratification. One of these preservice teachers noted that teaching is a profession and explained:

> For one thing, you have people in society itself who still look up to a teacher as being a profession. And that right there means a whole lot. ... Teachers still get, you know, a certain amount of respect, honor and prestige. (*James: 5–7–81*)

Another prospective teacher not only referred to status distinctions but also seemed to allude to class (market relations and the mental/manual dichotomy) divisions:

> I think that being a professional is having a set of abilities that most people around don't have. ... If you don't strive for that sort of thing, you're sort of like the guy who digs the ditches and, be there tomorrow or not, it's not going to make much difference. ... I think there are some jobs that are not professional, uh, although I guess in some sense everything has some

sort of professionality, because they all have some sort of abilities that are needed to be performed. But if you wanted to be clear-cut, this is professional [and] this is not, I think you probably could make a distinction. Maybe some of it's status. (*Nancy: 5–18–82*)

What can we say about the other eight respondents who did not unambiguously reference as legitimate the hierarchical division of labor and thus may have been challenging the class and gender divisions which are characteristic of (at least) capitalist and patriarchal social structures? We would be surprised if most of these offered a strong critique of the basic assumption of structured inequalities, given that only two prospective teachers in the sample communicated even an incipient radical critique of US society when discussing inequalities and the role of schooling.[20] The preservice teacher, quoted immediately above, provides an insight into the others' views. Indeed, had she *not* fully clarified her view, she would *not* have been classified as *un*ambiguously conceiving of professions as a part of a legitimate stratification system.

The point is *not* that most of the other eight respondents were *un*ambiguous in critiquing the structured inequalities connected with the concept of professionalism, but that their views, expressed even at different points of the same interview, were contradictory. Five of these preservice teachers discussed professionals as being on top of a legitimate hierarchy, but argued that one could exhibit professionalism in any type of work. For example, during the interview at the beginning of the program, one respondent stated:

Well, you know, something that is not a profession, maybe the skill of learning how to make shoes or whatever. ... [However,] I feel you can be a professional at shining shoes, if you are expert at it, if you know so much about it ... if you are doing well and you are happy doing it. (*Sonia: 9–16–80*)

The remaining three interviewees, while at times claiming teaching as a profession deserved higher income than some other workers, argued more forcefully against the invidious status distinctions. One, who was considering whether to pursue teaching or dentistry as his future profession and who dropped out of the preservice teacher preparation program at the end of the first semester (partly because of a low overall grade point average), commented on the issue raised in class of the mental/manual distinction between professions and other occupations:

140

It's not right to separate certain groups by whether they think or not. How does one determine and who determines when someone is thinking? It's like the arm and the brain, how does one weigh one against the other? (*Richard: 12–9–80*)

Another student, who dropped out of the program after the first semester (because she learned that she could not use Texas certification to teach in another country), also reacted to class discussions (mentioned above) on the topic of 'teaching as a profession':

We were talking about why teaching is a profession. ... And I was very hurt by that fact, because they listed [teaching] in the second column [of trades]. ... It made me feel like I'm something less than someone else. ... When the class put a plumber at the very end of the list [of trades as contrasted with professions], or a mechanic, I was very hurt about that, too. It's just like they're lower people. I consider people to be members of a profession if they are all professionals at their jobs, if they are masters at their job. (*Rachel: 9–19–80*)

The third, who did complete the program, exclaimed during an interview after one semester as a teacher:

Professionalism involves a dedication to task. ... It's the attitude of the person that's important. ... An auto mechanic or an assembly line worker can be a professional. ... I sense a distinction, a class distinction. ... that a professional is better than someone who isn't ... I resent that distinction. ... I don't see any job as non-essential, except for bureaucrats. (*Dana: 7–2–82*)

We now turn to examine more thoroughly some of the aspects of the ideology of professionalism which respondents drew upon and reproduced in making their claims about teaching being or not being a profession. We should keep in mind that these aspects were also employed concomitantly to critique and, more frequently, to provide legitimacy for the structured ineqalities characteristic of (at least) societies in which capitalist and patriarchal structures dominate.

Professionalism and Remuneration/Service Ideal

Eleven of the fifteen respondents mentioned issues of remuneration in their discussion of teaching and professionalism. However, the viewpoints expressed were heterogeneous. This appears to result because of the contradiction within the ideology of professionalism. On one hand, professionalism is identified with high incomes and, on the other, with a 'service ideal' in which remuneration is downplayed in importance, if not completely eschewed.

Six preservice teachers consistently stated that a high level of remuneration was a central feature of professionalism. This viewpoint was articulated by the one respondent, Mary, who did not believe teaching was a profession (see previous quote). The preservice teacher, who referred to teaching as a 'younger' or 'low status' profession, offered as part of his explanation:

> But I think part of the reason that it's hard for even teachers to think that they are a professional group is that we're not getting paid enough. ... You usually think of professionals as getting paid more than the average person, and we're making less than a waiter (laughs). I know because I'm a waiter [in a four-star hotel]. So I'm going to be taking a step down in teaching. ... [W]hen most unskilled or even uneducated people are making the same kind of money as teachers are making ... it's terribly unfair. (*Roberto*: 5–4–81)

He brought up the issue later in the same interview:

> Too many people are doing it for the vacation time. I think that's very unprofessional. ... And I think too many women in the profession, maybe not so much today, but I think in the past ... that maybe women that are married tend to use teaching as something to do while their husbands are making the big bucks or whatever. And so they don't take it [the level of remuneration] seriously sometimes. ... It's ok, you can call me a chauvinist pig.[21] (*Roberto*: 5–4–81)

Another respondent discussed the issue of pay level, not so much to explain a semi-professional label for teachers as to point out an inconsistency or contradiction.

> But the part that they're lacking so far is, you know, the financial part. And that part right there creates a kind of inconsistency for the teacher, uh, and a kind of strain on them, too. Because, you know, they can't keep preparing themselves and wanting to stay with the profession, if they're not given the support. ... Like people in say a grocery store ... maybe a cashier

or something, but no years of schooling, and come out making more money in one year than a teacher (*James: 5–7–81*).

This contradiction caused considerable consternation for other preservice teachers, sometimes based on comparisons with a sister who was making more without any college education working for Xerox than could teachers (*Allison: 9–12–80*). Other times the concern was stimulated by media coverage of labor disputes, e.g., the local meatcutters and four major grocery store chains.

> To be perfectly honest, I don't think (the meatcutters) deserved what they got. They shouldn't have struck. Most of the meat they get is prepackaged; therefore, they don't have any kind of preparation for what they do. There's no kind of real physical labor or mental stress that I can imagine; maybe, to some degree. And on top of that they go on strike for more money. And, of course, we saw the results: they got it. And I don't think they were justified in going on strike. Teachers deserve more money. There's a hell of a lot of difference! (*Richard: 12–9–80*)

Three of the interviewees, who mentioned financial issues, consistently articulated their viewpoint in relation to the notion of the service ideal. Their emphasizing the notion of an ideal of service, and thus derogating a concern for financial rewards, may also result from their encountering the contradiction (identified by the respondents quoted directly above) of conceiving of teaching as a profession, but one without the monetary rewards. One of these prospective teachers opined:

> Maybe they [the public] feel that teaching is not a profession because you don't make the most money in being a teacher. That's obvious; everybody knows that. But the fact that, if you know that and still want to become a teacher, it makes it a profession, because if they don't care about the financial rewards, then, you know, ... [otherwise] you're like skilled labor who's only doing that because of the money you can make. (*Sonia: 9–16–80*)

Finally, two respondents dealt with the contradiction, not by emphasizing consistently one aspect or the other, but by incorporating in their statements both aspects, even within the same interview. One of these preservice teachers discussed (at the beginning of the first semester) why she viewed teaching as a profession:

> Another aspect of it is that the teacher is supposed to care about the process and the result and become very concerned about it ... and spend a lot of energy on the process of teaching that you wouldn't necessarily spend ... in a regular or 8 to 5 job. ... [as opposed to not being able to] do anything else ... and ... needing some money. (*Dana: 9–15–80*)

Moments later, she emphasized during the interview the other aspect of the contradiction in explaining why she favored teacher organizations being involved in lobbying for pay:

> Because teachers, as compared to some of the other professions, are unable to set their own rates of pay. ... A person [i.e., a teacher] with that much education and training and dedication is at the mercy of the taxpayer. (*Dana: 9–15–80*)

At the end of the semester she indicated further the complexity of her perspective when she discussed her reactions to the meatcutters' strike:

> My first reaction: it's a strike, well, you know ... management is standing over them holding a whip. And then I saw how much they were making [without a college education] and I saw they were only working a 40-hour week, etc., And I became very resentful of the fact that they were asking for $27 thousand and they were being offered something like 22 or 23. ... I lost all my sympathy for them. OK, I do feel that people who have jobs on assembly lines or jobs that are tedious, jobs that are repetitive, jobs that don't require any use of their intellect [and] can be psychologically degrading and damaging to the person, ... that giving them a higher pay than certain other people, who might be called professionals, who are doing what they really want to. ... But I didn't feel as though they weren't being paid well in the first place. (*Dana: 12–15–80*)

The second respondent, who at different times emphasized different aspects of the contradiction connected with professionalism and remuneration, offered the following commentary at the beginning of the first semester in the program:

> Another thing, I don't think that teachers have ever been, they haven't been paid like professionals. So, in this materialistic, Philistine society we're living in, you know, you're worth what

> your paycheck says you are (sarcastic laughter). ... Society has put a lot more emphasis on things with a lot less responsibility, as far as how they are given economic rewards. ... Plumbers and construction workers make a lot more than teachers. (*Carol:* *9–22–80*)

She immediately countered, drawing on the other aspect of the contradiction:

> But teaching, on the other hand, has always been something that, in a way, you do it because you love it and because you would do it anyway. And, I think, unless you can say that, then you probably shouldn't, you probably shouldn't be there. (*Carol: 9–22–80*)

Then after a clarification probe, 'Does that, does that help make it a profession?' this preservice teacher raised the issue of the feminization of teaching, one to which she returned in subsequent interviews:

> I think so. ... I think it was a really valid point that was brought out in the seminar that, uh, too often it's been thought of as a second career and a female-oriented career ... a second job, a second income [for a family]. ... Maybe that's where we let ourselves in for getting less money and everything else. (*Carol: 9–22–80*)

At the end of the final semester in the program, this same respondent reported on one of several incidents she encountered during the program while attending dinner parties given by her husband's business associates. Notice, however, that this time when she raised the issues of gender and teaching, she focused more on exploitation of women than on how women voluntarily accept lower wages.

> I went to another one the other night. I had a guy who started pontificating about ... those who do, do, and those who can't, teach. ... I have a wonderful talent for running into these idiots. And I gave him my speech about the reason that you maybe don't run across super teachers all the time is because, for one thing, we're not paid enough. ... Also, I like to bring up the point that one of the problems, I think, in teaching is that it's been traditionally a female occupation, and that nursing has had the same problems — because they pay women less and expect more from them and get by with it. (*Carol: 5–26–82*)

Thus, as preservice teachers grappled with one of the contradictions in the ideology of professionalism — that professionalism involves significant financial rewards for practitioners, but at the same time implies an ideal of service without concern for personal gain — they reached different resolutions on the issues. Some of them emphasized one or the other aspect of the contradiction, while others incorporated in their conceptions both aspects, often in a compartmentalized manner that masked the relationship between the remuneration and service ideal aspects. It was also in the context of these discussions that social class and gender stratification emerged explicitly as issues, but not generally in ways that critiqued such unequal social relations.

Professionalism and Power

Thirteen of the fifteen interviewees raised the issue of power in their responses to questions about teaching, professionalism and teacher organizations. In five cases the focus was on the autonomy of the individual practitioner and in six cases collective or organizational power to obtain benefits or to influence policy was stressed; two respondents mentioned both aspects. Of the seven who emphasized individual autonomy in the workplace, one saw this as a negative feature of teaching as a profession, indicating a need for critical consumers with enough power to question what teachers say. Reflecting on some lessons he had taught during his second semester in the program, he stated:

> When I first started ... I taught something that was, that was a wrong viewpoint, whatever, you know. I didn't get the proper information to the students. ... After I finished I looked back on it and it kind of made me see how vulnerable the students were, you know. They, uh, look up to teachers. They respect teachers. They, uh, expect teachers to teach them what's supposed to be right, but they'll accept it anyway. And that kind of puts them in a vulnerable position ... if we force it upon them anyway without them being able to have time to critically think about it, whether that's what they want to accept or question it. (*James: 5–7–81*)

The other preservice teachers, who focused on autonomy, emphasized that power was a positive attribute of professionalism, although one

146

that so far had eluded teachers. Some blamed teachers for this state of affairs:

> Teachers have not wanted to place themselves in a position where they're saying, 'What I'm teaching in the classroom is right, totally right,' like the doctor. Generally a doctor does not come out with a diagnosis ... and then change his diagnosis (after discussion). But I think a teacher often does that. I think if teachers are expert in their field they shouldn't have to back down. Who should question them, but another expert? (*Cathy: 12–10–80*)

and others held the system or society responsible:

> I consider teaching a profession, but it still isn't treated like one, because of all the controls. ... [One of the reasons I'm dropping out of the program is because] administrators and parents are on [teachers'] backs and the state is looking over [teacher's] shoulders. It's hard enough to teach without this. (*Jerry: 12–15–80*)

Of the eight preservice teachers mentioning collective or organizational power to influence policy and benefits-related issues, four clearly favored such action for teachers as professionals. For example, at the end of his second semester in the program, one respondent reported on his views on the 'strike' by TAs in the University:

> I think the closest I've come to thinking about teacher organizations is the TA's organizing. I don't know, I think maybe for those purposes it would be a good idea to organize. There's strength in numbers, and for some things it's the only way you will get what you need, in this case, pay. (*Roberto: 5–4–81*)

Another interviewee expressed a similar view at the end of the first semester, in discussing a teacher collective bargaining bill which had recently been introduced in the State Legislature, she offered:

> I think it's a good idea. ... It appears to be the only way teachers can assert their rights, assert their own demands for salary increases or setting their own salaries and their own standards. ... You need some kind of consensus somewhere in the system and allowing the school board or the administration to set standards that are used in the classroom ... without giving teachers any input into the system ... doesn't seem to be

working. ... And teachers, to be able to feel as though they are teachers and they are professionals, they need to be able to assert themselves as individuals and as teachers ... to have some input into setting the salary ... or gaining input into the way the system is administered and curriculum, etc. (*Dana: 1–16–81*)

Four other preservice teachers expressed some ambivalence about the exercise of power by teachers as professionals. For instance, in discussing her reactions to the dispute between the Professional Air Controllers and the Reagan Administration one of these preservice teachers noted:

I have mixed feelings. On one hand, I can see, well, you know, other people, like other unions, have the right to strike. I mean, you know, that don't threaten, you know, like something like a policeman or fireman would do. Maybe ... [it would] pose a threatening situation. But then I look and see, you know, why is it some groups should have the right to strike and others not? ... [And in terms of teachers?] Uh, that's about the same thing to me. Um, I mean, it seems like, you know, ... why should others have the right? But then I don't know. Teachers, it's difficult for me to say because, I mean, something's missing out then. The students are hurting and it's a touchy subject there again. (*Jane: 5–27–81*)

Another of these respondents reported (at different phases of the program) that her father was an active union member, that she had friends who were teachers and friends who were on the governing board of a community college where unions had recently been banned from meeting on the campus, and that she had 'for the most part' supported the TAs who went out on 'strike' at the University. At the end of her first semester in the program, she expressed her ambivalence about exercising power in this manner:

I was approached in the teachers' lounge ... [by] one of the union members there. ... He had a thing for me to read about what happens to teachers their first year out. ... There's a lot of legitimate complaints. ... [T]he union is trying to do something about that. And, you know, I think he had a good point, but I can't see myself joining a union. ... The strikes still bother me. ... I was just a real liberal in the sixties and maybe I'm doing like everybody else and getting more conservative as I get older. And I think that, you know, a lot of economic problems we have are caused by unions. ... [However,] I know there's a real power struggle going on, you know ... especially with the economic situation being the way it is. But it's just something I haven't resolved yet. ... I think that [teachers] can have a voice, but I don't think it has to be through collective bargaining. (*Carol: 12–16–80*)

The power element of professionalism was drawn upon in different ways by the preservice teachers interviewed. For some it provided the foundation for claims to individual practitioner autonomy, although one respondent commented on the negative implications of such power by professionals. Other preservice teachers' conceptions evinced another contradiction within the ideology of professionalism — that the use of collective power is a central element of professionalism, while engaging in collective action is 'unprofessional'.

Professionalism as Individual Attitudes/Behavior in the Social Construction of Competence

Thirteen of fifteen interviewees referred to individual attitudes or behavior of practitioners in their discussion of teaching and professionalism. Here the concern was not with occupational group attributes (e.g., financial rewards or power) but with individual level attributes. For instance, one preservice teacher stated:

Oh, well, I haven't really thought of it as 'Ok, is this a profession?' but I think subconsciously I've been thinking, 'Are these people professional? ... Are they dressing professionally, are they behaving professionally?' (*Roberto: 5–4–81*)

The one respondent who did not view teaching to be a profession explained her view in part because 'teachers don't act like professionals ... they allow colleagues to use improper grammar, an incomplete sentence' (*Mary: 1–24–83*). Others, who expressed their belief that teaching is a profession, often qualified this point with reference to some individual teachers' lack of professionalism.

You know, as far as the education you need to get there ... I'm sure I would consider it a profession. But as far as other factors like ... attitude, I don't think so. Because teachers themselves don't act professionally, you know, and I don't even think they consider themselves professionals. (*Sonia: 12–9–80*)

For many of those interviewed the individualistic notion of a professional is highlighted as the path to professionalization of teaching.[22] As one respondent stated: 'Yes, it is a profession ... because, I think, I define a profession as something that one devotes time and energy to, and enjoys' (*Cindy: 5–14–81*). Unlike the issue of remuneration and power, about which many preservice teachers believe they can do little *as individuals*, exhibiting proper attitudes, dress and behavior are perceived to be within the realm of their control. It is an aspect of professionalism which, at least in the case of their individual practice, they can strive to achieve. This point was articulated concisely by the following preservice teacher:

> I personally think teaching is a profession. I don't think it is seen as a profession by the general public or by many people who are in it. I guess my approach is that I as a teacher ... think of myself as a professional because I was taking responsibility for what was going on. ... my own attitude makes it a profession. ... I may have restrictions by government agencies [and a relatively low salary] but it's still my responsibility. (*Nancy: 5–5–81*)

Interestingly, this emphasis on an individualistic approach was not only provided by those preservice teachers who were uncomfortable with collective action or who perceived striking to be 'unprofessional' (*Mary: 5–13–81*). For example, one of the preservice teachers, who frequently expressed a collectivist and activist position, discussed a contradiction she encountered in her school observations during the first semester of the program:

> I'm not really sure. I don't have any specific criteria for identifying a professional versus a non-professional right now. I can look at behavior and say, 'That's professional behavior and that isn't'. But, uh, for example, the one teacher who seemed least professional in the classroom was the one who was the most concerned about the future [status, pay, power] of the profession. And I found that a contradiction, very strange. ... His attitude towards the students doesn't [seem professional]. ... Well, I think ... a teacher's personality, or at least the way they present themselves, is more important than in any other profession, both physically and their personality, their physical appearance and various things like that. (*Dana: 12–15–80*)

In their discourse about teaching and professionalism, thus, the preservice teachers interviewed not only focused on structural features:

remuneration and power; they also drew upon individual attributes — teachers or other occupational incumbents were 'professionals' if they acted, dressed, and talked 'professionally'. In the next section, we will examine the implications of these conceptions of professionalism — their ideological functions *vis-à-vis* contradictions contained in capitalist and patriarchal societies.

Implications of the Ideology of Professionalism for Contradictions in Class and Gender Relations

These preservice teachers' conceptions of professionalism were relatively resilient as they encountered messages about professionalism in the formal and hidden curriculum. The one issue that challenged the previously constructed schema involved the public's critique or questioning of the degree of professionalization of teachers. For the most part, the messages encountered were in harmony with the views they brought to the program. Thus, a passive model of socialization, in which preservice teachers 'absorb' like sponges the messages of the program, is not appropriate, at least in this case.[23]

For some prospective teachers the program messages did provide 'academic' or 'scientific' reinforcement for their conceptions. However, because of the contradictions within the ideology of professionalism and, therefore, within the program messages and interviewees' conceptions, preservice teachers took on an active, interpretive stance toward the messages encountered; they filtered out or in different aspects of the contradictions in ways that usually sustained the equilibrium of the conception they brought in with them. Preservice teachers who conceived of professionalism as emphasizing high financial rewards and those who stressed the ideal of selfless service found corresponding (but also contradicting) messages. The same can be said of preservice teachers whose conceptions of professionalism stressed the exercise of power, individually or collectively, in contrast with those who viewed the exercise of power as 'unprofessional'.

It is nevertheless important to note that the conceptions of professionalism are not just random aggregations of ideas. They are dialectically related to — both constituted by and constitutive of — a broader, less ephemeral ideology of professionalism,[24] which has been constructed during different political economic periods, and which may be seen to both legitimate and challenge contemporary class and gender relations.

Preservice teachers deriving their conceptions from, and at the same time reproducing, the ideology of professionalism can be seen to mask/mediate or expose/challenge fundamental contradictions in (at least) capitalist political economies, for example, that although production is a social activity, the ownership and control of the means of production is privately concentrated. At the same time, their conceptions of professionalism may serve as a source to perpetuate and legitimate or critique and challenge unequal gender relations (and the attendant contradictions) at the school level, for example, that women teach and men manage, but also in society more generally.

The discussion below presents some of the implications of aspects of the ideology of professionalism, first, for class relations and then for gender relations. The three themes that were derived from the analysis of the fieldnotes, documents, interview data — remuneration/service ideal, power, and individual attitude/behavior — will serve as an organizing frame for the discussion of each form of relations.

Class Relations

Capitalist political economies not only contain the contradiction (as noted above) that although production is a social activity, the ownership and control of the means of production is privately concentrated. They also are characterized by the contradiction that production takes place for profit accumulation by capitalists rather than to satisfy the needs of workers, and that, because of the profit motive to reduce labor costs and increase productivity, many workers experience deskilling/proletaranization and thus become less expensive workers and more easily replaced by other humans or machines, while a few workers undergo reskilling/professionalization as they can be seen to enhance the design or control of the work process.[25] We will now discuss the potential relationships between these contradictions and the ideology of professionalism.

The remuneration/service ideal theme

The contradictory aspects within the ideology of professionalism — remuneration and an ideal of service as the driving force of professions — were evidenced in the program's curriculum and in the comments of prospective teachers interviewed. Emphasizing the remuneration aspect can help to mediate the contradictions in a class-based economy (outlined above). Inequalities in wealth, and thus private ownership of the means of production and private accumulation of profit, can be rendered unproblematic as 'true' professionals and other significant groups are seen to deserve more because of their rare skill or important and difficult function. At the same time, deskilling may become less visible or of less concern as attention is focused on reskilling of some workers, who are to be financially rewarded.

However, the remuneration aspect of the contradiction within the ideology of professionalism may also serve to highlight contradictions within the economy, and thus perhaps undermine the legitimacy of the extant political economy. One might be moved to question why, if wealth is the result of deserved remuneration, are some social groups wealthy without being highly educated, highly skilled, or performing essential tasks for society? Why are the means of production privately owned and controlled and oriented to creating profits for non-workers, rather than those who labor and deserve to be rewarded? Why are many workers being deskilled and receiving less remuneration; why are fewer workers being reskilled with added financial rewards?

The same can be argued for the service ideal aspect; it can both mediate and highlight contradictions within the economy. On one hand, the ideal of service and the attendant eschewing of financial rewards can operate to deflect concerns of exploitation; dedication to work regardless of personal benefit is an unproblematic given and, thus, who accumulates more money is of peripheral concern. The deskilling/reskilling contradiction is also mediated in that the issue is performing the assigned task as well as possible, not how much skill is involved or how much one is paid for doing the work.

On the other hand, if one stresses an ideal of service one might question why the system is characterized by private ownership and control of the means for performing the various productive and other services? Why are the needs of workers, both those directly and those indirectly involved in the service work, subordinated to the concerns of owners to acquire profit? Where is the service ideal among capitalists? In terms of the deskilling/reskilling contradiction, one might be tempted to ask how are people better served by the process of deskilling which fragments the work process and makes workers cheaper to hire?

The power theme

The element of exercising power being seen as either good/professional or bad/unprofessional could also mediate or highlight contradictions in the political economy. Conceiving that professionals should and deserve (because of their educationally acquired expertise) to be auton-omous or authoritative in their work may buttress the domination of workers, including many semi- and 'true' professionals, by political and economic elites.[26] In relation to economic elites, for instance, Larson explains that:

> historically, the core units of monopoly capital show strong affinities with experts, on whom their management depends, and with professionalism, which tends to be substituted for bureaucratic control in multidivisional structures. ... Expertise is implicitly proposed as a legitimation for the hierarchical struc-ture of authority of the modern organization; professionalism, in turn, functions as an internalized mechanism for the control of the subordinate expert.[27]

Following from this, a positive view of professionalism and power might even help to mediate the deskilling/reskilling contradiction, in that decisions about what jobs and which people to reskill or deskill would be seen to be made by superordinate experts.

Despite the symbiotic relationship between professionalism and organizational control noted above, for some people, favoring profes-sionals exercising power, individually or collectively, may expose and facilitate critique of the contradictions in the political economy. One might be stimulated to ask: Why should non-professionals own and control the means of production? Why should profit be the dominating motive of the economy when professionals ought to determine what the needs of the client are and how those needs are met?[28] Why are some forms of work being deskilled and thus reducing the need for experts?

A position opposing professionals' exercise of power, particularly of the collective variety, can also mediate contradictions within the political economy. If the use of power is conceived to be 'unprofess-ional', then that potentially leaves the domination by others, including owners, managers and state elites, unchallenged. Not only would 'professionals' avoid challenging the status quo either as 'professional' groups or in concert with other workers/citizens, but the articulation of this stance would undermine the legitimacy of other workers'/citizens' exercise of power to transform existing structural features of society.

It may also be, however, that denigrating the use of power may provide a basis for critiquing the concentration among a relatively small elite group of control and ownership of the means of production, benefits from productive activity, and decisions about reskilling/deskilling. This seems less likely, though, because elites' exercise of power is less overt, relying on the existing structures to realize it, and because given the smaller number of elites (compared to workers/masses) their use of power might be viewed as individualist rather than collectivist.

The individual attitude/behavior theme

This theme, which is partially linked to the service ideal aspect of another theme, appears to offer a very conservative position. By deflecting or ignoring the social, political and economic structural levels, and by focusing attention on how people should dress, talk, carry out with devotion the tasks assigned as well as what attitudes they should exhibit, this element of the conceptions and ideology of professionalism seems to render as unproblematic, and thus mediates the social production/private ownership and control, profit/worker needs, and deskilling/reskilling contradictions. In a sense, from this vantage point one need not worry about who owns and controls the means of production (or the state apparatus), whether economic activity is governed primarily by a profit motive or by a desire to satisfy human needs, or whether many workers are deskilled while some are reskilled. The concern instead is directed toward oneself and one's colleagues acting in a 'professional' manner and possessing attitudes which are consonant with professionalism.

We should note, nevertheless, that a position stressing individual, 'professional' attitudes and behaviors as the indicators of competence may lead preservice teachers to question the legitimacy of those with political and economic power to the extent that those in power do not exhibit 'professional' attitudes and behaviors seen to signify competence.

Gender Relations

When focusing on patriarchal structures in education, we note the contradiction that although education is predominantly a 'feminine' pursuit — school teachers, especially at the primary level, are predominantly women — the vast majority of those who control the means and who manage the process of educational production (school board members and educational administrators, respectively) are predominantly men. This contradiction is paralleled in society, in that although the females of the species constitute a numerical majority, political and economic power is concentrated in the hands of relatively few (elite) males. We should also consider the contradiction imbedded in the role of teacher, the 'requirement' of emotional detachment and the 'require-ment' of emotional engagement in relation to students as well as their parents.[29] We will examine the potential relationships between these contradictions and the ideology of professionalism.

The renumeration/service ideal theme

As discussed above some of the preservice teachers interviewed, both male and female, raised the issue of the relationship between the (semi-) professional status of teaching and the predominance of women in the field — an issue which was reinforced in one of the assigned readings[30] during the first semester of the program. The focus was primarily within the remuneration theme. Drawing on the remuneration issues associated with professionalism, they were able to both argue the legitimacy and offer an emergent critique of the fact that occupations such as teaching, which have a high proportion of women, have lower wages. It seems to depend on whether one assumes that women coming into the field somehow caused the status and remuneration to decline, or as Kelsall and Kelsall emphasize, that 'if this is true, it is a function of the status accorded to women in a given society, not simply to the presence of women'.[31]

The service ideal aspect of this theme also can mediate or highlight contradictions in gender relations. Stressing the ideal of service rather than financial rewards can deflect attention away from, and thus mediate, the contradiction that women workers are paid less. Equally, though, the ideal of service may prompt one to question whether educational administrators, school board members, or other predomin-antly male occupational groups are sufficiently motivated by a desire to serve the community, clients, etc., as opposed to being driven by self-interest or financial issues. Such questioning may lead to queries about the legitimacy of the superordinate status of such male dominated groups.

In connection with the detached authority versus emotionally engaged dilemma of the teacher's role, the remuneration aspect of the remuneration/service ideal theme appears to encourage an orient-ation of emotional detachment. Not only is one pursuing a career for economic rewards rather than committed service, one would also be buying into an ideology which operates to distance one from clients, especially of the working class, who are implicitly labelled as not deserving as large financial rewards. The service ideal aspect, in contrast, could reinforce an orientation of emotional engagement or one of emotional detachment, depending on whether the teacher viewed socializing/motivating or evaluating/controlling, respectively, as the major aspect of the role in which she or he were serving.

The power theme

To the extent that educational administrators were viewed as consummate professionals, those approving of professionals exercising power might help to mediate the women teach/men manage contradiction, in that the most expert group is seen to be in control. It is here where an examination of the nexus of bureaucracy, professionalism and patriarchy may be helpful. Recall first Larson's[32] claim (discussed earlier) about the symbiotic relationship between professionalism and bureaucratic control.[33] Given the predominance, especially in secondary schools, of male school administrators and female teachers, Larson's observation of how 'professionalism' can be used to subordinate 'professional workers' takes on a more complex meaning:

> Insofar as managers are recruited from the ranks of professional workers ... or if they themselves claim some kind of professional expertise, they are not likely to deny the ideology of professionalism, from which they too can derive legitimation.[34]

This domination of women workers may also be reinforced by drawing on ideological notions, such as that suggested by Simpson and Simpson, 'that women's personality characteristics require bureaucratic organizational control'.[35]

By way of contrast, people who concur with Kanter that 'many so-called sex difference findings about behavior in organizations can be more satisfactorily explained by differences in opportunities, numerical representation, and access to power that often coincide with sex',[36] and/or those who question whether educational administrators, let alone 'lay' school board members, are professional educators, may tend to expose and challenge this women teach/men manage contradiction. They could ask, why the 'true' professionals, the classroom teachers, are not the ones having the most to say about the content, structure and processes of schooling?

A position opposing professionals' exercise of power, especially of the collective variety, may also mediate contradictions in patriarchal structures. If the use of power is conceived to be 'unprofessional', then that leaves unchallenged the extant gender (and other) relations of domination and subordination, both in schools and society.

The contradiction within teaching — detached authority *vs.* emotional engagement — is also related to the power theme in the ideology of professionalism. Favoring or opposing the use of power by 'professionals' not only affects perceptions or relations with administrators and school board members; it also affects relations with clients: students and parents. Rather than encouraging people to seek a synthetic resolution in the gender-related contradictory role of teacher, the power theme in the ideology of professionalism may either lead teachers to, respectively, emphasize or de-emphasize the detached, authority aspect depending on whether they view the exercise of power as professional or not.

The individual attitude/behavior theme

As in the case of class relations, this theme in the ideology of professionalism could easily render unproblematic the structural inequalities between men and women in schools and society. With the primary concern about how individuals should dress, talk, carry out their assigned tasks, attention is deflected away from the larger issues of the unequal distribution of wealth and power. That in schools men manage and women teach or that in society men exercise more economic and political power than women is not a concern from this perspective; the issue in focus becomes do they perform their tasks well, with devotion and in concert with other appropriate attitudes and behaviors.

In relation to the detached authority/emotional engagement contradiction of the teaching role, this theme seems to facilitate people's emphasizing either or both of the aspects of the contradictions. 'Proper' dress and speech may tend to create an emotional distance between teachers and students and parents, particularly those of the working class. But 'proper' attitudes and devotion to work may be translated into greater or lesser emotional attachment to students or parents, depending on what aspect(s) of this dilemma of the teacher's role one stresses.

Conclusions

It has been claimed that in the United States, 'all intelligent modern persons organize their behavior, both public and private, according to "the culture of professionalism"'.[37] While this may be overstated, there is no question that professionalism as an ideology is important to consider at least in English speaking countries.[38] Based on our analysis and discussion here, however, it should be clear that the ideology of professionalism, which is drawn upon and reproduced by people, including preservice teachers, does not *a priori* have either a mediating or a critical undermining role in relation to the extant unequal class or gender relations.

On one hand, we identified aspects of the ideology that appear to provide a foundation of legitimacy for unequal wealth and power between social classes and between gender groups. Similarly, we noted how certain ways in which the ideology is drawn upon in preservice teachers' commonsense conceptions help to mask and mediate contradictions in both capitalist and patriarchal structures. On the other hand, we described aspects of the ideology of professionalism that could and were drawn upon to raise critical questions if not (as yet) to engender critical praxis (see Chapter 7). These aspects of the ideology helped illuminate contradictions in capitalist and patriarchal structures, pointing not only to problems, but also to places in which interventions might be attempted.

Some might argue that this type of conclusion — 'on the one hand' and 'on the other hand' — renders the study of the ideology of professionalism as worthless. If the ideology has no consistent impact on class and gender relations, they may ask, why spend the time theorizing and investigating its implications? In response to this we should first state that the absence of predictability of the relationship between the ideology of professionalism and structural features of society is only a problem if one assumes a non-diadectical account of society, where ideologies and social relations are usually in perfect 'correspondence' with each other. Second, the fact that there are contradictory aspects of the ideology of professionalism makes it more worthy of study, as a way to encourage reflection about other contradictions in society. Such contradictions are not only a source of consciousness raising; they also identify regions of social relations toward which progressive transformative action can be directed.

Finally, the contradictory nature of the ideology of professionalism means that those who subscribe to it as a rallying call run the risk of their efforts having unanticipated or opposite consequences.[39] This, of course, can be said of both those who use the ideology to mobilize individual and collective action to challenge unequal class and gender relations, but also those who employ the ideology to keep the proletariat (and the 'professional') in her or his place and/or to subordinate women in paid or unpaid work places. However, given the other ideological and structural resources available to the dominant groups, we should be very cautious even in our critical use of this ideology. The ideology of professionalism may in the immediate struggle help the cause, although in relation to other people's concurrent struggles and in one's own future struggles the one 'success' may translate into a major victory for those who would seek to benefit from the reproduction of unequal class and gender relations.

In the next chapter, we will discuss other ideologies upon which prospective teachers drew in their efforts to understand social inequalities and the role of schooling. These ideologies focus more specifically on individual social mobility or on social reproduction of unequal class, gender, and race relations.

Notes

1 This chapter synthesizes discussions presented in two earlier papers: GINSBURG, M., 'Reproduction, contradiction and conceptions of professionalism: The case of preservice teachers', in POPKEWITZ, T., (Ed.) *Critical Studies in Teacher Education: Its Folklore, Theory and Practice*, (Lewes, Falmer Press, 1987), pp. 86–129; and GINSBURG, M., 'Reproduction and Contradiction in Preservice Teachers' Encounters with Professionalism', paper presented at the American Educational Research Association annual meeting, New Orleans, 23–27 April, 1984. Some aspects of the discussion presented herein derive from collaborative work undertaken with Katherine K. Newman. Constructive criticisms on earlier drafts of this paper were graciously provided by Tom Popkewitz, Sheila Slaughter, and Linda Spatig. I want to thank Beatriz Arias-Godinez, Linda Spatig, Susan Stilley, and John York for their assistance in transcribing the interview tapes. Appreciation is also expressed to Rose Kassamali for typing some of the interview transcripts and to Dr. Tessa J. Shokri for word processing this manuscript.
2 LAWSON, D., 'What is a professional teacher?' *Phi Delta Kappan* (June, 1971), p. 589.
3 See, for example, LANGFORD, G., *Teaching as a Profession* (Manchester, University of Manchester Press, 1978); LEGATT, T., 'Teaching as a profession', in JACKSON, J., (Ed.) *Professions and Professionalization*, (Cambridge, Cambridge University Press, 1970), pp. 153–77; LIEBERMAN,

M., *Education as a Profession* (Englewood Cliffs, N.J., Prentice-Hall, 1956); LIEBERMAN, M., *The Future of Public Education* (Chicago, University of Chicago Press, 1960); LORTIE, D., 'The balance of control and autonomy in elementary school teaching', in ETZIONI, A. (Ed.) *The Semi-Professions and Their Organization*, (New York, The Free Press, 1964), pp. 1–53; LORTIE, D., *School Teacher: A Sociological Analysis* (Chicago, University of Chicago Press, 1975); RUHELA, S. (Ed.) *Sociology of the Teaching Profession in India* (New Delhi, National Council of Educational Research and Training, 1970); SEYMOUR, F., 'Occupational images and norms: Teaching,' in VOLLMER, H. and MILLS, D. (Eds.) *Professionalization*, (Englewood Cliffs, N.J., Prentice-Hall, 1966), pp. 126–29.

4   See for example COLLINS, R., *The Credential Society: A Historical Sociology of Education* (New York, Academic Press, 1979); GINSBURG, M., MEYENN, R., and MILLER, H., 'Teachers' conceptions of professionalism and trades unionism: An ideological analysis', in WOODS, P. (Ed.) *Teacher Strategies* (London, Croom Helm, 1980), pp. 178–212; JOHNSON, T., *Professions and Power* (London, Macmillan, 1972); MILLERSON, G., *The Qualifying Associations: A Study in Professionalization* (London, Routledge and Kegan Paul, 1964); OGZA, J. and LAWN, M., *Teachers, Professionalism and Class: A Study of Organized Teachers* (Lewes, Falmer Press, 1981); ROTH, J. 'Professionalism: The sociologist's decoy', *Sociology of Work and Occupations* 1(1) (1974), pp. 6–23.

5   The ideological nature of professionalism has been discussed by various writers. See for example, DINGWALL, R., 'Accomplishing profession', *Sociological Review*, 24 (1976), pp. 331–49; FINN, D., GRANT, N, and JOHNSON, R., 'Social democracy, education and the crisis', in CENTRE FOR CONTEMPORARY CULTURAL STUDIES, *On Ideology* (London: Hutchinson, 1977), pp. 144–85; FRIEDSON, E., *Profession of Medicine* (New York, Dodd Mead, 1970); GINSBURG, M., MEYENN, R., MILLER, I., KHANNA, I., and SPATIG, L., 'Teachers' Conceptions of Professionalism: A Comparison of Contexts in England and the United States', revised version of paper presented at the annual meeting of the Comparative and International Education Society, Vancouver, 19–23 March, 1980; HUGHES, E., 'The social significance of professionalization', in VOLLMER, H. and MILLS, D. (Eds.) *Professionalization* (Englewood Cliffs, N.J., Prentice-Hall, 1966), pp. 62–70; LARSON, M., *The Rise of Professionalism: A Sociological Analysis* (Berkeley, University of California Press, 1977). Professionalism has been referred to by George Bernard Shaw as 'a conspiracy against the laity' and Seymour (*op cit*). describes it as 'a state of mind, not a reality'. As an ideology, professionalism both distorts or only partially reflects social reality and serves to mobilize or immobilize individual and collective action in ways that support the interests of certain groups in society. More specifically, Larson (*op cit.*, p. 156) concludes, based on her historical analysis of 'the rise of professionalism' in England and the United States, that professionalism constitutes 'an important contribution to the ideological denial of structured inequalities'. This masking of the structural basis of inequalities in wealth and power is achieved by representing the school system and the political economy as

meritocratic [see also BARLOW, A., 'Review of M. Larson's *The Rise of Professionalism: A Sociological Analysis*', *Harvard Educational Review* 50(3) (1980), pp. 427–32] and by characterizing professionals as independent, neutral experts who serve the interests of all people — males and females, capitalists and proletarians, whites and people of color — through their roles as advisors to policy-makers [see POPKEWITZ, T., 'Social science and social amelioration: The development of the American academic expert', *Paradigm and Ideology in Educational Research: The Social Functions of the Intellectual* (Lewes, Falmer Press, 1984), pp. 107–27]. Nevertheless, we should also note, 'even if the idea of professionalism does have some role in maintaining the social system, this does not ... preclude its having some subversive role as well' [SCHUDSON, M., 'A discussion of Margali Sarfatti Larson's *The Rise of Professionalism: A Sociological Analysis*', *Theory and Society*, 9(1) (1980), p. 227].

6   See also JAMESON, F., *The Political Unconscious* (Ithaca, N.Y., Cornell University Press, 1981), p. 52.

7   For a more detailed discussion of the theoretical stance adopted in the analysis herein, see Chapter 1.

8   This section of the chapter is based on an analysis of fieldnotes and documents collected as part of a longitudinal ethnographic study at the University of Houston. See Chapter 1 for details.

9   Helsel and Krchniak share a similar observation. See HELSEL, A. and KRCHNIAK, S., 'Socialization in a heteronomous profession: Public school teaching', *Journal of Educational Research* 66 (1972), pp. 89–93.

10 RYAN, K. and COOPER, J., *Those Who Can, Teach*, 3rd Edition (Boston, Houghton and Mifflin, 1980), pp. 363–99: DARLAND, D., 'Professionalism in education', in MUSE, M. (Ed.) *Selected Readings for the Introduction to the Teaching Profession*, (Berkeley, McCutchan, 1970), pp. 220–33.

11 Ryan and Cooper, p. 371.

12 HOWSAM, R., CORRIGAN, D., DENMARK, G. and NASH, R., *Educating a Profession* (Washington, DC, American Association for Colleges of Teacher Education, 1976); Ryan and Cooper.

13 Howsam *et al.*, p. 18.

14 See Chapter 6 for discussions of messages about inequalities.

15 See also GYARMATI, G., 'The doctrine of professions: Basis of a power structure', *International Social Science Journal* 27 (1975), pp. 629–54; GYARMATI, G., 'Notes for a Political Theory of the Professions,' paper presented at the International Sociological Association meeting, Uppsala, Sweden, 14–19 August, 1978.

16 See FUSSELL, P., *Class* (New York, Summit Books, 1983).

17 This section is based on data collected through semi-structured, semesterly interviews of a sample of teacher education students as part of a longitudinal ethnographic study at the University of Houston. See Chapter 1 for details of sampling and other procedures. To ascertain how the fifteen preservice teachers, who were interviewed at least once after the beginning of the program, conceived of professionalism and its relation to teaching I drew primarily on comments made in response to two sets of questions asked during each interview:

162

1   Do you consider teaching a profession? Why do you say
    this? (and sometimes) What do you mean when you speak
    of profession, professional, and professionalism?
2   Do you plan to join (or have you joined) a teacher organiz-
    ation? (If yes) Which one(s)? Why?

A variety of probes for clarification and probes to encourage respondents
to elaborate on comments they had made during the relevant semester
were also used. In addition, interviewees were asked to express their
views on relevant events which had received media attention during the
semester. These events consisted of three 'labor disputes' — between the
Houston area meatcutters/meatwrappers and four supermarket chains,
between University of Houston teaching assistants and the campus
administration, and between the Professional Air Controllers and the
Reagan Administration — as well as a bill to authorize collective
bargaining for teachers which was introduced in the Texas Legislature.
Two magazines, *Texas Monthly* and *Time*, which during the research
period had cover stories dealing critically with education and teachers,
also provided stimuli for comments during the interviews.

18 NATIONAL COMMISSION on EXCELLENCE IN EDUCATION, *A Nation at
    Risk* (Washington, DC, US Department of Education, 1983).
19 See discussion in Chapter 3. It may be that college of education faculties'
    cries for the professionalization of school teaching is not unrelated to
    problems they confront in the university setting. The subordination of
    colleges of education (experienced in terms of lower status and salaries)
    within institutions of higher education might be seen to be reversed if they
    were the training and research arms of a 'full profession'. On the
    importance of professionalism in the history of teacher education, see
    Chapter 2. While the concern with professionalization emerged as a
    central concern to teacher educators in the US during the nineteenth and
    twentieth centuries, there is evidence that the concern was not a new one.
    For example, the Englishman Richard Mulcaster (1530–1611), head-
    master of two famous academies in London, St. Paul's and Merchant
    Taylor's wrote, in *Positions* (1582) words that were echoed three centuries
    later across the Atlantic: 'Why should not teachers be well provided for,
    so they can continue their whole lives in the schools, as divines, lawyers,
    and physicians do in their several professions? ... I consider, therefore, that
    in our universities there should be a special college for the training of
    teachers' [WEISS, R., *The Conant Controversy in Teacher Education* (New
    York, Random House, 1969), p. 11].
20 See Chapter 6. Interestingly, James, one of these two 'incipient radicals',
    who discussed inequalities and schooling from a perspective focusing on
    institutional and societal structure, had no reservations about hier-
    archically differentiating professions from other occupational groups (see
    above). The other, Dana, began with an ambiguous view on the issue of
    professionalism — a view that, as she moved into teaching, became more
    clearly critical of the invidious status and class distinctions associated with
    certain notions of professionalism (see discussion below).

21 See Carol's comments (quoted later) which raise the issue of the impact of the feminization of teaching, at times from a more critical perspective.
22 See discussion above of a similar emphasis in the formal and hidden curriculum of the teacher education program.
23 For elaboration on this point, see Chapter 1.
24 For details on issue of the ideological nature of professionalism, see note 5.
25 See discussion of contradictions in class relations in Chapter 1.
26 See Barlow, p. 431.
27 Larson, *The Rise of Professionalism*, p. 193.
28 See; Johnson, *Professions and Power*, for a discussion of issues of who determines clients' needs and how those needs are met.
29 See discussion of contradictions in gender relations in Chapter 1.
30 See Howsam *et al.*
31 KELSALL, R. and KELSALL, H., 'The status, role and future of teachers', in KING, E. (Ed.) *The Teacher and the Needs of Society in Evolution*, (Oxford, Pergamon, 1970) quoted in ACKER, S., 'Women and teaching: A semi-detached sociology of a semi-profession', in WALKER, S. and BARTON, L. (Eds.) *Gender, Class and Education*, (Lewes, Falmer Press, 1983), p. 131.
32 Larson, *The Rise of Professionalism*.
33 See also Ginsburg *et al.*, 'Teachers' conceptions of professionalism'.
34 Larson, 'Proletarianization of educated labor', p. 161.
35 SIMPSON, R. and SIMPSON, I., 'Women and bureaucracy in the semi-professions', in ETZIONI, A. (Ed.) *The Semi-Professions and Their Organization*, (New York, Free Press, 1969), quoted in Acker, p. 131.
36 KANTER, R., *Men and Women of the Corporation* (New York, Basic Books, 1977), quoted in Acker, p. 132.
37 Bledstein, p. ix.
38 See GINSBURG, M. and CHATURVEDI, V., 'Teachers and the ideology of professionalism in India and England: A Comparison of cases in colonial/peripheral and metropolitan/central societies', *Comparative Education Review* (1987).
39 See GINSBURG, M., WALLACE, G., and MILLER, H., 'Teachers, Economy and the State: An English Example,' revised version of paper presented at the 10th World Congress of Sociology, International Sociological Association, Mexico City, 15–21 August, 1982; DENSMORE, K., 'Professionalism, proletarianization and teacher work', in POPKEWITZ, T. (Ed.) *Critical Studies in Teacher Education* (Lewes, Falmer Press, 1987), pp. 130–60.

Chapter 6

Ideologically Informed Conceptions of Social Mobility and Social Reproduction[1]

Democracy asks individuals to act as if social mobility were universally possible. ... But democracies also need selective training institutions ... [in which] increasingly fewer persons succeed at ascending levels. Thus democratic societies need not only to motivate achievement but also to mollify those denied it in order to sustain motivation in the face of disappointment and ... blocked opportunity.[2]

Introduction

Societies characterized by inequalities in wealth, status and power contain a major contradiction:[3] each generation of workers/citizens must both be 'warmed-up' and 'cooled-out'. This contradiction, especially in industrial societies, is evidenced most clearly in the context of the educational system.

In sum, at every level and through every route within the total selection process, an educational system must strive, on one hand, to warm up some of its students [to motivate them to fill essentially superordinate roles], and, on the other hand, to cool out those who are rejected for further training. ... This contradiction generates pressure for social change, both within the educational system and in its relation to other institutions, but even if changes occur, the nature of the dilemma remains constant, as do pressures for further change.[4]

Moreover, although in stratified societies, the warming-up–cooling-out contradiction cannot be 'resolved ... with complete success',[5] I argue that this contradiction can be masked and thus mediated or exposed and thus challenged by differing combinations of pairs of ideologies of social mobility/reproduction: sponsorship versus contest and particularistic versus universalistic.[6]

In this chapter, we will examine how a group of preservice teachers conceive of the nature and legitimacy of extant class, race and gender relations in schools and societies in an effort to better understand how these ideologies of social mobility/reproduction may relate to this warming-up–cooling-out contradiction. In turn, the messages in the formal and hidden curricula of their teacher education program will be scrutinized for sources of influence or reinforcement of these pre-service teachers' ideologically informed conceptions of unequal social relations.

That is, interview, participant observation and documentary data collected as part of a longitudinal ethnographic study[7] in one college of education will be drawn upon to illuminate how, at the micro-level, human thought and action can be seen to be related to macro-level, structural and ideological features of society.

As noted above, two contradictory pairs of ideologies are relevant to our discussion here with respect to mediating or challenging the warming-up–cooling-out contradiction. These ideologies have been delineated by Hooper[8] in his analysis of ideologies of implementation and ideologies of legitimation, which he built on Turner's[9] earlier work on 'folk-norms' associated with different mobility systems.[10] The two pairs of ideologies can be distinguished by the basic question concerning selection each is seen to address: sponsorship vs. contest and particularism vs. universalism.

The *sponsorship vs. contest* ideologies of implementation concern the questions of how and when selection should occur. Hopper discusses the tenets of what I term a sponsorship ideology as emphasizing that people should receive education commensurate with their 'future ability to contribute to the economic productivity and to other social goods'; in contrast, he identifies the basic elements of the contest ideology as stressing that 'the maximum amount of education is the right of every citizen regardless of his future ability to contribute to the economy and other social goods'. In addition, as distinguished from a contest ideology focus on effort-based achievement, emphasizing 'survival of the fittest' in an open competition common to all, a sponsorship ideology specifies that those with different futures should be identified early (based on their ability to contribute) and schooled differently in segregated settings.[11]

The contradictory pair of ideologies of legitimation, *particularism vs. universalism*, pertain to the question of who should be selected. Within a particularistic ideology, according to Hooper,[12] 'pupils should be selected primarily on the basis of their diffuse skills and only secondarily on their technical skills'; whereas, from a universalistic viewpoint, achieved technical skills are emphasized rather than ascribed diffuse skills. Thus, under a particularistic (versus a universalistic) ideology, selection is based on the performance of skills or other characteristics which not everyone or even most people have an opportunity to acquire, for example, particular sociolinguistic codes, personalities, values, world views, or other aspects of culture.

Views of Preservice Teachers [13]

Issues of social stratification were not often stressed by those interviewed during the first semester interviews, in which questions posed provided space to discuss such issues, but did not explicitly raise them. There were also only a few references to education's selection function. Sonia, who observed that one of the ways that teachers help the local community was 'to educate future leaders', also noted that one of the abilities teachers need to be successful beyond the classroom was 'not to pass on judgments of students to other teachers' (*9–16–80*). Usually, however, their responses to various questions about schools and teaching omitted any references to stratification or even to education's selection function. As interview questions during the second semester became more focused on issues of stratification and education's selection function, it became more apparent how they conceived of these issues as well as what ideologies of social mobility/reproduction these perservice teachers drew upon and reproduced.

As discussed elsewhere,[14] based on an analysis of the data collected during the early phases of the fieldwork, the perspectives of preservice teachers interviewed could be categorized into three general orientations to issues of social inequalities and the role of schooling. First, there was a pair of respondents who emphasized schooling's role in reproducing inequalities. For example, Dana stressed structural dynamics of reproduction when discussing why inequalities in wealth and power exist.

It's part of the structure of the US. ... Some will have power and others won't. ... Wealth is a by product of power. ... [Being wealthy and powerful depends on] what family you're born into, whether you're male or female. ... Society is not set up to include people of color. And, therefore, if you are born a person of color, you are automatically excluded from success. ... [Schooling's effect on inequalities?] One of the things is it totally ignores that inequalities exist. I mean it isn't in the history books. ... [And] by ignoring inequalities, it tends to reinforce them. (*Dana: 5–12–81*)

A second perspective evidenced by prospective teachers in our sample highlighted social mobility (as opposed to social reproduction) and offered an image of individuals freely (without structural constraints) choosing whether or not to be wealthy or powerful. Roberto's comments about why inequalities in wealth and power exist are illustrative of this perspective:

Well, I think, being a capitalist society, those differences have to exist in order for the system of work. ... What the teacher might want to do is just make the students understand what capitalist society is and then let them choose whether or not they want to be a part of whatever status they want. And, believe it or not, people do choose to be poor and people do choose to be rich. ... I think if the individual seeks social mobility he's going to find it, whether it be in school or somewhere else. The school facilitates it, but only if the student wishes it to. (*Roberto: 5–4–81*)

The third group of respondents, although they also framed their answer around the question of mobility, did not treat social stratification — or at least the extant relations of subordination and domination — as almost totally unproblematic in the way that those with a perspective similar to Roberto did. However, their primary concern was with individual attitudes and prejudice, and not with structural forces as was the case for the first perspective discussed above. From this perspective, Carol explains:

Well, I think it's because if you start out behind, you can never really catch up. ... And I think education is the key. But, I think, we started out in this country as unequal, and we still are. ... That's what's happened with minorities and women. ... I think that education is a two way street: not only education of the people who start out behind, but also the people who start out ahead. I'm just talking about things like prejudice. ... Well, I think [schooling] should contribute to upward mobility, because as I said earlier about education and the cycle of poverty thing. (*Carol: 5–21–81*)

As we shall see below, each group's perspective is built upon a different combination of the two contradictory pairs of ideologies: contest versus sponsorship and particularistic versus universalistic. That is, these preservice teachers' conceptions of schooling and class, race, and gender relations are not idiosyncratic, but rather patterned constellations of ideas drawn from ideologies of social mobility and social reproduction available in the broader culture.

Contest Versus Sponsorship

The preservice teachers interviewed gave voice to a contest ideology, expressing a preference for delayed selection and delayed segregation of future elites and non-elites on the assumption that all can benefit from the maximum amount of education as well as from continued interaction with different strata of people. However, a fairly strong representation of elements from a sponsorship ideology was also reflected in their remarks.[15]

One way in which contest and sponsorship ideological elements were combined was evidenced by Dana and James, the two respondents whose conceptions of social inequality and the role of schooling reflected a 'societal level structural reproduction' position. These preservice teachers drew critically upon sponsorship ideological elements in their description of the current situation. They identified that selection was undertaken early, that segregated education obtained, and that such stratification was a function of social origin as well as social destiny. As an example, in discussing social inequalities and the role of schooling during a second semester interview, James commented on the problem of 'racism':

We have different practices and policies that keep this in effect. ... It kind of set up an unequal opportunity, so everybody didn't have an equal chance to get the best out of the system so far as education and opportunities. (*James: 5–7–81*)

In their normative analysis, though, James and Dana manifested elements drawn primarily from a contest ideology. For example, James indicated satisfaction with a process consonant with a decentralized, effort-based system reflective of a contest ideology.

> I am very impressed with this notion of mastery learning: that if you do not learn the material the first time, you can retake it. It takes the stress out of [the learning experience] and allows you to compete with yourself. (*James: 5–7–81*)

And at the end of the first semester Dana expressed a preference for mixed ability classes because the segregation of 'bright' kids and those 'performing less well' would 'stigmatize' the students (*12–15–80*). Another semester into the program, she discussed why inequalities in wealth and power exist:

> I feel that there is a certain tradition that we are taught that success in our own culture will be rewarded with recognition, power, status; that success can only be achieved through competition with others. And personally, I do not feel that is true or needs to be true. ... Success can be the situation where nobody fails. ... [School's effect on inequality?] I think that the ways schools are now set up, they identify the elite, the successful people. ... But I don't think that is necessary. (*Dana: 5–12–81*)

For other preservice teachers, especially those stressing the role of historical and contemporary attitudes, their normative views contained a mixture of elements of both the contest and sponsorship ideologies. For instance, drawing on elements of a contest ideology, Carol expressed a preference for teaching mixed-ability classes during the interview at the end of the first semester in the program, mentioning problems of ability group segregation: 'not being rewarded for effort' and 'lowering of student's self-expectations'. Carol interjected, though, that ability grouping would be 'nice for a literature course ... it would be fun to work with a high ability group, but I'm not sure I agree in principle. ... Life is more mixed' (*12–16–80*). After two semesters of coursework and school observations, Carol appeared to take for granted the existence of ability grouping — an element central to a sponsorship ideology. In discussing how she would envision deciding what content to teach, Carol noted that her curriculum decisions would depend on 'if I am teaching major works or basic English', expressing her preference as before: 'I would love to teach a major works class in literature, because literature is still my main interest' (*5–12–81*).

170

However, during the interview following her student-teaching experience, Carol gave voice to an element of a contest ideology, stressing the importance of *not* segregating different groups, primarily because integration was perceived to improve students' attitudes towards other groups.

> I don't see [schools] reinforcing the divisions that are there. ... Just the fact that they ... put ... together students from different ethnic backgrounds, I see that in the long run, that's going to make a difference in the attitudes these kids have toward different ethnic groups. ... There's a lot of prejudice there amongst the students. (*Carol: 5–26–82*)

Another respondent, Donald, drew on contest ideology and emphasized the role of attitudes when explaining how teachers could inappropriately influence the stratification process, by communicating their prejudices, attitudes or expectations to students.

> Q: Why do you think certain social classes do better or worse in school?
> A: I think part of it is because they're told to do better or worse. ... And an awful lot of the times if you've told somebody they could do it, whether you thought they could nor not, ... they'd give it a good shot. Uh, and if you told somebody they couldn't, then they didn't. (*Donald: 5–27–82*)

A third pattern of combining sponsorship and contest ideological positions was evidenced most strongly by preservice teachers who represented a 'free choice in a neutral system' perspective. In this pattern, the contradictions between sponsorship and contest ideologies, whether drawn on for descriptive or normative commentary, were glossed by using terms such as 'potential'.[16] These terms operated to render compatible positions promoting equal education for all students and unequal, segregated education for different students depending on their 'potential' to achieve or contribute to society. As an illustration, excerpted from the end-of-the-second-semester interview, Jane articulated her understanding of why inequalities in wealth and power exist:

> I know in my own mind that ... I've associated wealth with drive and ambition and a little luck ... similarly [for political power]. ... [And in terms of racial and ethnic groups?] ... I'm not saying I believe this myself, but laziness with certain groups and things like that. You know, ideas that have been put upon you: No drive. (*Jane: 5–21–81*)

and later in the interview, commented during a discussion focused on the role schools have *vis-à-vis* social inequalities:

> I think they [schools] should facilitate mobility, to give every-
> one a chance to become something. ... Schools should try to
> help every student, and not ignoring those at the lower levels ...
> and help him [or her] reach his [or her] *potential*. (*Jane:
> 5–21–81*)

Particularistic Versus Universalistic

When preservice teachers discussed social inequalities and the role of schooling they consistently drew upon elements of a universalistic ideology when engaging in a normative analysis. This was the case for those interviewed regardless of their overall perspective. For example, James, who tended to view the issues in terms of societal level structural reproduction, offered the following universalistic ideology informed analysis, critiquing selection based on ascribed, diffuse skills rather than achieved, technical skills.

> Q: How do social inequalities in society affect schooling?
> A: Well, for one, like, you have the taxes, the way they are
>   collected, you have different regions. ... One area may be
>   economically lower. ... And so far as getting resources for
>   the schools, they'd probably get less, rather than more.
>   Whereas the school from the more affluent areas, where
>   they have a higher tax base and everything, they'd prob-
>   ably get more and they'd probably attract better teachers.
>   ... So far as learning, what they're going to be taught in the
>   lower economic areas is mainly such things as respect for
>   people in authority, then, you know, you're going to be
>   punished. But they are not actually instructed in some
>   essential things that they need to be learning, you know,
>   instructed to think ... to be on your own. (*James: 5–7–81*)

Preservice teachers, who conceived of social inequalities and schooling in terms of free choice in a basically neutral system, also drew upon elements of a universalistic ideology of implementation. As an illustration, Roberto criticizes some teachers who would select out for less positive attention and concern certain students because of their ascriptive characteristics, such being Hispanic and female. Drawing on his own experience as a son of a Mexican born, working class, mother and father, who each had three years of formal schooling, he goes on to explain:

> I think I experienced some of it [prejudice] when I was in high school. And, as soon as I found out what a self-fulfilling prophecy was it changed everything. Because I decided, okay, this is what it is, and I know I've been following the rule ... and I'm just not going to be doing it anymore. I think a lot of it is: just tell the kids what things are and they decide for themselves whether or not they want to be part of that self-fulfilling prophecy or whether they want to be better. (*Roberto: 5–4–81*)

Note, however, that above Roberto is not deviating strongly from his 'free choice in a basically neutral system' perspective. This emphasis on individual choice and effort, although consonant with a universalistic ideology's concern with achievement (vs. ascription), manages at a descriptive level to deflect in-depth consideration of structural biases on ascribed, diffuse (vs. achieved, technical) skills.

Preservice teachers, focusing on historical and contemporary attitudes in their analysis of social inequalities in the role of schooling, also denounced selection based on ascriptive characteristics or diffuse skills. For instance, Nancy exhibited a universalistic ideology informed view at the end of the student-teaching semester when dealing with the question: 'Why do you think certain social classes do better or worse with our current school system?'

> I think there are two sides to that. One of them is the expectation of the teacher in the classroom. ... I had an experience as far as the teacher expected students who came from good, quote-unquote, middle class families ... to do well. She expected that students who were dressed poorly, who were in the druggy group, to do poorly. ... And they fulfilled all of her expectations ... even though she never said it. It wasn't a verbal thing; it was just an attitude. ... [Also,] I worked with one [Mexican American] student who has a ... teacher who ... is prejudiced against Mexican Americans and [who] refuses to let her do things like go to district contests and things like that, which is hurting the girl in the area that she'd like to work in. (*Nancy: 5–18–82*)

The other 'side' to Nancy's explanation, however, indicates that we should not overly-romanticize the universalistic ideological orientation evidenced in these preservice teachers' remarks. Nancy went on in her explanation of unequal school achievement by different social classes to focus on:

> family environment. ... One of my students ... his father has been in and out of jail for years. ... And ... [the student] doesn't have much of a chance because ... the only people interested in him going to school and succeeding in school are a few of his teachers. ... His father certainly doesn't care about what happens to him. (5–18–82)

Similarly, Carol, who critiqued selection decisions based on ascriptive characteristics, explained the unequal academic performance among students of different social class origins in terms of 'home environment'.

> I think it goes back to the basic, you know, home environment and whether or not they've had enough stimulation. ... I think if the parents put ... education as a priority. ... And I think the stability of the family has a big influence. (*Carol*: 5–26–82)

The unreflexive and uncritical juxtaposition of elements from a universalistic ideology and explanations of inequality, highlighting the contribution of family background, reflects a potential for internal contradiction in preservice teachers' conceptions.[17] While normatively they decried educational selection decisions based on ascriptive features, they have developed a descriptive theory that could provide a rationale for selection based on such criteria. That is, they have positioned themselves ideologically to stratify students based on academic achievement, which on one hand was seen as based on technical skills, and on the other hand understood to be directly related to ascribed characteristics such as family-derived cultural capital.

Messages in the Formal and Hidden Curriculum

Given the variation in preservice teachers' perspectives on inequalities and the role of schooling and given the tensions and internal contradictions evidenced in some of their ideologically informed views, it is important to examine the messages they encountered in their teacher education program. This is because it is in relation to the messages in the formal and hidden curriculum that these prospective educators' ideas were consolidated or altered. Their perspectives were not originally developed in the context of the program, though the conceptions they held when they began their formal teacher preparation experience interacted with ideas they encountered during that time.

The first point to be made is that although issues concerning social class, race/ethnicity, and gender inequalities surfaced in the secondary education program, they really did not receive sustained, indepth treatment except during three class sessions devoted to 'multicultural education' during the first semester of the program. During the multicultural education class sessions students were informed briefly about dominant and minority racial/ethnic groups, and that multicultural issues apply not only to race but also social class differences, and unequal gender relations: 'male domination ... if you don't confront it, you support it' (*Fieldnotes: 9–9–80*).

Even in this case, the impact of the messages may have been muted by the course instructor introducing the three sessions, organized and implemented by guest instructors, as being 'required by the State' and by the course instructor announcing to the students at the end of the third class session that 'we will be back at it for real on Tuesday'. Similarly, one of the students commented during an interview at the end of that semester:

> When we moved out of our classroom for the multicultural sessions, it interfered with the progression of the course. People didn't know where it fit in for the exam. ... There [were] at least ten pages of material and there ended up being one [multiple choice] question related to multicultural on the exam. (*Dana: 12–15–80*)

Besides holding the class in different space, the sessions were marked off from others by the fact that they were taught by the guest instructors, the majority of whom constituted the only people of color that the students encountered in an official capacity in the entire three semester program.

Explicit messages about social stratification also were infrequently encountered at other points in the program. For example, one of the handouts distributed in preparation for a 'cultural imprint paper' assignment during the second semester listed several categories of 'forces which impact one life':

> *Societal Polarizations*: What were the issues, conflicts and prejudices which kept people apart or unequal? How did these polarizations affect you? *Examples*: White *vs.* Black ... Poor *vs.* Rich.

During this semester, several of the group presentations by students also directed attention to unequal social relations.[18] In one of these, the students conducted a

> simulation portraying Xians in a Greek Cafe who meet two journalists from the United States. ... The journalists attempt to interact with the Xians while dining, but find it very difficult because their values and assumptions do not correspond to the Xians: For one thing, female Xians are dominant, not the males; and although men are cherished in Xian society, they can't go out of the house except to work in the garden. (*Fieldnotes: 4–2–81*)

Other times the issues about inequalities were not given explicit, let alone critical, attention; the issues merely seemed to occupy the 'natural' background in front of which other issues could be placed for highlighting. For instance, in a handout, 'Strengthening Desirable Behaviors', which was distributed in the second semester course, unequal class relations appear as background to a discussion of 'reinforcement':

> Alas, people are not completely controlled by the consequences others provide — only mostly. ... But we are bound to an arrangement (Work = $$$$) that requires our devoting a large segment each day to working for reinforcers that other people give out. (p. 18)

Unequal gender relations, too, appear in the background in the handout on 'Strengthening Desirable Behaviors' as an example of consequences affecting behavior. Note that although the illustration raises the issue of negotiation and exchange governing the domestic division of labor between men and women, it does so in a way that suggests uncritically a quite unequal basis for the parties involved.

> Similarly, wives cook breakfast for crabby husbands — when consequences are right. If hubby doesn't come through with proper consequences, however, breakfast probably stops or at least gets worse. On the other hand, if hubby remembers anniversaries, birthdays, and Mother's Day, breakfast probably continues or maybe even gets better. (p. 15)

Perhaps, given the strong classification or boundaries between curriculum content areas in this teacher education program,[19] we should not be surprised to find limited attention paid to the topic of

176

social stratification in the 'generic' teacher education courses. Such issues might appropriately be raised in the multicultural education 'module' (as they were), but also could be examined in the sociology 'module' in the Foundations of Education for Teaching course. However, issues of social inequalities were not treated in any sustained fashion in the foundations course either.[20] One significant indicator is that the general objective for the sociology section of the Foundation course highlighted 'socialization', made no reference to structural inequalities, and even appeared to offer an uncritical view of social reproduction:

> *Sociology — General Objective*: Students will develop an understanding of the socialization process and the impact it has on the developing child. ... The discussion should emphasize that socialization provides the [means for] individual adaptation to the environment and a means for society to perpetuate itself. (Foundations of Education for Teachers course description, requirements and objectives handout)

Not only were general issues of social stratification a rare focus in the formal curriculum, but the question of education's selection function was also accorded little attention. The above noted objective of the sociology component of the Foundations course is indicative, but overall in the program the instruction and socialization functions of education or roles of teachers were highlighted. Even when focusing on the teacher's evaluation role, the formal curriculum accorded greater attention to providing 'formative' evaluation and obtaining feedback to enhance instructional process than to engaging in summative evaluation, which would be tied more to the selection and sorting function. For example, one of the modules used in the first semester course discussed 'three aspects of instructional evaluation: monitoring student progress, determining student achievement, and assessing instructional effectiveness' (*Instructional Modules 3304*: 65). The first and third aspects pertain more to instruction than to selection of students.

Clearly, a whole variety of messages were available in the hidden curriculum about these issues — students encountered peers whose academic performance and/or degree program opened-up or closed-off 'opportunities' for careers with different levels of income, power, and status; they were informed how their own 'credentials' compared with education students at other institutions or with engineering, science, and art students at their own university (see further discussion below). But in the formal curriculum of the program, one found few explicit allusions to selection. This obtained, of course, at least in part because of the psychologization and individualism which dominates in teacher education programs, but there is more to it than that in this particular case.

During the middle of the first semester as a participant observer I wrote the following observer comment in my fieldnotes:

> Why don't these [readings] raise questions about the inequality implications of maintaining or changing the predominant use of certain teaching strategies? Material either laments or celebrates strategies in terms of their (implied) ineffectiveness or effectiveness for ALL students. Some mention is made that only a few students may be able to respond [to questions posed by the teacher] if the 'wait time' is too brief, but no attempt is made to raise this issue in its wider context ... [e.g.,] cultural capital. ... Generally, skills seem to be dislocated from the value or socio-political aspects implied by or informed by them. (*Fieldnotes: 10–21–80*)

There was some discussion in the multicultural education sessions of these issues. And they received some attention as well during a guest instructor's remarks about 'mastery learning' in the second semester of the program:

> Students come in with differences, and if instruction is the same, then the outcomes will be different. Mastery learning is based on the premise that one needs to differentiate instruction so all can achieve the objective. (*Fieldnotes: 2–19–81*)

This illustration involving concepts of mastery learning is not only one of the few examples in which the issue of education's selection function was raised. It also provides part of the answer as to why the issue was accorded so little emphasis. If mastery learning, which the same guest instructor introduced as the 'rationale for why we tell you to do the things we do in courses in education' (*Fieldnotes: 2–19–81*) and which was indicated several times to be a basic assumption of this competency-based teacher education program, offers the promise that 'all can achieve the objective', then education's selection function becomes not a reality, but merely an unfortunate consequence of ineffective instruction. Especially, if, as we have discussed above, issues of structural inequalities are downplayed or ignored, the promise of all students achieving mastery serves to deflect attention from issues of how teachers and the process of schooling sort and select students

178

(perhaps based on gender, race, and social class of origin) for future unequal positions in the social structure.

The way in which education's selection function and even society's system of social stratification managed to escape sustained scrutiny within the program is perhaps best illustrated by a quote from an untitled handout excerpted from a book chapter by Benjamin Bloom and colleagues, which was distributed in conjunction with the mastery learning session in the second semester:

> Some societies can utilize only a small number of highly educated people in the economy and can provide economic support for only a small proportion of the students to complete secondary or higher education. ... Such societies invest a great deal more in predicting and selecting talent than in developing it. [However,] the complexity of skills required by the work force in the United States and other highly developed nations mean that we can no longer operate on the assumption that completion of secondary and advanced education is for the few. ... If school learning is regarded as frustrating or even impossible by a sizeable proportion of students, then little can be done at later levels to rekindle a genuine interest in further learning. (p. 44)

Thus, even while students in the program were being warned that mastery learning is more of an ideal than a real possibility,[21] they were still presented with a basis for focusing on instruction and socialization and ignoring issues of selection and sorting.

The excerpt from Bloom *et al.*, quoted above is also the only explicit allusion to the warming-up–cooling-out dilemma, that it may be impossible to 'rekindle' the motivation of those who previously had been discouraged from or frustrated in academic achievement efforts. It is to illustrations from program messages concerning the ideologies which may serve to mediate or challenge this contradiction that we now turn. We will examine the two contradictory pairs of ideologies: contest vs. sponsorship and particularistic vs. universalistic.

Contest Versus Sponsorship

The dominant message in the formal curriculum of the program offered the basic elements of the contest ideology of implementation — that, because effort should be the basis of achievement, the maximum education is the right of all people and that segregation during schooling of future elites and non-elites is not desirable. In the hidden curriculum of the program, however, the dominant message coincided with a sponsorship ideology.

The quote (above) from the Bloom *et al.*, mastery learning handout provides an indication of the formal curriculum dominant message: 'we can no longer operate on the assumption that completion of secondary and advanced education is for the few'. The 'module' on mastery learning also provided messages consonant with a contest ideology's stress on the importance of 'effort' as opposed to 'ability' in educational (and other) stratification. In the second semester course, a guest instructor launched one of the rare discussions about the evaluation/selection aspect of the teacher's role, asking: 'How will you grade?' This guest instructor explained how under a mastery learning framework, which provides the 'rationale for why we tell you to do the things we do in courses in education':

> Aptitude must be redefined; we must challenge the definition of aptitude as something a person has versus the time it takes to learn something. ... [And we should stress the] importance of a child's perseverance, time on task. (*Fieldnotes: 2–19–81*)

But the topic of mastery learning was not the only one that served as a channel for messages relevant to contest and sponsorship ideologies. During a student-teaching seminar devoted to teaching reading in secondary schools, the guest instructor stressed the goal of increasing the test performance of all students:

> A lot of people are ... intelligent, but can't read textbooks. ... For comprehension to be effective there needs to be a match between students' ability [reading level] and the demand of the material. ... You may need to change the reading level of text [or use other techniques to make material comprehensible]. ... You will always have problems with the higher achiever. ... Find out what your average is. Normally, teachers teach to the upper ten percent of the class, then you're an elitist. (*Fieldnotes: 2–19–82*)

Similar points were offered during the multicultural education unit during the first semester of the program. A handout, 'Understanding Culture: A Learning Experience for Teachers in a Multicultural Society', distributed and referred to during this unit states:

> For decades, unfortunately, educators have drawn heavily from inaccurate assumptions that all learners, regardless of their life

experiences, their cultural and ethnic diversities, their personal needs or goals or the varied learning styles would achieve at very similar rates, in similar amounts, through the same methods or instructional strategies. (p. 1)

Another topic in the formal curriculum of the first semester course in the program, 'Public Law 94–142: Education of the Handicapped Act (1975)', offered a similar message that all students could benefit from a maximum amount of education. The topic also highlighted the concern within a contest ideology to avoid segregating students with different 'abilities' and/or different future roles. Appendix A of Module 11, which was devoted to this topic, informed the reader that: 'The intent of the law is to meet children's educational *needs* in the mainstream — regular classroom — rather than in segregated settings'. The discussion about 'mainstreaming', however, also offered messages which are more ambiguous in their connection to either a contest or sponsorship ideology. For example, in Appendix A of Module 11, PL 94–142 is described 'as one of a number of Public Laws extending equal opportunity to all members of our society in developing their individual *potentials*'. Similarly, a guest instructor during the multicultural education component during the first semester course argued that 'people of all backgrounds should achieve at an *optimum* higher *level*' (*Fieldnotes: 9–16–80*). But just as the notion of 'needs' can become the basis for legitimating unequal access to curriculum knowledge, the concepts of 'equal opportunity' and 'potential' or 'optimum' can mask stratifying kinds of actions.[22]

This may be particularly the case when elements of a sponsorship ideology are flowing in the formal curricular stream along with the higher concentration of contest ideological elements. For instance, in discussions about teaching as a profession, the notions that some individuals do and should receive higher levels of education than others, and that it is at least partly this differentiation which helps account for the power, wealth, and status hierarchies stratifying professions and other workers, were for the most part treated unproblematically.[23] Such a message is more consistent with a sponsorship ideology in that it stresses that the maximum education should be given based on ability to contribute economically or socially in the future. That some students deserve more education than others was also stressed in the first semester course module in 'Public Law 95–561 Gifted and Talented Children's Education Act (1978)', which read in part:

> The purpose of the management plan for Gifted/Talented [in contrast with other] students is to assure a program which teaches, challenges, and expands the students' knowledge while stressing the development of the independent learner. (*Instructional Modules 3304: Module 11, Appendix F*)

The element from a sponsorship ideology that segregation of students by ability or anticipated future contribution was preferable was also at times included in the messages in the formal curriculum of the program. At the beginning of the semester, student teachers were told matter of factly by their instructor that they would undoubtedly encounter ability grouping or tracking in the student-teaching assignment (*8–28–81*). And during the first semester course, one of the case histories presented in Appendix C of Module 4, also treats unproblematically, and thus apparently approvingly, the issue of tracking:

> Situation 9. You have a boy in one of your *accelerated classes*. He is *incapable* of doing the work. You talk to him about transferring to another class where the work is less demanding. (*Instructional Modules 3304:48*; emphasis added)

While messages in the formal curriculum were dominated by a contest ideology, the hidden curriculum of the program communicated primarily elements of a sponsorship ideology. In their school observations and student-teaching activities in local public schools, preservice teachers frequently encountered examples of educational stratification — the separation of students according to some measure of 'intelligence' or 'educability' and an unequal provision of educational programs and resources. Prospective teachers were exposed to 'ability' level tracking in almost all subjects in the high school, e.g., math, English, drama, social studies, and science. They were introduced to (or reminded of) the terminology employed to label different class types: Fundamentals of Mathematics students (FOMs), major works or honors students, etc. This, taken for granted, backcloth of educational stratification within schools was complemented by educational stratification between schools and districts. During their three semesters preservice teachers may have observed or student taught in different schools, and even if they stayed with one institution throughout the three semesters, they had their own school experiences and the observation and student teaching experiences of peers to draw upon for comparison. Besides the inter-district differences apparent in this setting as in most metropolitan areas, students also encountered the

182

strong message about intra-district inequalities between magnet and regular school programs, which were being stressed by the major urban school district as its path to racial desegregation.

On the university campus, students encountered similar messages. The University has an Honors Program for undergraduates with special 'ability' and 'potential' who have access to special facilities, seminars, and an enriched curriculum in a variety of major areas. Furthermore, preservice teachers had access to messages concerning inequalities between the education program and other programs at the University. Such messages were available directly to perceptive preservice teachers or indirectly through comments by other students and by faculty in and outside the College of Education. These messages focused on the 'ability' level of students enrolled, the 'quality' of and level of requirements in the programs, the extent of financial and other resources.

Within the College of Education there was no evidence of ability group tracking for students, except perhaps for the distinctions between undergraduate and graduate programs, which especially for educational administration, tended to have a higher proportion of male students. However, there also were points when decisions were made about who could benefit from further education offered by the program. The strength of these sponsorship ideological messages were muted somewhat by the aspects of contest ideology in the competency-based program, in that students were normally informed only that they were *not yet* ready to benefit, rather than that they could never benefit from what the program had to offer. Students could sometimes retake course exams, revise and resubmit assignments, or take additional courses in a subject to improve their grades. Nevertheless, entry into the program, access to a student-teaching assignment, and successful completion of the program (and, thus, recommendation for certification) were all based in part on meeting the 2.5 grade point average standard in various breakdowns of accumulated coursework. The point here is not that large numbers of students were deselected on this criteria of 'educability', but that the message was conveyed prominently in various program documents and forms that not all people could or should benefit from further education in the secondary certification program. Moreover, although not always stressed in public discussions related to the programs, course instructors played a visible part in selecting or deselecting students — they graded assignments and assigned course grades, as well as provided students with more informal feedback, positive and negative — which was not always stressed. For instance, one of the other instructors of another section of the first semester course articulated in some detail a view shared by other colleagues involved in the program. In discussing a student who had recently 'dropped out of the program', this instructor commented:

> that he was pleased that some people dropped out of the program, despite the College's need for students [so as not to lose additional faculty positions]. He felt that some people shouldn't be teachers and that a gradual process of letting them know what it takes to be a teacher would 'weed out' those who weren't right. He prefers the students to reach this decision themselves, rather than being told by faculty right away or abruptly, since with the former procedure the student isn't as likely to be disgruntled with the program. (*Fieldnotes: 10–14–81*)

Note, as well in this case, that the contest-like selection process is preferred because it seems to accomplish what a sponsorship-like, early selection approach would, but in a manner rendering the selection as more legitimate in the eyes of the student, who might otherwise be 'disgruntled'.[24]

Another aspect of the hidden curriculum that sent a sponsorship ideological message involved inter-university comparisons. First, the existence of Texas Southern University, a historically black institution, located three blocks from the predominantly white University of Houston, where my research was undertaken should be noted. The funding disparity between these two state universities was apparent to any observer who drove by the campuses — a situation which contributed to the federal government's threat to cut-off post-secondary education funding to Texas until a revised remedy plan (in conjunction with a desegregation case) was submitted during the 1983–84 academic year. This comparison yielded an image of historical and contemporary racial segregation of higher education institutions correlated with unequal facilities and other resources.[25] A similar message, but one that highlighted social class rather than race, was provided by comparing the University of Houston with Rice University, an elite private institution of higher education located a few miles from both Texas Southern University and the University of Houston. Rice's reputation as a highly selective, high tuition institution with 'outstanding' faculty and programs or at least facilities is supported visually by a drive by the campus, and thus a sponsorship ideology message was also available to the casual observer.

Particularistic Versus Universalistic

In the formal curriculum of the program messages consonant with an ideology of universalism were frequent and emphatically communicated. That academic (and occupational) selection should be based primarily on achieved, technical skills rather than diffuse skills, which are either ascribed characteristics or attributes, that only a few groups have an opportunity to acquire, is first of all promoted by the competency-based rhetoric of the program.[26] The competency-based theme was stressed from the first day of class in the first semester — the competencies were listed in the preface to the *Instructional Modules 3304* booklet, through the second semester of the program — where the course was titled 'Generic Teaching Competencies', and to the final event of the students' program experience — an evaluation of student-teaching based on the nineteen competencies. As an illustration, the *Secondary Student Teaching Handbook*, distributed to all student teachers, stated that:

> The teacher education program at the University of Houston is based on nineteen competencies deemed essential to effective teaching. Through campus courses and field experiences students work to achieve each competency, and during student teaching students demonstrate their proficiency in classroom settings. (p. 2)

Concomitantly, instructors and assigned reading materials emphasized that evaluations should be based on skill performance and not ascribed characteristics. During the multicultural education unit in the first semester's course a guest instructor discussed issues of bilingual education and criticized 'the cultural bias of tests and some (less than successful) efforts to overcome this problem' (*Fieldnotes: 9–18–80*). Later that semester the class viewed a slide-tape presentation on Public Law 94–142 which exhorted that 'tests must not be culturally discriminatory' (*Fieldnotes: 11–18–80*). Another illustration is from a handout, 'Cultural Assumptions and Values Affecting Interpersonal Relationships', distributed as required reading for the second semester course, which juxtaposed the 'assumption or value held by the majority of Americans' (A) and the 'assumption or value held by the majority of persons of a 'contrast-American society'; that is, one which is opposed [in contrast] to American society in its assumptions and values' (C–A):

2 What do we value in people?

> A: What people can achieve through special skills.
> C–A: A person's background, family connections, tribal affiliations.

Contradicting the above noted universalistic ideological messages in the formal curriculum were other messages promoting a particularistic ideology of implementation. Particularistic ideological notions that selection should be based on diffuse skills or ascribed characteristics was sometimes evidenced in comments about students in school settings. For instance, an ascribed characteristic, 'home situation', was proposed as an explanation for unequal academic performance by a guest speaker during a large group, student-teaching seminar session entitled 'Teaching as a Profession':

> As secondary teachers, you need to visit with elementary teachers. ... Don't think that elementary teachers aren't doing their jobs if your students aren't prepared. ... Instead, you should look to their home situation for the explanation. (*Fieldnotes: 9–22–81*)

More often messages consistent with particularistic ideology were contained in discussions about who should be selected as a teacher. For instance, diffuse skills and ascribed attributes were accorded salience during the large group student teaching seminars devoted to interviewing, resume development and other aspects of the 'job search'. The recommendation forms given to students by the Career Planning and Placement Center, whose staff were guest instructors during these seminars, asked the person acting as a reference for the student to rate the prospective teacher on a 'superior' to 'poor' scale on the following dimensions, some of which allude to diffuse (rather than technical) skills: 'scholarship, ability to express thoughts (by speaking and/or writing), cooperativeness, reliability, leadership potential, poise (self-confidence and group interaction), work habits (constant application to assignments and duties'. These written messages were paralleled in the various guest instructors' oral presentations to the students in attendance. One school district personnel director, for example, when asked what kinds of things 'turn off' job interviewers, replied:

> We try to train interviewers to not be biased. But candidates can be disqualified if they indicate they are not really interested in the job (by their clothing, not shaving, not being informed about job and work setting, having canned or artificial

speech ...). You have to communicate in standard English.
(*Fieldnotes: 11–10–81*)

Within the hidden curriculum there was a frequent and strong message consonant with what can be seen as a particularistic ideology. This concerned the use of the grade point average (gpa) as a major criterion for selecting and stratifying students in the program and later in the job market. Individual assignments or course grades were sometimes questioned. Cathy, for instance, in explaining at the end of the first semester in the program what she thought she still needed to learn as teacher, related her unfortunate experience of having professors who graded 'based on my personality' (*12–10–80*). Nevertheless, this mathematically produced and seeming objective and scientific symbol,[27] the gpa, was rarely the target of validity questions or criticisms.[28] As one of the readings assigned during the first semester course articulated it: 'letter grades have come to have relatively universal meaning'.[29]

The grade point average was a salient feature in the hidden curriculum of the program.[30] Entry into the program, acceptance for a student-teaching assignment, and successful completion of the program (and, thus, recommendation for certification) all depended upon meeting a grade point average standard. For example, the 'Secondary Student Teaching Handbook, 1981–82' identifies the following among the 'prerequisites to student teaching':[31]

3   Demonstration of acceptable grade point averages:
    a. 2.5 overall on all courses taken
    b. 2.5 in English (except where the student has declared
        English as a teaching field; the required gpa is then 2.67)
    c. 2.5 in professional education courses (p. 3)

During a large group student-teaching seminar, those present were informed that the 'grade point average is used as an initial screening device' as districts decide when to interview for job openings (*Fieldnotes: 2–16–82*).

The prominence in the program's hidden curriculum of the grade point average as a symbol is important because such 'performance' indicators may be more of a reflection of students 'cultural capital'[32] and other diffuse skills and ascribed characteristics than it is an indication of technical skills or capability. To the extent this view is accurate, then the hidden curriculum of the program provided a strong message in line with a particularistic ideology of legitimation.

Concluding Remarks

What do these patterns of messages and conceptions tell us about ways in which societal contradictions are either masked/mediated or exposed/challenged? We will examine this question primarily in relation to the warming-up–cooling-out contradiction, and only indirectly in terms of other contradictions of capitalist, patriarchal and racially/ethnically stratified societies.[33] Certainly, these prospective teachers encountered the warming-up–cooling-out contradiction. In the formal curriculum, there was the one explicit reference to this contradiction, quoted above from the mastery learning handout excerpted from a book chapter by Benjamin Bloom and colleagues: 'If school learning is regarded as *frustrating* or even *impossible* by a sizeable proportion of students, then little can be done at later levels to *rekindle* a genuine interest in further learning' (p. 44; emphasis added). In the hidden curriculum, moreover, there were various messages relevant to the warming-up–cooling-out contradiction. They experienced directly, as well as vicariously, efforts to encourage or discourage teacher education students about remaining in the program and/or pursuing a career as a teacher. (Recall that there was a significant role of non-continuation in the program between the first and second semester.) They also were exposed to the contradiction as they engaged in their school observations — the different atmospheres characteristic of the 'major works' and 'regular' classes and the differences in the way in which teachers interacted with various groups of students. Finally, they became directly involved in this contradiction as they undertook the role of student teacher, primarily in the efforts to warm-up groups of classed, gendered, and raced students, who had previously been either cooled-out or warmed-up in the school system. This was sometimes expressed in terms of preferring to teach upper-track versus regular-track or mixed ability classes.

These encounters produced some concerns and traumas, but for many of the preservice teachers they were able to construct an ideologically derived explanation that tended to deflect the concerns and minimize the traumas, if not totally mask, and therefore, mediate, the contradictory nature of their experiences. This was not always a smooth intellectual/emotional process, and the tension produced provided the base for some exposure and challenge to contradictory social relations. Moreover, there were two preservice teachers who began the program with a critical stance and (at least for Dana, who finished the program) tended to sustain and even strengthen this during the program, thus indicating a possibility for exposing and challenging contradictions. In the quote below from an interview conducted after her first semester as a teacher, Dana articulated one of her goals as a teacher and later explained how she viewed others who had been in the teacher education program with her.

> [goals affecting the community?] ... to make movement through different [social] structures — class, sex, age, race barriers — easier. ... [What ... is your best guess in terms of the views of others in the program?] Well, it's clear to me that many of my colleagues in the classroom are aware that inequalities exist ... but the impression I get is that there is nothing that they can do. ... We have to, all you can do is wait 'til the old people die. (*Dana: 7–2–82*)

While the tension in their conceptions, especially that attributable to contradictions, meant that the picture obtained from interviews was not static, there was also no clear direction in the movement of the views of those preservice teachers who participated in the interviews.[34] This was the case not only for those students in the program whose perspective mirrored that which was dominant in the formal curriculum, but also those whose ideas contrasted to varying degrees with these dominant messages. Clearly, these teacher education students were not passive agents internalizing the program's dominant explicit messages.[35] This is, however, more than a question of individuals filtering messages from the program curriculum. There is also the point that messages in the formal *and* the hidden curriculum not infrequently provided elements of ideologies which contradicted those which dominated in the formal curriculum.[36]

The availability of contradictory ideologies in the message channels meant that preservice teachers could select to incorporate in their own views only those elements which were viewed as compatible with their perspective. This did seem to occur. However, given that some of their conceptions already contained elements from contradictory ideologies and given the lack of sustained, in-depth treatment in the program of the issues of social inequalities and the role of schooling, it was possible for some preservice teachers to accumulate separately elements from different, contradictory ideologies. The infrequent and superficial treatment of the general issues did not facilitate students' critical examination of their own perspectives or those in the message systems of the program. So, for example, contest and sponsorship ideological notions could coexist in a compartmentalized manner, almost as if they were unrelated, to be drawn upon at different times depending on the issues raised. In addition, it meant that terms like 'potential' and 'self-actualization' could be employed to patch over tensions or cracks which obtained when contradictory ideologies were uncritically drawn upon at the same time. We should also note the way in which many preservice teachers drew on universalistic ideological elements in their normative statements about who should be selected, while concomitantly espousing descriptive theories which could be used to rationalize selection based on ascriptive features of students.

From the above discussion we should not conclude that the program had little effect, but rather that it tended to reinforce and perhaps give legitimacy to the preservice teachers' ideologically informed conceptions. Of particular importance is the scant attention in the formal curriculum to issues of social class, gender, and ethnic/racial group relations generally and to education's selection function more specifically. The lack of sustained, in-depth, and integrated treatment of these issues limited all preservice teachers' opportunities for reflection and development. It meant for those whose perspective stressed societal level structural reproduction, that their understandings remained somewhat overly deterministic and simplistic. Conceptions focusing on 'free choice' and 'individual attitudes' were also for the most part left unchallenged.

What might this mean for their practice as teachers, assuming (as was the case for the three interviewed after a period of employment) that they would not initially shift in perspective? Entering a situation in secondary school settings, where warming-up and cooling-out have already been experienced by different classed, gendered, and raced groups of students, and where teachers must continue to engage in these processes associated with educational (as well as political and economic) stratification, these individuals will presumably draw on their ideological perspectives to both interpret what is going on and to develop strategies for action. For example, if one has a normative theory consonant with a contest ideology, that all should receive the maximum education, but posits a descriptive theory, emphasizing individuals freely choosing to be wealthy and powerful in some sort of an open contest, then one may tend to do one's best instructionally, but not be overly worried if educational (and political economic) inequalities result. This may be especially possible if they and their immediate colleagues do not seem to act upon social class, gender, or race/ethnicity-related prejudices. Sonia is one of the people whose ideologically informed perspective fits this pattern. She confided early in her program experience:[37]

> I used to think that a teacher could help all students to succeed. ... I'm less idealistic now. I can't be every student's friend and help them with their problems. ... If you think you [as a teacher] are going to be terrific, it could be real traumatic if you're not. ... If you go in and try your best, then you [as a teacher] are not going to die about it if all students don't succeed. (*12–9–80*)

For Sonia, however, this is not a comfortable resolution, just one that seems realistic. In another interview she stressed her contest ideological position about effort being the major contributing factor to social inequalities, but at the same time criticized those who have succeeded personally, but failed to help others to do the same.

> It just happens that you are born into a poor situation. ... You just have to have the opportunity, and if you have it, I think just about everybody will strive to get out. ... Because some people want to get out of that situation; but that doesn't mean that they want to help other people get out of it or anything like that. ... They just, you know, want to help themselves. Once they're comfortable they may forget about the rest, you know, of the people. (*Sonia: 5–28–81*)

Similar statements could be made about those preservice teachers who viewed the contest mobility system as partly tainted by the impact of biased attitudes. For instance, Donald, who subsequently after successfully completing student teaching opted not to pursue a teaching career because of a desire for a higher income, commented at the end of the second semester in the program how social inequalities affect schooling:

> It affects the school because ... in a better [higher socio-economic population] district [the schools] have a better choice of getting better teachers. ... Because ... unless you've got this thing that you want to change the world ... you want to achieve the best for yourself that you can ... whether it's in salary or working environment. (*5–15–81*)

Here, some of the preservice teachers confront a problem derived from their reliance on an ideology of individualism: the notion of an open contest mobility system functioning for some individuals may ensure that inequalities are perpetuated and (perhaps) legitimated.

This may especially be the case when messages in the hidden curriculum provide an uncritical backcloth to the ideological tapestries that these preservice teachers were engaged in constructing. Concerns about whether social inequalities are/should be fostered in segregated or desegregated settings (sponsorship vs. contest), or are/should be derived from perceived differences in diffuse or technical skills (particularistic vs. universalistic), is perhaps less important than beginning to see inequalities in wealth and power as problematic, rather than as given and natural features of society. In that sense, all the ideologies of social mobility and social reproduction (separately) can be seen to mediate societal level contradictions. But when critically counterposed, they may unmask the contradictions and provide a basis to challenge the structure and ideologies which contain them.

The views of Dana and James provide examples of preservice teachers who have begun the process of critically counterposing contradictory ideologies of social mobility and social reproduction. In their developing *descriptive* 'theories' of inequality and the role of schooling they draw critically on sponsorship and particularistic ideologies. Much of the time, though, they juxtapose these with their *normative* 'theories', built primarily from elements of contest and universalistic ideologies. This should be seen as development toward critically counterposing ideologies not because of the specific construction of their descriptive and normative theories, although I happen to prefer their conceptions. Rather, it is because they have gone somewhat further than many of their peers in clearly contrasting the contradictory ideologies and in distinguishing their perceptions of what is versus what ought to be. Nevertheless, during the program, they were not encouraged to systematically develop their perspectives.

In the next chapter, we will discuss how educators of teachers committed to critical praxis might engage prospective teachers in a process that facilitates their involvement in critically counterposing ideological and structural contradictions. We will also examine this and other issues in relation to current debates and proposals for reform in teacher education.

Notes

1 Revised version of paper presented at the Annual Meeting of the American Educational Studies Association, Atlanta, 6–9 November, 1985. This paper presents a reanalysis of some of the data drawn upon in Ginsburg and Newman (1985) as well as an extension of the analysis of other data collected during prior and subsequent phases of my longitud-

inal ethnographic study focusing on a program for secondary education students. I want to express my gratitude to Katherine Newman for her collaboration on aspects of this project. I also want to thank Beatriz Arias-Godinez, Linda Spatig, Susan Stilley, and John York for transcribing many of the interviews. Appreciation is also given to Rose Kassamali for typing some of the transcribed interviews and to Tessa Jo Shokri for word processing this manuscript.

2 CLARK, B., 'The cooling-out function in higher education', *American Journal of Sociology* 65 (1960), p. 569.

3 The warming-up–cooling-out contradiction can be seen to be related to other societal contradictions. For discussion of these other contradictions in class, gender, and race relations, see Chapter 1. These other contradictions all depend upon social selection within which the warming-up–cooling-out dilemma or contradiction arises. The ideologies of social mobility and social reproduction, discussed below, therefore, not only serve to mask and thus mediate or expose and thus challenge the warming-up–cooling-out contradiction, but must be seen as potentially operating similarly in relation to the other societal contradictions.

4 HOPPER, E., 'A typology of the classification of educational systems', in HOPPER, E., (Ed.) *Readings in the Theory of Educational Systems*, (London, Hutchinson, 1971), pp. 162–63. See also BERLAK, A. and BERLAK, H., *Dilemmas of Schooling: Teaching and Social Change* (New York, Macmillan, 1981).

5 HOPPER, E., 'Educational systems and selected consequences of patterns of mobility and non-mobility in industrial societies', in HOPPER, E., (Ed.) *Readings in the Theory of Educational Systems*, (London, Hutchinson, 1971), p. 326.

6 See GINSBURG, M. and GILES, J., 'Sponsored' and 'contest' modes of social reproduction in selective community college programs', *Research in Higher Education* 21 (1984): 281–300; STILLEY, S., 'The Sponsored Mode of Social Reproduction and the Primary School Classroom in the Federal Republic of Germany', (Ed. D. diss., University of Houston, 1986).

7 For details on the ethnographic research approach undertaken, see Chapter 1.

8 Hopper, 'A typology of the classification of educational systems'; also HOPPER, E., *Social Mobility: A Study of Social Control and Insatiability* (Oxford, Basil Blackwell, 1981).

9 TURNER, R., 'Sponsored and contest mobility and the school system', *American Sociological Review* 25 (1960): 855–67.

10 Although Turner stresses mobility, I have argued elsewhere (see Ginsburg and Giles) that these folk-norms and systems are at least as relevant to the issue of social reproduction. Persell also comments on the greater attention paid to mobility, as compared to reproduction, among sociologists in the United States. See PERSELL, C., *Education and Inequalities* (New York, Free Press, 1977).

11 Hopper, *Social Mobility*, pp. 164–65. In fact, Hopper employs two labels (contest and egalitarian) for what I term a 'contest' ideology, and two other terms (sponsorship and elitist) for what I call a 'sponsorship'

ideology. My choice of terms is influenced by Turner, but also because of the close association of each pair of the ideologies collapsed into one.

12   *Ibid.*, pp. 165–66.

13   The views of preservice teachers presented in this section are derived from interviews collected as part of a longitudinal ethnographic study at the University of Houston — see Chapter 1 for details of fieldwork and data analysis strategies. Most of the interview data discussed in this chapter was collected in response to questions designed to elicit preservice teachers' ideologically informed conceptions of inequality and the role of schooling. The following questions are quoted from the interview schedules used during different phases of the study, but it should be noted that the actual questions asked represented paraphrasings rather than verbatim readings of these words. At the beginning of the Fall 1980 semester, students were asked about 'Functions (actual consequences) of Schooling and Teaching':

>   1   Imagine, for the purpose of this question, that there are no schools and no teachers in society. What do you think would be different? ... for children and young people? ... for their parents? ... for the local community? ... for society in general?
>
>   2   In what ways are teachers a help (or hindrance) to: children and young people? Their parents? The local community? The society more generally?

At the end of Fall 1980 interviewees were presented with a list of the 'functions that schools (and teachers) do *or* should accomplish', which were derived from information provided at the beginning of the semester in response to the above noted questions. Then they were asked something like:

>   a   Which of these functions do you still think *are actually accomplished* by schools and teachers? Are there any other functions that schools and teachers actually accomplish?
>
>   b   Which of the functions (that you mentioned at the beginning of the semester) do you still think *should be accomplished* by schools and teachers? Would you mention any other functions that schools and teachers should accomplish?

Interviewees were also asked to reply to the following questions later in the interview conducted at the end of the Fall 1980 semester:

>   9   At this point in your teacher training experience, how do you feel about teaching students who are from a different cultural background than your own? Why do you say this?
>
>   10 How do you feel at this point about teaching students of high, medium, or low levels of measured ability or past achievement? Would you prefer to teach any particular ability/achievement level(s) of students? How do you feel about students being grouped according to ability?

At the end of the Spring 1981 semester, part 'C' of the interview schedule read:

>   1   Some people claim that in the United States there are differences among people in economic wealth and political power. Why do

you think differences in wealth and power exist? What do you think accounts for such differences?

2 (If not discussed above) Do you think different ethnic or racial groups (blacks, hispanics, whites, etc) have had the same or different extent of wealth and power? Why do you think this is the case?

3 Let's talk more specifically about education. Do you think schools and/or teachers currently play any role in relation to the above noted inequalities in wealth and power?

    a Is what happens in school affected by these inequalities? Why do you say this? How?

    b How do you see schooling's effect on inequality in our society? Does schooling facilitate mobility, reinforce existing inequalities, or have no effect on who has wealth, power and status from one generation to the next? Why do you say this? How?

    c What role *should* schools and/or teachers play in relation to these inequalities: facilitate social mobility, reinforce existing inequalities or not have any effect on who has wealth and power from one generation to the next? Why do you say this? How would this work?

Finally, the interview schedule employed after the end of the student-teaching semester indicated the following questions to be asked. (Unfortunately, as in previous interviews, the issue of unequal gender relations was not given an explicit focus.)

8 Last semester during the interview you discussed your view on how what goes on in schools relates to inequalities in wealth and power in the society. Let's look at some of the issues under this topic.

    a Why do you think certain social classes do better or worse in school?

    b Why do you think certain ethnic or racial groups do better or worse in school?

    c Do you see a person's success in school as related to their future wealth and/or power as an adult in society? Why do you say this? How and why does this occur?

    d Do you think the process of schooling facilitates social mobility, reinforces existing inequalities, or has no effect on who has wealth and power in society? Could you explain?

14 GINSBURG, M. and NEWMAN, K., 'Social inequalities, schooling and teacher education', *Journal of Teacher Education* 36 (1985): 49–54.

15 Turner's characterization of the dominant folk-norms in the United States would lead us to expect the contest ideology to be more heavily reflected. For further evidence on the relevance of sponsorship ideology among educators in the US., see Ginsburg and Giles.

16 During interviews and more informal discussions, I strove to clarify the meaning(s) of ambiguous terms such as 'potential', had for the respon-

dents. Such efforts were not fully successful in that the terms were not problematic for many of them. 'Potential' was 'what one could be or do', and it seemed strange to them that I would not know the meaning of straightforward, frequently used educational terms like this. Moreover, it appeared that many students entered the teacher education program already employing terms like 'potential' in an unproblematic fashion. Messages available in the formal curriculum, nonetheless, provided additional reinforcement for such practice. For example, under the 'societal needs' category of 'Program Assumptions', distributed as a handout during the first semester course, it was expressed that:

> The institutional system must reflect those values of a pluralistic society which holds that individuals must be provided an opportunity to reach their fullest potential. (Attachment Three, p. 2)

See also subsequent discussion on the program's effect in challenging or reinforcing prospective teachers' ideologically informed conceptions of inequalities and the role of schooling.

17 This uncritical juxtaposition was also exhibited by some of those reflecting a 'free choice in a neutral system' perspective. For example, Sonia expressed concern about teachers selecting students for unequal treatment based on ascriptive characteristics, she also explained, 'Why ... certain social classes do better or worse in school', by drawing upon a descriptive theory that might legitimate such selection decisions.

> Well, I think ... it has a lot to do with your upbringing at home [before] ... your first year in school. ... If you grew up with a ton of books around your home, and you saw your parents reading and your parents read to you. (*Sonia: 5–27–82*)

18 See also Ginsburg and Newman, pp. 50–51.
19 See Chapter 4.
20 Although I did not undertake participant observation in any section of this course, informal conversations with several of the teaching fellows who taught the Foundations course, and my examination of the syllabus and other handouts, provided strong evidence for this conclusion, which was originally based on comments made by students during interviews.
21 In the Bloom *et al.*, excerpt, which was handed out in the second semester course, a cautionary note is offered: 'Were it not so costly in human resources, the provision of a good tutor for each student might be an ideal strategy' (p. 51). Similarly, the course instructor commented in the class session immediately following the guest instructor's lecture on mastery learning that: 'You can do mastery learning if you have thirty students and only one class, but you can't pull it off with five classes of thirty students ... it's not workable'. (*Fieldnotes: 2–26–85*)
22 See Chapter 4 concerning functioning of term 'needs' and see earlier discussion in the present chapter of students' comments in which the term 'potential' serves to mask contradictory elements in their viewpoints.
23 See Chapter 5.

24 See also Clark; Ginsburg and Giles; Hopper, 'Educational systems and selected consequences ...'

25 For additional details, see Ginsburg and Newman.

26 Given the behaviorist psychology implicit in the competency-based movement (see APPLE, M., 'Behaviorism and conservatism: The educational views in four of the "systems" models of teacher education', in JOYCE, B. and WEIL, M., (Eds.) *Perspectives for Reform in Teacher Education,* [Englewood Cliffs, NJ, 1972]), this emphasis on performance versus non-behavioral attributes is not surprising. The reliance on behavioral indicators for competence also makes it appear as if anyone can acquire the competencies, because they can be spelled out so clearly. In Chapter 5, I describe how students in the program were given the behavioral indicators of the nineteen competencies and coached in how to demonstrate these competencies during student-teaching. This approach was also recommended to students in their program as one to follow in their future instructional work with their own students. For example, during the first semester course, the instructor commented during a class session, which had been introduced by the question, 'How do teachers decide what to teach?'

> We use behaviors as indicators to infer learning. ... The criteria for judging the quality of instructional objectives are that they communicate clearly, focus on outcomes, are student-oriented, and specify observable performances. ... You need to specify what is to be learned and how the student is to demonstrate that he or she has learned that. Be sure to inform the students about this. (*Fieldnotes: 9–30–80*)

27 See BLEDSTEIN, B., *The Culture of Professionalism: The Middle Class and the Development of Higher Education in America* (New York, W. W. Norton, 1976), pp. 123–24.

28 The grade point average can be seen to be part of the organizational structure that helps to 'symbolically redefine people and make them eligible for membership in categories in which specific rights are assigned'. See KAMENS, D., 'Legitimating myths and educational organizations: The relationship between organizational ideology and formal structure', *American Sociological Review* 42 (1977), p. 47.

29 TENBRINK, T., 'Evaluation', in COOPER, J. (Ed.) *Classroom Teaching Skills: A Handbook,* (Lexington, MA, D.C. Heath, 1977), p. 442.

30 See also BECKER, H., GEER, B., and HUGHES, E., *Making the Grade: The Academic Side of College Life* (New York, Wiley, 1968).

31 The image of the grade point average as being a scientific, neutral and objective measure of technical skill or capability is perhaps buttressed when the following prerequisite is listed in a manner to suggest its equivalence with the three gpa prerequisites: 'evidence of a negative tuberculosis test (completed within 120 days of the start of student teaching)' (*Secondary Student Teaching Handbook, 1981–82,* p. 3).

32 See Bourdieu and Passeron.

33 See Note 3 for comment on the relationship between the warming-up–cooling-out contradiction and other societal contradictions.

34 It is not possible to trace easily change or stasis in preservice teachers' conceptions of social inequalities and the role of schooling. This is the case because of the change in the nature of questions asked being confounded with the shifts in the interview sample. The major change in the interview sample occurred at the beginning of the second semester, which was also the time when interview questions on this topic became much more explicit and focused. Nevertheless, none of the three preservice teachers (Dana, Sonia, and Carol) who were interviewed during the entire length of their program experience evidenced any clear movement in one direction. With less confidence I can say the same for the five other preservice teachers who were in the first semester class in which I was a participant observer, but who were not members of the formal interview sample until the second semester. Moreover, none of those interviewed commented on significant shifts in their thinking on these issues, though some did with respect to issues of curriculum and professionalism (see Chapters 4 and 5).

35 See discussion in Chapter 1 and also LACEY, C., *The Socialization of Teachers* (London, Methuen, 1977); LeCOMPTE, M. and GINSBURG, M., 'How students learn to become teachers', in NOBLIT, G. and PINK, W. (Eds.) *Schooling in Social Context: Qualitative Studies* (New York, Ablex, 1987); SPATIG, L., GINSBURG, M., and LIBERMAN, D., 'Ego development as an explanation of passive and active models of teacher socialization', *College Student Journal* 16 (1982): 315–25.

36 On the importance and potentially contradictory nature (in comparison to the formal curriculum) of the hidden curriculum in teacher education, see BARTHOLOMEW, J., 'Schooling teachers: The myth of the liberal college', in WHITTY, G. and YOUNG, M., (Eds.) *Explorations in the Politics of School Knowledge*, (Nafferton, Driffield, England, Nafferton Books, 1976); DALE, R., 'Implications of the rediscovery of hidden curriculum for the sociology of teaching', in GLEESON, D. (Ed.) *Identity and Structure in the Sociology of Education*, (Nafferton, Driffield, England, Nafferton Books, 1977); MARDLE, G. and WALKER, M., 'Strategies and structures: Some critical notes on teacher socialization', in WOODS, P. (Ed.) *Teacher Strategies*, (London, Croom Helm, 1980).

37 Although Sonia's idealism actually began to wane prior to entering the teacher education program, she did encounter some messages in the formal curriculum that may have reinforced this process. For instance, a guest instructor during a multicultural education class session exclaimed:

> Too often we apologize for being a teacher. We must feel good about ourselves and transmit that feeling to others. ... Remember there are people who don't get well when treated by doctors, and there are clients who lose court cases despite having a lawyer, so teachers should not be so down on themselves because students aren't learning enough. (*Fieldnotes*: 9–9–80)

Chapter 7

What Is To Be Done? Critical Praxis
by Educators of Teachers

The resolution of theoretical contradictions is possible only through practical means, only through the practical energy of [human beings]. This resolution is by no means, therefore, the task only of understanding, but is a real task of life, a task which philosophy was unable to accomplish precisely because it saw there a purely theoretical problem.[1]

Introduction

In this chapter, I will initially, briefly discuss the theoretical issues introduced in Chapter 1, indicating how they have been addressed in the ensuing chapters. As evidenced by the title of this chapter, employing the words of Lenin,[2] and as concisely explained in the quote above from Marx, however, I want to go beyond merely theorizing. Pursuant to this, I will sketch some ideas of how educators of teachers can and should orient their careers, and their lives, toward what needs to be done, what I refer to as critical praxis. These ideas are organized around three areas: intervening in the teacher education reform debates, engaging preservice teachers in critically counterposing contradictions, and becoming activist intellectuals in struggles for social transformation.

Summary of Theoretical Issues in Relation to Historical and Ethnographic Observations

I began this book by arguing that we must consider teacher education as involved in the reproduction or transformation of unequal class, gender

199

and race relations. In the foregoing chapters, hopefully, I have developed and documented this argument drawing on both historical and ethnographic data. We have seen evidence of how at the structural and ideological levels social inequalities help to constitute and (in part) are constituted by the organization, content and processes of teacher education.

Early on in Chapter 1, I suggested that the concept of contradiction should be seen as useful not only in countering what sometimes becomes an overly-deterministic model of reproduction, but also in clarifying debates concerning passive versus active models of socialization of teachers. Chapter 2 represented an attempt to illustrate how contradictions in class and gender relations have informed historical developments in teacher education. Contradictory class and gender structures and their attendant ideologies provided, in part, the rules and resources that constrained and enabled teacher educators and others in their efforts to develop and shape institutionalized forms of preservice teacher preparation. At the same time, such actions, although sometimes illuminating and thus providing the basis for confronting and challenging such contradictions, more often masked and thus mediated contradictions in class and gender relations.

Chapter 3 offered a more detailed analysis of a specific case in the more recent history of teacher education. Therein we observed how efforts to professionalize teaching by reforming a teacher education program were experienced by different sets of university faculty members. One of the major structural contradictions (and its associated ideologies) of social class relations — proletarianization versus professionalization — was relevant to consider in this case, in analyzing the actions of both the 'elites' and 'masses' of the professoriate. The former group of professors experienced varying degrees of professionalization and accumulated varying amounts of 'academic capital', while the latter became the target of a proletarianization process. Nevertheless, the latter group's clinging to individualist notions and other cultural forms linked to the ideology of professionalism operated to limit the effectiveness of their critique and resistance locally as well as to deflect their consideration of solidarity with other groups similarly affected outside the professoriate.

Within the discussion of the ethnographic data in Chapters 4–6, I sought to demonstrate how the concept of contradictions in class, gender and race relations could inform our analysis of the formal and hidden curriculum of a preservice teacher education program and the socialization of prospective teachers, who were often actively working to construct their occupational and more general identities. Curriculum dilemmas or contradictions, *viz.*, knowledge as given versus problematical, public versus personal knowledge, and knowledge as molecular versus holistic, were examined in Chapter 4, particularly in relation to preservice teachers' developing conceptions of curriculum knowledge and their future roles as curriculum decision-makers or curriculum delivery service workers. For the most part, we witnessed a process termed 'anticipatory deskilling'. This process can be seen as masking and thus mediating the deskilling/reskilling contradictions as most (but not all) prospective teachers were never really helped to develop curriculum decision-making skills, while at the same time, they were not oriented toward viewing such skills as integral to the teacher's role.

Contradictions in conceptions of professionalism in programmatic messages and in preservice teachers' views was the focus of Chapter 5. Three themes — remuneration/service ideal, power, and individual attitude/behavior in the social construction of competence — provided the basis for linking these conceptions to a broader ideology of professionalism and for indicating how such conceptions contained the potential for masking, and thus mediating, as well as illuminating, and thus providing the basis to challenge, contradictions in class and gender relations.

As in the previous and subsequent chapter, I indicated how, given the contradictory nature of the messages in the formal and hidden curriculum, preservice teachers could be perceived as actively constructing an identity for their anticipated career, although often orienting themselves in directions that appeared to model the dominant messages of the program. Meanwhile, other prospective teachers were able to construct alternative occupational identities, based partly on conceptions developed prior to entry in the program and partly on their selective incorporation of ideas encountered during the program.

Chapter 6 presented an analysis of ideological informed conceptions of social mobility and social reproduction. The concern was with how prospective teachers initially conceived the nature and legitimacy of extant class, gender and race relations in school and society and how they continued to develop such conceptions as they encountered contradictory messages in the program's formal and hidden curriculum. I presented evidence of the warming-up–cooling-out contradiction characteristic of capitalist, patriarchal, and racially stratified societies being mediated as well as questioned. I also suggested how critically counterposing the evidenced descriptive and normative theories, concerning contest versus sponsorship and particularistic versus universalistic issues, seemed to illuminate this and other contradictions, thus creating a basis for challenging and confronting the attendant unequal social relations.

Critical Praxis and Educators of Teachers

We will now turn to a discussion of critical praxis and how such might be pursued by educators of teachers. Critical praxis is the process of combining critical theorizing and critical practice. The issue here is to retain a critical stance toward society, schooling and teacher education, while developing and refining strategies for action, for intervening in political, economic and ideological arenas. It is not just a question of theory informing practice, but also a practice informing theory, while concomitantly holding onto the language and commitments of critical traditions. In some ways, the distinction I am making here between critical theory and critical praxis is analogous to the one that Aronowitz and Giroux[3] make between 'critical intellectuals' and 'transformative intellectuals', respectively. They argue that as individuals, 'Critical intellectuals are ... critical of inequality and injustice, but they often refuse or are unable to move beyond their isolated posture to the terrain of collective solidarity and struggle'.[4] By way of contrast, transformative intellectuals help to 'analyze various interests and contradictions within [education and] society' and collaborate with others in 'articulating emancipatory possibilities *and* working toward their realization'.[5]

I want to emphasize, though, that critical praxis implies more than abstract theorizing and action directed at broad, long-term goals. It also necessitates what Noddings has labelled an 'ethic of caring'.[6] Whereas, concern, compassion and caring for people stimulate the theorizing and strategic action; they must also be evidenced to those with whom we come in contact, directly or indirectly, in what we say and do. As Noddings articulates in discussion of the teacher education reform proposals:

> [T]he self does not grow [by becoming] more individually powerful, more cruel in the pursuit of highly valued goals, more unlike the human beings it seeks to dominate. Rather, the self is surpassed in relation, in the realization of interdependence and the joy of empowering others.[7]

Throughout the remainder of this chapter, I will outline the aspects of such critical praxis in which educators of teachers and others may engage. I should clarify that the term 'educators of teachers' is broader than that of teacher educators. As educators of teachers, I include people in universities who teach generic and subject-specific teaching methods courses, educational psychology and social foundations of education courses, and arts and sciences courses comprising prospective teachers' major and other coursework. Most, if not all, university faculty, are thus, educators of teachers. The label also applies to all educators — administrators and teachers — whom preservice teachers encounter during field observations and other assignments as well as during student teaching.

Intervening in the Teacher Education Reform Debates

One aspect of critical praxis by teacher educators involves entering into policy debates and ideological work. Media coverage of the 'crisis' in education and teaching was apparent during the period of fieldwork, 1980–82, but considerably more public attention was focused on this 'crisis' in conjunction with the publications of *A Nation At Risk* and other reports in 1983.[8] And, as might be expected from the descriptions in Chapter 2 of other periods of crisis, concerns about teachers and teacher education were soon to emerge. In 1985 and 1986, several reports[9] were published, offering similar analyses of the 'problems' in teacher education and proposing an overlapping set of 'solutions'. The major thrust of these proposals can be summarized as follows:

1 develop more and earlier, centralized testing to raise standards, i.e., to become more selective in screening who will and will not become a teacher;

2 extend the time required in training before becoming a teacher;

3 further stratify the educational workforce by creating a formal hierarchy of teacher positions and tie those positions to different kinds and amounts of teacher preparation;

4 make the education of teachers intellectually, or at least academically, more challenging;

5 restructure school organizations so that teachers have more autonomy and receive greater remuneration.

What would educators of teachers committed to critical praxis do in this context? To start, one would write in 'scholarly' journals for audiences of teacher educators and other academics. Articles in journals and periodicals, such as *Education Week* and the *Chronicle of Higher Education*, read by a broader range of educators and educational policy-makers, would also be useful, if not unusual, outlets for such writing efforts, as would outlets possessing a more 'popular', general audience readership — national and local newspapers and magazines, newsletters of educators' and other workers' organizations, religious, political and civic groups. Radio and TV programs and editorial opportunities should not be overlooked either.

However, there is a need to go beyond the intellectual's scribe role. On both an individual and, preferably, a collective basis, educators of teachers committed to critical praxis need to enter into the debates about the 'problems' and the efforts to formulate and implement 'solutions'. The scope of such activities can focus on one's institution, the local community, state, region, nation and world. Groups with which one could become involved include university and public school committees, educators' organizations, PTAs, legislative bodies, government or foundation panels, political parties, unions, ethnic groups and women's organizations. The task here is to raise questions, make proposals, take on assignments, and otherwise help shape the discourse and policy/practice outcomes.

Such efforts should not be conceived merely as providing a critique, pointing out the limitations and contradictions in others' analyses and proposals. Critical praxis also contains a more proactive component. For example, not only should contradictions be identified, but suggestions should be offered on how to exploit the theoretical and political space they provide in order to move toward more liberatory or emancipatory ends for educators and other people.

What kinds of issues and concerns would a teacher educator devoted to critical praxis bring to these various, admittedly vaguely described activities? First, given our discussion in Chapter 2, we would want to focus attention on whether the 'reform movement' is indeed generated out of a 'crisis' in education or whether the movement constitutes the result of more fundamental political and economic crisis in the United States and globally, generated itself out of con-tradictions in class, gender and race relations. Certainly, similar education debates and reform efforts in Britain during the mid- to late-1970s have been shown to represent more of an ideological discharge, deflecting attention away from economic crisis and fiscal crisis of the state, than comprising an outgrowth of citizen or edu-cational community concerns.[10] Moreover, it is difficult to treat as unproblematic the claim in the introduction of *A Nation at Risk* that 'The Commission was created as a result of the Secretary's concern about the widespread public perception that something is seriously remiss in our education system',[11] when in 1982, according to a Gallup poll, 'an increasing percentage of the American people ... consider[ed] the public schools to be excellent, above average, or average'.[12] We cannot devote space to delineating the issues here, but fortunately others have begun the task of analyzing the 'crisis' and what it reflects and how some of the discourse surrounding (and perhaps creating) it have served ideological functions.[13]

Second, we must examine how the analyses of the 'problem' and proposed 'solutions' not only depend upon, but also appear to reinforce, unequal class, race and gender relations. To illustrate this point, I want to focus attention on the proposals for differentiating teacher education programs in terms of their location (in research universities or not), their level of delivery (graduate or undergraduate), and the occupational rank of their graduates (professional teachers or instructors).[14] The parallels between these proposals and what we discussed in Chapter 2 in relation to the distinctions between administrator versus teacher, secondary versus elementary teacher, and university versus normal school programs should be enough of a warning of how at least class and gender relations are penetrating these discussions. Thus, it is more than just competition for control of teacher education between research-oriented universities with graduate programs in education and institutions emphasizing undergraduate teaching as Tom argues.[15] We should probe concerning how the social class, gender and racial composition of teacher education students, university instructors, and 'professional' or 'lead' teachers would change if these proposals were implemented. In Texas, for instance, the implementation of standardized testing as a criterion for entry into and exit from teacher education programs has had the effect of screening-out a higher proportion of black and hispanic than white candidates, and has threatened the continued existence of some programs that attract a predominantly 'minority' population.[16] Similar trends of decreased racial minority entry into teaching have been noted for the US more generally.[17] We know, furthermore, that the class and racial composition of research universities is different from other institutions of higher education and graduate programs tend to be more masculinized than undergraduate programs. Will the 'professional' or 'lead' teacher category contain a higher proportion of white, male, relatively economically advantaged educators compared to instructors?

Nevertheless, the fact that both the Carnegie Task Force and the Holmes Group raise concerns about the potential negative effect of the reforms on ethnic minority (but not social class or gender differentiated) access to teaching careers, may provide some basis for countering what otherwise may be very regressive developments. Apple, for one, applauds this attention in the Holmes Group report, but cautions that such rhetoric must be matched with 'extensive financial support'[18] to become a reality.

In addition, we need to scrutinize the discourse employed in the debates. Is there an assumption of superiority of the liberal or theoretical over the technical or the practical in teacher education and is there a preference implied for 'mental' versus 'manual' or 'emotional' labor? These latter questions may be particularly difficult for those of us in the foundations of education to notice and raise concerns, since our occupational identities are so firmly planted in the liberal arts, disciplinary traditions. Does the language of debate and reform have to legitimate unequal social relations or to mediate contradictions in class and gender (as well as race) relations? Is it not possible to speak of improving teacher education without implying a hierarchy in ways of experiencing the world — liberal versus technical traditions of knowledge, analytic versus intuitive ways of knowing, mental versus emotional and manual forms of labor? I concur with Martin, who argues, pointing to both class and gender contradictions linked to notions of liberal education, that

> Instead of unreflexively endorsing education that divorces not only head from hand and the productive from the reproductive processes of society, but also reason from feeling and emotion and self from other, [we] should be seeking ways to overcome the dualisms inherent in the historic tenets of liberal education.[19]

In examining the debates and reform proposals, it is clear that a major goal is the professionalization of teaching. As Murray explains on behalf of the Executive Board of the Holmes Group, for example: 'The Consortium wishes to see nothing less than the transformation of teaching ... into a genuine profession'.[20] Given what we discussed in Chapter 3, the teacher educator committed to critical praxis should be wary of what such efforts might mean for the autonomy and skill utilization among the professoriate. We might pose the question and monitor developments around the issue of which segments of the faculty in education and other units in the university may be proletarianized and which will be professionalized and acquire greater amounts of 'academic capital'?

Also, based on the discussion in Chapters 3 and 5, we should be cautious about the firmly grounded assumptions of occupational and social inequalities inherent in most discourse and struggle about professionalism and professionalization. It is not just how appropriating elements of the ideology of professionalism may help to mediate contradictions in class, race, and gender relations, and thus help to perpetuate and legitimate social inequalities in society and the world generally, it is also how the ideology of professionalism may justify internal stratification among educators.

We should thus be vigilant regarding the proposals to create formal hierarchies, differentiated staffing, in the quest for professionalizing the teaching force. A number of educators have commented on the Holmes Group's proposal to create the positions of Instructor, 'who would be prepared to deliver instruction under the supervision of a Career Professional Teacher'; Professional Teacher, 'who would be prepared as a fully autonomous professional in the classroom'; and the Career Professional Teacher, 'who would be capable of assuming responsibility not only within the classroom but also at the school level'.[21]

Shive and Case[22] as well as Sedlak,[23] in promoting the concept of differentiated staffing among teachers, make clear that while some educational workers might be professionalized, others would be deskilled and proletarianized, in order to reduce costs by making a subset of the teaching force, in this case, Instructors, less expensive more easily replaceable workers. Dreeben criticizes this approach, in my view arguing that Instructors would equate in Marxian terms to a reserve army of surplus labor, in that they will be easily 'laid off and hastily hired'.[24] Raymond is also critical of such differentiated staffing proposals because: 'The Division manages the job of splitting-up teacher related functions into three distinct levels of role and status, but it does so at the cost of denying the two lower levels functions essential to maximal performance'.[25] That this is, at its heart, a deskilling process is indicated by Zumwalt, when she notes that the Instructor would be 'an implementor of curriculum created by someone else'.[26] And Apple reminds us that the issues pertain to gender relations as well as class and race:

Any call for greater control over the teaching profession, any attempt to change teachers' work, is also a call to control the labor process of what is largely 'women's work' and needs to be seen in the context of the frequent attempts to rationalize women's paid work in the past.[27]

Now, it may very well be as Conley and Bachrach argue, that contained in the Holmes Group recommendation for differentiated staffing are two contradictory models: one that emphasizes hierarchy for purposes of control and one that stresses hierarchy for purposes of education or internship.[28] Thus, this ambiguity may provide space for progressive interventions in discourse and action. Nevertheless, one might want to challenge the notion of vertical relations even if the focus is on education of novice teachers.

Therefore, we may wish to pose the more general questions: What would be the implications of focusing on further developing educational programs for all educators (and all people) rather than trying to find a strategy that would seem to upgrade the status, if not the competence, of a minority — who, I would predict, would be disproportionately male, white and from economically privileged backgrounds? Perhaps the 'problem' with the caliber of teacher education students and teachers should not be seen as one where the solution involves trying to attract a larger proportion of those successful in the current system and then providing this select group with a more elite-like educational experience in a teacher preparation program and with more autonomous and skilled work roles in the schools. Maybe the 'problem' lies in the fact that the organization and processes of schooling, whether designed to or not, do not help most students to gain access to a broad range of knowledge or to achieve competence in skills associated with mental, manual and emotional labor.

The issues raised here are not just about the lives of other groups, but also of educators of teachers. Even if we wanted to ignore the implications of our discourse and actions for other groups, we may want to, from a selfish perspective, get off the teacher-education-reform-through-status-enhancement bandwagon. The critical analysis of historical studies of teacher education presented herein indicated that similar previous efforts have usually failed dramatically to enhance the status, power, and wealth of educators associated with the more desirable programs and students. Moreover, such strategies have helped to solidify ideologically the unequal relations within which educators find themselves subordinated compared to arts/sciences faculty and other groups. Perhaps the individualist and professionalist strategies of teacher educators must be eschewed in favor of collaborating in a broader struggle with the groups who have even less power, wealth and status than we do. There have been hints in the history of teacher education that such an orientation is plausible, if not always followed to its logical conclusion.

We must also consider the impact these 'reform' proposals would have on the socialization of teachers. In terms of conceptions of curriculum (discussed in Chapter 4), we may want to draw attention to the messages that would be sent by the implementation of some of the proposed reforms in terms of curriculum knowledge as given versus problematical. If some, but not all, educators became more involved in curriculum decision-making in schools, then perhaps preservice teachers would be less likely to understand curriculum knowledge as given. We should be cautious here, however, because curriculum decision-making could be conveyed as a technical activity undertaken by 'experts', without reference to its political and cultural dimensions, thus, muting the message of curriculum knowledge as problematic. We must identify the implications of reinforcing messages about the molecular (versus holistic) conception of curriculum that would occur if the notion that 'teaching technology is subject matter-specific'[29] is implanted more firmly in teacher education programs.

In addition, messages relevant to conceptions of professionalism (discussed in Chapter 5) are certainly contained in proposals to provide higher salaries to 'professional' or 'lead' teachers and to give more work-related power and autonomy to such teachers as contrasted with their lower status 'colleagues'. And as Judge notes, we should examine the extent to which a 'nakedly hierarchical' notion of professionalism in teaching rests primarily on 'the mysticisms of academic status'[30] rather than on any clear evidence of competence and expertise.

With respect to ideologies of social mobility and social reproduction, the recent reports on the 'crisis' in education can also be seen as strongly reinforcing the sponsorship and particularistic ideologies already in the hidden curriculum of the teacher education program as discussed in Chapter 6. The moves toward both greater selectivity for those aspiring to become teachers and increased stratification within the occupational group could have different effects ideologically. On one hand, the implementation of earlier and centralized, standardized screening of future teachers — a reinforcement of a sponsorship ideological message in the hidden curriculum of teacher education programs — may encourage preservice teachers and other educators to incorporate these elements of a sponsorship ideology in their perspective, thus perhaps making it easier for them to accept proposals for greater educational stratification for students with whom they work.

On the other hand, such developments, if critically connected to their strongly held contest ideologically informed perspective, may prompt them to ask, 'Why such warming-up and cooling-out must occur?'

Efforts to improve the quality of teacher education programs by reducing the number of institutions that offer them is also of interest. Such efforts, if achieved, would provide sponsorship ideology messages in the hidden curriculum of teacher education programs. Contest ideological elements would be signalled by the greater homogeneity in the 'quality' of programs for prospective educators, perhaps eliminating the kind of sponsorship messages currently available in contrast between more and less well-funded programs. However, some of the proposals by the Holmes Group of Deans of 'leading research institutions seems to be directed toward insuring at least a two-tiered stratification in teacher education'.[31] Sponsorship elements would be contained in messages about the increased centralization of decision-making regarding which institutions should be allowed to offer programs and, therefore, which students should be encouraged to enroll in teacher certification programs. Preservice teachers might be swayed by these messages or they might critically juxtapose them with other messages.

Finally, moves to further stratify the educational workforce (e.g., with the introduction of formal hierarchies among teachers) may help preservice teachers and others to feel more comfortable with other aspects of a sponsorship ideology at play in the schools — that the maximum benefits (education or otherwise) should be given to those few who because of (cultural or genetic) heredity are seen to be able to make the most significant contribution to the economy and other social goods. Critically examining these elements along with the elements from a contest ideology, which they have incorporated in their conceptions, however, may expose some of the contradictions in capitalist, patriarchal and racially/ethnically stratified societies. I hope it is not too optimistic to imagine educators concluding: 'If invidious distinctions of status, wealth and power among teachers is inappropriate and unnecessary, then perhaps analogous forms of stratification among people more generally are equally indefensible'.

Engaging Preservice Teachers in Critically Counterposing Contradictions

Educators of teachers concerned with critical praxis, clearly, must intervene at the programmatic level of curriculum, pedagogy, and evaluation as well as at the level of policy. I argued at the end of Chapter 6 that one of the main focuses of such programmatic efforts is to engage prospective teachers (and others) in a process that facilitates critically counterposing ideological and structural contradictions. How can we do this? First, we must provide the students in our courses with the requisite analytical skills and conceptual tools to critically reflect and inquire about their own and the broader experiences of school and society. This step in some ways parallels the call by the Holmes Group and other reform proposers to make the education of teachers more intellectually challenging. What I am calling for is similar to the development of what Feinberg terms 'the interpretive and normative skills required in order to understand the larger social context of [teachers' and others'] work'[32] or what Shor calls 'critical literacy ... in order to provoke conceptual inquiry into self, society and the discipline itself'.[33] As Britzman explains: 'Prospective teachers need to participate in developing critical ways of knowing with which they can interrogate school culture, the quality of students' and teachers' lives, and the particular role biography plays in understanding these dynamics'.[34]

Second, more of the 'life space' of courses and programs must be devoted to using such analytical skills and conceptual tools to examine issues relevant to social class, gender and race relations. This does not imply more 'ghettoized' curricular units on social foundations or multicultural education. It entails instead stressing the use of such skills and tools in an integrated way throughout the various phases and components of the program. This means focusing on the fundamental contradictions discussed in Chapters 1 and 2 that are reflected in (at least) capitalist, patriarchal, and racially-stratified societies. It entails, moreover, engaging students in a dialogue about how educators and other workers encounter the proletarianization/professionalization and deskilling/reskilling contradictions, around which Chapters 3 and 4 revolved. The curriculum knowledge dilemmas or contradictions — knowledge as problematical versus given, knowledge as personal versus public, and knowledge as holistic versus molecular — as well as the contradictions within the ideology of professionalism (e.g., remuneration versus service ideal), discussed in Chapters 4 and 5, respectively, could also serve as the focus for critical dialogue. Finally I would encourage attention to the contradictions in ideologies of social mobility and social reproduction — contest versus sponsorship and particularistic versus universalistic — as analyzed in Chapter 6.

Third, the curriculum content of teacher education programs and other courses must become not only a purveyor of these and other relevant skills and tools, but also the focus of critical examination. This would entail instructors and students identifying and discussing what messages are evidenced, and those which are not evidenced or are only part of the taken-for-granted background, in a given reading, handout, lecture, school/community observation. Moreover, the content of any specific message in the formal curriculum would have to be analyzed in relation to other messages in the formal curriculum, as well as those in the 'hidden' curriculum — that constituted by the social relations of the teacher education program, the university, and school/communities. Such a process, of course, is not likely to be a comfortable one for instructors or students. From the instructor's perspective, this makes what they say, what they may decide upon as curricular materials, and their routine practices — including admission decisions, grading, and interaction outside of class — subject to critical inquiry and reflection. For students, not only would they be placed in the awkward position of publicly discussing the contradictory elements of a program organized by instructors who may be gate-keepers for their projected careers in teaching, but they would also have to interrogate their own actions and statements and those of their peers.

Fourth, contradictory ideologies and social relations should become a terrain of critical action and reflective practice. Thus, I am not proposing that these issues be subject merely to in-depth thought and discussion by liberally educated, reflective students of education. What I am suggesting is a form of critical praxis by students of education. To really come to terms with the complexity of the issues involved and to avoid becoming merely followers of others' orders or unwitting collaborators in mediating contradictions in class, race and gender relations, preservice teachers and educators of teachers will have to actively confront their reality — to engage in critical praxis. They will have to avoid compartmentalizing normative and descriptive theories of social mobility and social reproduction or other ideologically informed notions that contain contradictions. They will need to critically analyze situations (i.e., seek to discover and expose contra-dictions) and then with others, collaborate in challenging such ideo-logies and social structures in universities, schools, and elsewhere.

Clearly, the complexity and the range of relevant issues mean that the task is enormous and that only some aspects can be undertaken at one time. Furthermore, such a development and implementation of critical praxis by prospective teachers and those involved in the education of teachers would need to occur while prospective teachers are learning enough about what may be expected of them in schools and society as they are now being constructed, while at the same time strategies are being developed to transform such social relations. Here I am not merely theorizing about the complexities and difficulties involved. Rather I am also reflecting on my own experience with colleagues and undergraduate students at the University of Houston during 1985–87 in efforts to build a 'Reflective Inquiry Teacher Education' program. I do not want to really describe the program here, since others have begun to do so at least for early phases of the on-going efforts.[35] What I want to suggest is that even trying to do even some of the things suggested here involves a real struggle. The struggle entails avoiding curriculum development efforts that tend to proletarianize colleagues who become involved later; preventing the program's curriculum[36] and the more general education experience of preservice teachers from being organized molecularly, from stressing only public knowledge, or from being treated as given; encouraging students, both verbally and through our actions (especially in grading assignments and exams), to treat reflective inquiry as a process with potentially multiple outcomes, rather than as a search for the right answers as determined by university instructors, state proficiency examiners, or the school-based educators with whom they come in contact; deflecting tendencies to discourage prospective teachers from entering the field because it is so complex and problematic; and avoiding treating success in the program as the result of a fair and open contest based only on universalistic criteria when, in fact, often skills in reflective inquiry are closely associated to different forms of cultural capital that are differentially distributed currently among groups of students entering a program.

Recognizing such challenges is not a reason for abandoning the need to confront reality. While our efforts to transform schooling and society through critical praxis in teacher education alone will not be sufficient, I want to argue it is a necessary contribution. The alternatives — to accept things as they are or to assume we cannot have an impact — render us impotent, ironically, at the same time unequal social relations are reproduced. As Shor posits, we need to direct our efforts toward 'critical desocialization' through 'egalitarian pedagogy' or what I have termed 'critical praxis' in the education of teachers. 'Individual classrooms cannot change an unequal social system; only political movements can transform inequality. In working for transformation, egalitarian pedagogy can interfere with the disabling socialization of students'.[37]

Becoming Activist Intellectuals in Struggles for Social Transformation[38]

In the above quote, Shor reminds us that no matter how vigilant and energetic we are with respect to intervening in reform debates and engaging in critical praxis in our curricular, pedagogical and evaluation work in educational institutions, this is not sufficient. As educators of teachers, we must also operate as activists in broader struggles for social transformation. In answer to Bruce Joyce's[39] question — Should educators 'see themselves as aloof from the global issues whose resolution will determine the future of human kind?' I offer a resounding NO! This is because these broader structural and ideological struggles are, as I have tried to show in this book, dialectically related to the struggles within teacher education; because we need to be models for the people we seek to educate as teachers; and because becoming involved in such political activity will help us to establish relations with others whose lives are similarly constrained and enabled by these broader structures and ideologies. As Maxine Green observes, the type of community, society and world that

> we cherish is not an endowment, ... it must be achieved through dialectical engagements with the social and economic obstacles we find standing in our way. ... We cannot neglect the fact of power. But we can undertake a resistance, a reaching out toward becoming persons among persons.[40]

Through such collective action not only can we increase mutual understanding of the parallels between our own and others' experiences, but also we can attract allies for our efforts in the education of teachers, while concomitantly serving as allies in others' more specific or local struggles.

There are a wide variety of political parties and movements, and optimistically, even the possibility of one united progressive movement, in which we can and should become involved directly, and not just acting as an 'advisor' or provider of the 'instruments of analysis'.[41] Despite the contradictions in the role of professors or other intellectuals as activists, we must enter the fray and not remain on the sidelines on issues of racism, sexism, economic exploitation and imperialism in our local communities, the nation and more globally. My own recent efforts have focused to varying extents on issues of apartheid (i.e., exploitation without representation) in South Africa, US intervention in Central

214

America, peace and justice in the Middle East, and jobs and justice for people of all colors and both sexes in the United States.[42]

Many readers, I am sure, may have reservations about such explicit politicization of the educator's role. Is it not possible, one may ask, to remain as objective and neutral observers and commentators, helping others to understand and act more intelligently? I hope that the earlier chapters have tempered such beliefs in the feasibility of such a role within educational institutions.[43] But I suspect even those who may agree with me that there is a need to make the 'pedagogical more political',[44] and to confront the issues directly in our work, may be less sanguine about going outside the boundaries of more generally under-stood roles of educators and intellectuals.[45]

Certainly, for those of us in universities there is a rather explicit difference in the protection provided by the 1940 AAUP 'Statement of Principles' as they apply to discourse and action in the classroom versus in the community, with really only the former being covered under provisions of academic freedom.[46] Moreover, as Silva and Slaughter conclude, even in the context of the ivory tower,

> academic freedom, as it is presently constituted, far from being [always] the liberating right to test the limits of thought and deed, is in fact the very chain that immobilizes university-based intellectuals, always separating their thoughts from their deeds and keeping their ideas from reaching systematic limits.[47]

Perhaps the issues of why we must become activist intellectuals can be clarified by confronting the implications of not speaking and not acting for social transformation. I have attempted earlier in this chapter to make the point, drawing on Aronowitz and Giroux's distinction between critical and transformative intellectuals,[48] but here let me turn to a major source for their conceptualization, Antonio Gramsci. For me, Gramsci's discussion, perhaps significantly included in his *Selections from the Prison Notebooks*, about 'organic' and 'traditional' intellectuals helps to clarify this question. He posits that:

> Every social group, coming into existence on the original terrain of an essential function in the world of economic production, creates within itself, *organically*, one or more strata of intellectuals which give it homogeneity and an awareness of its own function not only in the economic but also in the social and political fields.[49]

In contrast with this category of 'organic' intellectuals, who may be connected to dominant or subordinate social groups, Gramsci identifies what he terms 'traditional' intellectuals. The 'traditional' intellectuals are those whose origin and organic connection is with a (normally dominant) group associated more clearly with a previous social form-ation, for example, those who were 'organically bound to the landed aristocracy'[50] in the current epoch of monopoly capitalism.

Gramsci goes on to explain, 'Since these various categories of traditional intellectuals experience through an *esprit de corps* their uninterrupted historical continuity and their special qualification, they thus put themselves forward as an autonomous and independent group'.[51] This notion of autonomy or neutrality has already been mentioned, and thus I want to push further into Gramsci's theorizing. He develops the discussion further by stating that:

> One of the most important characteristics of any group that is developing towards [or attempting to maintain] dominance is its struggle to assimilate and conquer 'ideologically' the 'tradi-tional' intellectuals, but this assimilation and conquest is made quicker and more efficacious the more the group in question succeeds in simultaneously elaborating its own organic intel-lectuals.[52]

From Gramsci's analysis, then, the implications of *not* speaking out and *not* acting are clear. Not only do we facilitate our colleagues' and our students' organic links with current and emerging dominant groups—with respect to race and gender as well as class relations—but we thus hasten the day for our own assimilation and conquest. The question is not whether we can remain neutral, but how we can exploit the space provided by contradictory social relations and ideologies to struggle for a more equitable, just, and peaceful world system, one in which critical praxis in the education of teachers might be appropriately concerned with relatively minor imperfections in schools and society, rather than the more fundamental structural problems that we must confront now.

Notes

1 MARX, K. [Economic and Philosophical Manuscripts (1844), Marx-Engels Gesamtausgabe 1/3, p. 121] in BOTTOMORE, T. and RUBEL, M. (Eds.) *Karl Marx: Selected Writings in Sociology and Social Philosophy*, (Har-mondsworth, Middlesex, England, 1961), p. 87.

2   See LENIN, V.I., *What Is To Be Done? Burning Question of Our Movement* (New York, International Publishers, 1969).

3   ARONOWITZ, S. and GIROUX, H., *Education Under Siege: The Conservative, Liberal and Radical Debate Over Schooling* (South Hadley, MA, Bergin and Garvey, 1985).

4   *Ibid.*, p. 37.

5   GIROUX, H. and MCLAREN, P., 'Teacher education and the politics of engagement: The case for democratic schooling', *Harvard Educational Review* 56 (1986), p. 215. I have edited the text here to clarify that 'intellectuals' can and should contribute more than the fruits of their intellectual labor. See also KRETOVICS, J., 'Critical literacy: Challenging the assumptions of mainstream educational theory', *Journal of Education* 167 (1985), pp. 50–62; LIVINGSTONE, D., *Critical Pedagogy and Cultural Power* (New York, Bergin and Garvey, 1987).

6   NODDINGS, N., 'Fidelity in teaching, teacher education and research for teaching', *Harvard Educational Review* 56 (November, 1986), pp. 496–510.

7   *Ibid.*, p. 501.

8   For examples of media attention in the 1980–82 period, WILLIAMS, D. 'Why public schools fail?', *Newsweek* (20 April 1981), pp. 62–65; WILLIAMS, D., 'Teachers are in trouble', *Newsweek* (27, April 1981), pp. 78–84. Reports issued in 1983 include: NATIONAL COMMISSION ON EXCELLENCE IN EDUCATION, *A Nation at Risk: The Imperative for Educational Reform* (Washington, DC., US Department of Education, 1983); TASK FORCE ON EDUCATION FOR ECONOMIC GROWTH, *Action for Excellence: A Comprehensive Plan to Improve Our Nation's Schools* (Denver, Education Commission of the States, 1983); TWENTIETH CENTURY FUND TASK FORCE ON FEDERAL ELEMENTARY AND SECONDARY EDUCATION POLICY, *Making the Grade* (New York, Twentieth Century Fund, 1983); CARNEGIE CORPORATION OF NEW YORK, *Education and Economic Progress: Toward a National Educational Policy* (New York, Carnegie Corporation, 1983).

9   Some of the more widely discussed reform proposals are included in CARNEGIE TASK FORCE ON TEACHING AS A PROFESSION, *A Nation Prepared: Teachers for the 21st Century* (Hyattsville, MD, Carnegie Forum on Education and Economy 1987); HOLMES GROUP, *Tomorrow's Teachers: A Report of the Holmes Group* (East Lansing, MI, Holmes Group, Inc., 1986); NATIONAL COMMISSION FOR EXCELLENCE IN TEACHER EDUCATION, *A Call for Change in Teacher Education* (Washington, DC., NCETE, 1985); NATIONAL CONSORTIUM FOR EDUCATIONAL EXCELLENCE, *An Agenda for Educational Research: A View From the Firing Line* (Nashville, TN, Vanderbilt University, 1985).

10 For example, see GINSBURG M., MEYENN R., and MILLER H., 'Teachers, the "Great Debate" and education cuts', *Westminster Studies in Education* 2 (1979), pp. 5–33.

11 National Commission on Excellence in Education, p. 1.

12 HODGKINSON, H., 'What's still right about education?' *Phi Delta Kappan* (December 1982), p. 231.

13 See, for example, ALTBACK, P., KELLY, G. and WEISS, L., (Eds.) *Excellence*

in Education (New York, Prometheus Books, 1985); APPLE, M., 'Will the social context allow a tomorrow for tomorrow's teachers?' *Teachers College Record* 88 (1987), pp. 330–37; Aronowitz and Giroux; GIROUX, H., 'Public philosophy and the crisis in education', *Harvard Educational Review* 54 (1984), pp. 186–94; Giroux and McLaren; SHOR, I., 'Equality is excellence: Transforming teacher education and the learning process', *Harvard Education Review* 56 (1986), pp. 406–26.

14 Both the Holmes Group and the Carnegie Task Force on Teaching Profession reports propose creating a formal hierarchy among teachers with attendant distinctions in how those occupying these ranks would be prepared. The Holmes Group proposes a three-tier system of instructors, professional teachers, and career professional teachers; while the Carnegie Task Force suggests a two-tier one, differentiating between teachers and lead teachers.

15 TOM, A., 'The Holmes Group Report: Its latent political agenda', *Teachers College Record*, 88 (1987), pp. 430–35.

16 'Group wins stay against Texas teacher exam', *Education Week* (4 September, 1985), p. 4; RODMAN, B., 'US claims Texas teachers' skills test is legal', *Education Week* (16 October, 1985), pp. 5 and 16.

17 RODMAN, B., 'Teaching's "endangered" species: Minorities said opting out, or being screened out, just when profession "sorely needs" their influence', *Education Week* (20 November, 1985), pp. 1 and 11–12.

18 Apple, 'Will the social context ...' p. 333.

19 MARTIN, J. ROLAND, 'Reforming teacher education, rethinking liberal education', *Teachers College Record* 88 (1987), p. 407.

20 MURRAY, F., 'Goals for the reform of teacher education: An executive summary of the Holmes Group Report', *Phi Delta Kappan* 68 (September 1986), p. 28.

21 Holmes Group, p. 65.

22 SHIVE, R. and CASE, C., 'Differentiated staffing as an educational reform response', *Educational Policy* 1 (1987), pp. 57–66.

23 SEDLAK, M., 'Tomorrow's teachers: The essential arguments of the Holmes Group Report', *Teachers College Record* 88 (Spring, 1987), pp. 314–29.

24 DREEBEN, R., 'Comments on tomorrow's teachers', *Teachers College Record* 88 (Spring, 1987), p. 361.

25 RAYMOND, M., 'Tomorrow's teachers and today's schools', *Teachers College Record* 88 (Spring, 1987), p. 414.

26 ZUMWALT, K. KEPLER, 'Tomorrow's teachers: Tomorrow's work', *Teachers College Record* 88 (Spring 1987), p. 440.

27 Apple, 'Will the social context ...,' p. 330.

28 CONLEY, S. and BACHRACH, S., 'The Holmes Group Report: Standards, hierarchy, and management', *Teachers College Record* 88 (Spring 1987), p. 343.

29 JOYCE, B., 'Reflections on tomorrow's teachers', *Teachers College Record* 88 (Spring, 1987), p. 392.

30 JUDGE, H., 'Another view from abroad', *Teachers College Record* 88 (Spring, 1987), p. 395.

31 CURRENCE, C., 'Major universities adopt tougher teacher-training requirements', *Education Week* (12 June, 1985), p. 5.

32 FEINBERG, W., 'The Holmes Group Report and the professionalization of teaching', *Teachers College Record* 88 (Spring, 1987), p. 373.

33 SHOR, I., 'Equality is excellence: Transforming teacher education and the learning process', *Harvard Educational Review* 56 (November, 1986), p. 420.

34 BRITZMAN, D., 'Cultural myths in the making of a teacher: Biography and social structure in teacher education', *Harvard Educational Review* 56 (November, 1986), p. 454. See also Giroux and McLaren, p. 223; BEYER, L. and ZEICHNER, K., 'Teacher education in cultural context: Beyond reproduction', in POPKEWITZ, T., (Ed.) *Critical Studies in Teacher Education: Its Folklore, Theory and Practice* (New York, Falmer Press, 1987), pp. 298–334.

35 See CLIFT, R., MARSHALL, F. and NICHOLS, C., 'The RITE Program: A Close Look at Students' Perceptions'. Presentation at the annual meeting of the Association of Teacher Educators, Houston, February, 1987.

36 It should be noted that various colleagues with whom I have collaborated in designing and teaching in the RITE program have different organizing constructs and, perhaps, political agendas besides what I have termed critical praxis. Thus, the program should be understood as a terrain for my own critical praxis rather than as a model of what a group of educators of teachers all committed to critical praxis might hope to create.

37 Shor, p. 413.

38 This section draws heavily on GINSBURG, M., 'Contradictions in the role of professor as activist', *Sociological Focus*, 20 (April, 1987), pp. 111–22.

39 B. Joyce, p. 393.

40 GREENE, M., 'In search of a critical pedagogy', *Harvard Educational Review* 56 (November, 1986), p. 440. See also WHITTY, G., BARTON, L. and POLLARD, A. 'Ideology and control in teacher education: A review of recent experience in England,' in POPKEWITZ, T. (Ed.) *Critical Studies in Teacher Education* (New York, Falmer Press, 1987), p. 187.

41 Foucault seems to reject the former and promote the latter role. See FOUCAULT, M., *Power/Knowledge: Selected Interviews and Writings, 1972–1977* (C. Gordon, trans.) (New York, Pantheon Books, 1980), p. 126.

42 For an indication of some of these activities see Ginsburg, 'Contradictions in the role of professor as activist'.

43 For an excellent discussion debunking the notion of the university social scientist intellectual as neutral and somehow independent of broader power relations, see also POPKEWITZ, T., 'Social science and social amelioration: The development of the academic expert', in *Paradigm and Ideology in Educational Research: The Social Function of the Intellectual* (Lewes, Falmer Press, 1984), pp. 107–27.

44 Aronowitz and Giroux, p. 36.

45 It is true, as Lenin reminds us, that there are 'not two forms of the great struggle of social-democracy (political and economic) ... but three, placing the theoretical struggle on par with the first two' (p. 27). However, I

propose that this means we attend to all three aspects, and not just engage in theoretical forms of struggle, thus delegating the political and economic forms.

46   See SILVA, S. and SLAUGHTER, S., *Serving Power: The Making of the Social Science Expert* (Westport, CT, Greenwood Press, 1984).
47   *Ibid.*, p. 303
48   Aronowitz and Giroux, *Education Under Siege.*
49   GRAMSCI, A., 'The intellectuals', in *Selections from the Prison Notebooks* (New York, International Publishers, 1971), p. 5.
50   *Ibid.*, p. 7.
51   *Ibid.*, p. 7.
52   *Ibid.*, p. 10.

Index

370.71
G435
1988

120808

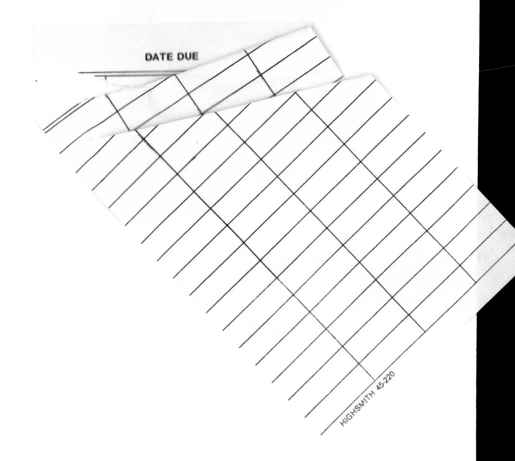

DATE DUE

HIGHSMITH 45-220